IN THEIR OWN WORDS

IN THEIR OWN WORDS

TRUE STORIES AND ADVENTURES
OF THE AMERICAN FIGHTER ACE

James A. Oleson

iUniverse, Inc.
New York Lincoln Shanghai

IN THEIR OWN WORDS
TRUE STORIES AND ADVENTURES OF THE AMERICAN FIGHTER ACE

iUniverse books may be ordered through booksellers or by contacting:

iUniverse
2021 Pine Lake Road, Suite 100
Lincoln, NE 68512
www.iuniverse.com
1-800-Authors (1-800-288-4677)

ISBN: 978-0-595-47116-4 (pbk)
ISBN: 978-0-595-70912-0 (cloth)
ISBN: 978-0-595-91396-1 (ebk)

Printed in the United States of America

This book is dedicated to my wife, Karen, and my sons, Patrick and Scott. Without their love, support, computer skills and artistic ability this book would only exist in the inner workings of my mind and would never have been compiled, completed and published.

Contents

FOREWORD

BY
STEVE PISANOS
COL. USAF (RET.)

I know Jim Oleson and his gracious family, long time loyal "FRIENDS OF THE AMERICAN FIGHTER ACES ASSOCIATION", through the exchange of correspondence. I have been impressed with the sincere friendship and appreciation he has shown over the years for America's heroes of the air, the brave aviators who fought America's enemies gallantly in the skies over territories far from home.

Jim Oleson is a true American patriot who highly values the American ideal of freedom. He believes strongly that freedom is not free and should never be taken for granted. Freedom must be defended because it has always been threatened by an endless bombardment from everywhere. He believes that America must be ready to defend this gift of God by all means. We must be ready to fight for, and if necessary, die for it.

In this book, Jim Oleson has written what he believes with great enthusiasm. He illustrates the love, respect and admiration he has for America's fighter Aces who fought America's adversaries in the skies with determination and courage, for one purpose only, to defend America's ideals of freedom.

I am a believer of Jim Oleson's thinking and views on freedom and I believe in America, my adopted country, and for what it stands for.

It is this reason why I admire this dedicated American. I am certain the reader will find this book not only interesting, but also fascinating reading.

ACKNOWLEDGEMENTS

In Their Own Words-True Stories & Adventures of the American Fighter Ace is a tribute to our remarkable and heroic aviators and their fallen comrades.

I wish to give special thanks to Colonel Steve Pisanos for writing the forward for my book and Captain George Chandler and Commander Willis (Bill) Hardy for their help, inspiration and friendship. Also of great help were Robert Miller and Thomas Neale from the Southern and Northern California Friends of the American Fighter Aces, Cheryl Dart, Harold Rubin, Phil Schasker, John Sarkesian and especially Gregg Wagner.

I gratefully acknowledge the information, kindness and encouragement from the following American aces and renowned fighter and test pilots. Without their generosity and help this book would not have been possible.

Maj. William H. Allen, USAAF
Lt(jg) Benjamin C. Amsden, USNR
Col. Clarence E. Anderson, USAAF
Capt. William Y. Anderson, USAAF
Lt Col. Stanley O. Andrews, USAAF
Lt Col. Richard W. Asbury, USAAF
Maj. Richard S. Becker, USAF
Capt. Norman R. Berree, USNR
Lt. Richard Bertelson, USNR
MGen. Frederick C. Blesse, USAF
Lt Col. Wayne K. Blickenstaff, USAAF
Maj. Stephen J. Bonner Jr., USAAF
Cdr. Clarence A. Borley, USN
Lt Col. Lowell K. Brueland, USAAF

Lt Col. Donald S. Bryan, USAAF
Capt. Clinton D. Burdick, USAAF
Capt. Daniel A. Carmichael Jr., USNR
Maj. George Carpenter, USAAF
Capt. Nial K. Castle, USAAF
Col. Dean Caswell, USMCR
Capt. George T. Chandler, USAAF
LtGen. Charles G. Cleveland, USAF
Capt. Robert C. Coats, USNR
Col. Jerry D. Collinsworth, USAAF
Col. Harold E. Comstock, USAAF
Cdr. John T. Crosby, USNR
Albert S. "Scott" Crossfield NACA
Capt. William J. Cullerton, USAAF

Lt Col. Donald M. Cummings, USAAF
Maj. Robert C. Curtis, USAAF
Col. Perry J. Dahl, USAAF
Col. Barrie S. Davis, USAAF
Cdr. Robert H. Davis, USNR
Capt. Michael Dikovitsky, USAAF
Capt. Robert W. Duncan, USN
Lt Col. Roy W. Evans, USAAF
Col. Arthur C. Fiedler Jr., USAAF
Lt Col. Charles R. Fischette, USAAF
Capt. Richard H. Fleischer, USAAF
Col. Cecil G. Foster, USAF
BGen. Frank L. Gailer Jr., USAAF
Maj. Frank L. Gaunt, USAAF
Adm. Noel A.M. Gayler, USN
MGen. Francis R. Gerard, USAAF
Lt Col. Robert J. Goebel, USAAF
Capt. Donald Gordon, USNR
LtGen. Gordon M. Graham, USAAF
Cdr. Lester E. Gray Jr., USNR
Col. Herschel H. Green, USAAF
Capt. Joseph H. Griffin, USAAF
Capt. Clayton K. Gross, USAAF
Capt. Fred E. Gutt, USMC
Lt. Everett C. Hargreaves, USNR
Cdr. Charles H. Haverland Jr., USNR
Col. David L. Hill, USAAF
Cdr. Harry E. Hill, USNR
Lt Col. Frank D. Hurlbut, USAAF
Lt Col. James C. Ince, USAAF
Col. Julius W. Ireland, USMC
F/Ldr. Kenneth A. Jernstedt, AVG
1st Lt. Dale E. Karger, USAAF
Lt. George N. Kirk, USNR

Cdr. Philip L. Kirkwood, USNR
Maj. John A. Kirla, USAAF
Col. Frank W. Klibbe, USAAF
Capt. Kenneth B. Lake, USNR
Capt. Marlow J. Leikness, USAAF
Lt Col. Brooks J. Liles, USAF
Lt Cdr. Elvin L. Lindsay, USNR
Lt Col. Donald S. Lopez, USAAF
Lt Gen. George G. Loving Jr., USAAF
Maj. James F. Low, USAF
Capt. Walter A. Lundin, USNR
Col. Morton D. Magoffin, USAAF
Capt. Thomas E. Maloney, USAAF
BGen. Bruce J. Matheson, USMC
Cdr. William R. Maxwell, USNR
Cdr. Richard H. May, USNR
MGen. Charles M. McCorkle, USAAF
Lt Col. Donald C. McGee, USAAF
Ens. Donald M. McPherson, USNR
Cdr. Hamilton McWhorter III, USNR
Lt Cdr. Norman Mollard Jr., USN
Col. James B. Morehead, USAAF
Lt Col. James M. Morris, USAAF
Capt. Paul C. Murphy Jr., USAAF
Lt Cdr. Robert E. Murray, USNR
Capt. William R. O'Brien, USAAF
Maj. Edwin L. Olander, USMCR
BGen. Robin Olds, USAAF
1st Lt. Paul E. Olson, USAAF
Col. Charles P. O'Sullivan, USAAF
Lt. James L. Pearce, USNR
Lt Col. Sammy A. Pierce, USAAF
Col. Steve N. Pisanos, USAAF
Lt. Tilman E. Pool, USNR
Col. Robert B. Porter, USMCR

Capt. Tony D. Porter, USAAF

Lt. Vincent A. Rieger, USNR

Maj. Alden P. Rigby, USAAF

BGen. Robinson Risner, USAF

Cdr. LeRoy W. Robinson, USNR

Col. Edward F. Roddy, USAAF

Col. Herbert E. Ross, USAAF

BGen. Robert L. Scott Jr., USAAF

BGen. Leslie C. Smith, USAAF

Capt. Richard E. Smith, USAAF

Col. Walter E. Starck, USAAF

Lt(jg) John D. Stokes, USNR

MGen. Donald J. Strait, USAAF

Capt. Robert C. Sutcliffe, USAAF

Col. James B. Tapp, USAAF

Lt Cdr. William P. Thayer, USNR

Lt Col. David F. Thwaites, USAAF

Capt. Harrison B. Tordoff, USAAF

Lt(jg) Franklin W. Troup, USNR

Capt. Stanley W. Vejtasa, USNR

Cdr. Alexander Vraciu, USNR

Maj. Ralph H. Wandry, USAAF

Lt Cdr. Charles E. Watts, USNR

Col. Darrell G. Welch, USAAF

Cdr. Edward G. Wendorf, USNR

Lt Col. William H. Wescott, USAF

Cdr. John M. Wesolowski, USNR

Capt. David C. Wilhelm, USAAF

Capt. Robert P. Winks, USAAF

Capt. Theodore H. Winters Jr., USN

Lt. Earling W. Zaeske, USNR

* Photos used in this book are from the individual aces shown in picture, the National Archieves or the author's personal collection of nearly 4,000 8x10" autographed military aviation photographs and framed prints, letters, documents, signed books, and related memorabilia from over 500 ace pilots. The den in Oleson's home has been transformed into a mini-air museum to honor the American fighter ace. A large portion of the author's extensive collection of nearly 1,100 die-cast military model aircraft is also on display.

INTRODUCTION

This book is a tribute to America's fighter Aces of World War II and Korea. Though many people know of the achievements and accomplishments of the legendary Eddie Rickenbacker, few know or remember much of the other fighter Aces from the First World War. This must never happen to the men I grew up most admiring, the courageous and heroic fighter pilots of World War II and Korea.

As a life long Military Aviation Historian my one burning desire and goal is to share my admiration of America's fighter Aces and their accomplishments.

Even though I entered the writing of this book knowing it would be a daunting and compelling journey, I am driven to acquaint the reader with many of our overlooked and unheralded American Aces. My hope is that both the novice and advanced aviation enthusiast will finish this work with a better understanding of what it took to become an American fighter Ace. The term *ACE* became a common term during World War I by the French to describe experts in aerial warfare. Public morale was at an all time low and a new hero was desperately needed. The brave knight's of the past riding their colorfully clad mounts and displaying their individual coat of arms were replaced by gallant and dashing young aviators with their daring aerial escapades and colorful fighter aircraft.

Thus was born a new breed of hero.

Originally ten victories were required to qualify as an ace. This was later dropped to five and became standardized by most nations to determine the number of "kills" required to achieve Ace status.

In my mind all fighter pilots were 'heroes'. To fly in combat may seem exciting and noble, but it was also extremely dangerous and deadly. All fighter pilots regardless of their personal victory tallies are deserving of great respect and credit for what they endured.

The odds of engaging or even having the opportunity for an aerial victory depend on many factors. Early in the war America had only marginal planes to fight with. The early European Theatre was 'target-rich' for all involved. As the war wore on and German and Japanese resources were diminished, it became hard to find a target to destroy. Many fighter pilots were assigned ground support or strafing missions. My close friend Tony Porter was a prime example of this. He flew P-47 Thunderbolts in Europe and told me "The only enemy combat planes I ever saw were attached to the ground". As the war progressed in the Pacific Theatre our pilots gained experience and received an endless supply of superb and advanced fighter aircraft and their opposition fielded a greatly depleted pilot force. Gone were Japan's highly experienced warriors of China and Pearl Harbor fame. In their place were youthful flyers whose training was at best minimal and in many cases nearly non-existent. Many impressive victory totals were achieved by our fighter pilots during the later stages of the Pacific War. Much the same could be said about the huge victory totals rung up by German pilots on the Eastern Front early in the war fighting the Russians.

Confirmation of an aerial victory usually required visual and sworn statements by fellow pilots or ground personal. Gun cameras were later installed but this method of determination was not always foolproof.

Nearly all combatant countries gave one victory tally for each plane shot down and verified. America adopted the split victory credit giving a fraction to each pilot responsible for an enemy aircraft's destruction. Interesting and odd fractional scores were obtained by some American Aces. USMC Ace Colonel Phil DeLong was credited with 13.166 victories. (You figure the math!)

In France a victory was given to every pilot involved in downing an enemy aircraft.

Germany had very strict rules governing how a downed enemy plane would be credited.

There were no assists or partial kills. One pilot was given each victory claimed. At times it was left up to the individual pilots to work out who would get the credit if more than one person was involved in downing the aircraft.

In Germany, the elite or ace fighter pilots needed to score ten or more victories and were then considered 'experten' or experts in aerial combat.

Regia Aeronautica (Royal Italian Air Force) rules governing victories granted were similar to those in France.

Italian pilots were only given a full share of a victory. Partial or shared kills were granted as a complete victory. As can be imagined, this often led to inflated victory counts for Italian and French flyers.

Russian fighter pilots in World War II could have 'personal' as well as 'shared' victories. This same system of computing kills was later used by the Soviets, North Koreans and Chinese during the Korean War.

In Japan, especially late in the war, downing an enemy bomber was given the status of ten victories over fighter aircraft.

Often the *Bukoshi* (the Japanese equivalent of the Medal of Honor and the Victoria Cross), was given out to each pilot that shot down an American heavy bomber over home soil.

Similarly, German pilots were given four points for downing allied bombers versus a single point for shooting down a single engine aircraft. When forty points were accumulate Luftwaffe pilots were awarded the fabled *Knight's Cross*.

The Allied and Axis countries utilized their best pilots in different ways.

Japanese and German pilots were left on the front lines throughout the war. The only sure way to get out of combat was to be severely wounded or killed. Many Axis Aces ran up huge victory totals for this reason.

The allies had many more aces with less impressive victory records. Aces were often rotated home for publicity reasons or to help teach new recruits how to succeed and survive fighter combat.

QUALITIES OF AN ACE PILOT

It is hard to pinpoint the exact qualities that separate a good and a great fighter pilot. Surely it must consist of a fighting inner spirit and a motivation and determination to survive and succeed at any cost, with a measure of opportunity and luck added to the mix.

Perhaps, eleven victory P-51 Ace **Lt Col. Robert Goebel** said it best: "Not all pilots that flew fighter-type aircraft were fighter pilots.

Some were more interested in trying to live up to the fighter-pilot image than in being a fighter pilot.

I believe that the proper fighter pilot was first and foremost a fighter who happened also to be a pilot.

The aces had the confident air of the hunter, the steely eye. All knew instinctively the right moves to make in a combat situation, anticipating the actions and reactions of their adversaries. All were cool and decisive in action.

They had lightning quick reflexes and aggressively sought out the enemy wherever he could be found. Having these attributes wasn't an act, nor did they come out of a bottle. The ace's instinct and attitude were what General Adolph Galland of the Luftwaffe so eloquently described as the *spirit of attack*. And, of course, luck played a small part, too. Luck took the ace where the action was and assigned him a good machine." Eight victory Ace **MGen. Francis Gerard** further described the necessary attributes of an ace pilot as: "Good eyesight (20/10), athletic ability and guts!"

*   *   *

The following are stories and personal remembrances about and by the Aces themselves. Over 120 patriotic and courageous pilots contributed to this book. These recollections consist of true accounts from their combat careers. Sometimes exciting, sometimes humorous, sometimes tragic, but all are from the heart and gut.

I wish to thank every Ace pilot that I interviewed and received encouraging and informative correspondence from. All have been supportive of my efforts and many have in fact urged me to tell their story. I am proud to be able to do so. This book is my tribute to America's Ace pilots, those that lived to see fame and those who tragically died defending our freedom.

Finally, I wish to share with you the words of renowned ace **Captain William (Bill) Cullerton**, "Thanks for honoring American fighter pilots. Honor me, you honor my fallen comrades. I pray for them every day".

PART I
FIRST PERSON COMBAT
EXPERIENCES OF AMERICAN
FIGHTER ACES

Lt. VINCENT RIEGER
VF-15   F6F Hellcat
5 Victories

<u>NO COWS TODAY</u>

"The date was June 1944, location Marianas Islands-Saipan, Tinian, Guam and Rota a string of islands south to north (similar to the Hawaiian Islands) within reach of Japan by our B-29 bombers.

Navy fighters destroyed all Japanese aircraft. Then the Marines, with Navy support, secured the islands using the airfield on Tinian to base the Air Force B-29 used to bomb Japan. The location of the airfield allowed us to make round trip missions without refueling. Subsequently, the atomic bombs were dropped on Japan ending the war in 1945.

We were routinely flying in and bombing the airfields with 500 pound bombs carried by our Hellcat Navy fighter, in addition to machine gun ammunition. On one mission I and three other pilots flying F6F Hellcats, were sent in to drop napalm incendiary bombs on the Japanese facilities. We were assigned to fly north to the island of Rota. Rota was an R & R facility for

Japanese senior officers and families with rows of small bungalows homes with yards filled with animals and poultry, all without anti-aircraft defense.

Upon arriving, we were able to drop down to low altitude, slow down and observe the facility. There were no humans to be seen but a lot of animals and poultry were running and flying about. It was clear that the people were hiding in their basements after being alerted to our arrival by the sound of the plane engines.

Having six .50 caliber machine guns loaded and nothing to shoot at but houses, we each took a row of bungalows and strafed them. Our mix of shells was 20% tracers, 40% armor piercing shells and 40% incendiaries. The incendiaries set fire to bungalows and we blew the roofs off of four rows of about 20 houses each.

Upon leaving the area to go back to the aircraft carrier, I observed a cow galloping down a dirt road. So, I throttled back, dropped flaps and got the cow in my gun site. Then I fired a short burst from the .50 calibers. Needless to say, the animal somersaulted and dropped to the ground. I joined up with my division and we flew back to the carrier. Not a word was spoken by me or my squadron buddies to the C.O. at the carrier's interrogation, post-mission briefing.

The next day upon being assigned to another mission over Guam and upon boarding my aircraft, I observed a cow painted on the side of my fighter. I taxied up to the catapult for launching and observed all flight deck hands as they attached the cable. They were grinning and giving me a *'thumbs up'* signal and the flight director on the radio said, 'Number 22, no cows today. Save ammo'. That was one credit I was never given or acknowledged by the Navy."

Capt. DAVID C. WILHELM
31 FG   P-51/B Mustang
5 Victories

THE GLYCOL LEAK

"One amusing incident happened over Ploesti when one of our pilots took a leak in his pilot relief tube, got jumped immediately after relieving himself, and during the ensuing chase by the Kraut, the urine from the tube backed up because of inverted flight and spilled all over the windshield. All of a sudden over the radio: 'I've been hit and I have a glycol leak'(radiator fluid). 'Going to have to bail out.' The flight leader told the harried pilot to stay with it. The true reason for the yellow liquid on the windscreen was realized! He returned home totally humiliated."

OUR LEADING ACE

"Pilots differed in their abilities, their aggressiveness, their tactics, their abandonment and their caution in performing their duties. Sam Brown was our leading Ace in the theater who flew for the 309th squadron. He would just dive headlong into a swarm of enemy fighters and usually come out unscathed with kills to his credit. Not long after one of his many victories, he had an engine quit on takeoff and his plane hurtled at 200 mph through trees, but the seat of his plane remained intact even though the plane was junk. I had rushed to the scene in my jeep to find him, only to see the plane's carcass remaining. Apparently, he had escaped and was unhurt. He returned to the squadron headquarters before I did!"

Col. DEAN CASWELL
VMF-221   F4U-1D
7 Victories

AN ILL-FATED ATTEMPT

"Most of our carriers had been at sea and in combat for sixty days or more. Our Corsairs turned in stunning performances against the enemy air forces, many of which were kamikazes. We all suffered from physical fatigue and increasing mental strain. The ever-frequent Kamikaze attacks, with their fighter cover of Zekes and Tonys constituted one of the largest attacks of the period on our carriers and escort force.

My part of the action involving successful air combat occurred around the island of Kikai Shima where Viceroy 15, my flight, was attacking a Japanese airfield. The enemy fighters were taking off and coming up to meet us. Give them credit. They were fighters and not giving up.

The twisting, turning and tight high-G pullouts were thrilling and scary as we chased our opponents at low altitude. I finally used my head and pulled in behind a Zero and was able to get a good lead on his tight turn. All six .50-caliber machine guns were working and began blowing bits and pieces off the Zero. His canopy came back and he attempted to bail out. He did not succeed.

One of the awful sights of combat took place. I am now 50 feet behind him, seeing his ill-fated attempt when he sagged back into his cockpit, minus his head. A sight I have never forgotten as his plane then exploded into many fragments, which I flew through."

MGen. FREDERICK (BOOTS) BLESSE
4 FIW Korea   F-86 Sabre
10 Victories

MY FIRST AERIAL VICTORY

"My first aerial victory pumped a combination of anxiety, thrill, eagerness and maybe even a little fear into me. We spotted two MiG's, higher than we were, that obviously didn't see us. Above 25,000 feet, the MIG-15 had double the f-86's rate of climb and was a little faster, so I tried to cut to the inside and gradually gain on them. I realized there, in that moment of time, I saw him, he saw me and one of us was not going home. The world's most dangerous game had begun.

I was anxious, eager, excited and scared all at once. I'd come all this way to do this single thing, yet I wasn't sure I was prepared. How good was the MiG-15? All I knew was what I had been told. Now I was about to find out for myself. We closed rapidly, me climbing and the MiG turning and diving slightly. We passed within a few hundred yards-our combined speeds about 1,000 miles per hour. I slid in behind him and began shooting into that MiG-15 but nothing happened. No pieces, no fire, no bail out-nothing! He was accelerating away from me and in a second or two was out of gun range and climbing for the Yalu. I was crushed! So close and nothing! I began the painful duty of transferring my thoughts to the business of getting home. Suddenly my wingman shouted: There he goes, Red Lead, he punched out. I whirred around in time to see the MiG in a deep descending spiral and a beautiful white parachute. That MiG pilot made two or three really dumb decisions in our brief encounter. As a result, my first fight left me confident, elated and a little bit shaky."

Col. HERBERT E. ROSS
14 FG   P-38 Lightning
7 Victories

ANOTHER MACCHI 202

"Our standing orders were to stay with the bombers and I think the enemy pilots were aware of this. They knew they could make passes and we would not go after them. My philosophy was simple. Shoot him down today and he could not come back up tomorrow to shoot you down again. I did not like the order, and told General Doolittle after several missions. He would fly over to our strip in his Martin B-26 to listen to the debriefing. He was the 15th Air Force Operations Officer under General Spaatz and Vandenburg. He said both of them were very pleased with the job we were doing protecting them from enemy fighters. Most of the losses were from anti-aircraft ground fire.

We were not shooting down enemy fighters as I thought we should. I wanted permission to go after them. General Doolittle agreed with me and said he had discussed this with both of his bosses. He said their philosophy was: If it works good, don't change it. On this mission not a single enemy fighter got a shot at a bomber, but two of our fighters had been hit. One had been hit on the rudder and the other on the tail boom. The pilots did not know it until we got back on the ground. The bombers had made their run and were headed back home when I spotted a lone Macchi 202. My flight was to the extreme left of the bombers and about a mile behind and this Macchi was directly ahead and about 200 feet higher. All I had to do was pull up behind him in his blind spot, put the piper on him and pull the trigger. It is amazing what four .50 caliber machine guns and one 20 mm cannon can do to an airplane. I must have hit the fuel tanks because the explosion was huge. I had to pull up sharply to miss the pieces and not fly through the fireball. A victory cannot be claimed without verification from another pilot, and usually a wingman or another pilot sees the plane hit the ground or the pilot bail out. All eleven guys behind me saw this one."

Capt. FRED E. GUTT
VMF-223   F4F Wildcat
8 Victories

GREAT MINDS

"I never quite understood the Japanese tactics in coming down from Rabaul on bomb runs against us at Guadalcanal. Their fighters would accompany the bombers allowing us an over head run on the bombers, which essentially broke up their formations and pretty much negated the purpose of their mission. I used to wonder why they didn't send the fighters in about ten or fifteen minutes earlier coming in higher than we could go, get us engaged and give the bombers a free run. Later, when we were making bomb runs on Rabaul, we were doing the same thing. I concluded that the great minds doing the planning all had gone to the same school."

Maj. JOHN KIRLA
357 FG   P-51 Mustang
11.5 Victories

HITLER YOUTH TESTIMONY

"On the day before Christmas 1944 we were escorting B-17's down to Leipzeig Germany and after the bombers dropped their loads they turned and headed back home to England. Out of our three Squadrons, two continued to escort bombers back to England and one Squadron was allowed to go down to look for targets of opportunity. That was ours, the 362nd. We descended down to 22,000 feet and headed east looking for trouble and someone spotted Bogies in the distance. Heading east and slightly above we came into a gaggle of Me-109s and FW-190s.

My wingman Willey Gilbert went into them first and the rest of us followed. There was only sixteen of us and over seventy of the enemy. We lost two of our Mustangs. Willey Gilbert called and said he got two and then was shot down by the last of the Me-109s. He eventually bailed out and ended up in a tree but died there from his injuries. The other pilot was named Mooney and he landed safely and surrendered to a Hitler Youth. He was taken into the nearest town. A German civilian came and tried to take Mooney away but the Hitler Youth refused. The German civilian returned later and shot Mooney in the back of the head and killed him. After the war the Graves Registration Unit came down to the area and interviewed the young Hitler Youth. With his help they found the civilian in Berlin. After a trial that included the Hitler Youth's testimony the German civilian was found guilty of murder and promptly hanged."

BGen. FRANK GAILER JR.
357 FG   P-51 Mustang
5.5 Victories

BLUE NOSES

"I only flew the P-51 in WW II and my observation was that it was at least the equal of the FW-190 and Me-109 because of its speed and turn capability. I feel that because the war was coming to an end and when I was with the 357th (August-November 1944), that we were then matched against far less experienced German pilots-giving us an even greater capability to win the big air to air battles. On 27 November 1944 I downed two FW-190s. I aimed at the element leader's wingman and he flipped over and crashed into his friend. Both exploded and blew up. WOW! Two victories and lots of ammo left. I had lost my own wingman earlier and now had a young lad from the 55th FG latched on to my wing. We started to climb back up from 3,000 feet to around 10,000 feet looking for any enemy stragglers. I saw what looked like two Me109s coming head on and descending towards us. It then appeared to me that their air-scoops were not under their wing but under their fuselage, obviously they were P-51s. Then my engine and canopy were smashed and I saw the two solid blue noses of the 352nd Fighter Group go by. When my prop froze I bailed out at 3,000 feet landing near Kassel Germany (The geographical center of Germany I was told). The story of my bail out is a riot. You'll have to get that another time!"

Cdr. CLARENCE (SPIKE) BORLEY
VF-15   F6F Hellcat
5 Victories

A LIFE RAFT IN A TYPHOON

"My most memorable experience in the Hellcat involved a five day event. After shooting down four Japanese aircraft I was shot down myself. Landing in the water only ½ mile from the Formosa shore, I threw away everything except my life jacket and swam toward the open ocean. About eight hours later one of the Hellcats spotted me and dropped me his life raft. A true hero I was never able to identify. After drifting for two days a typhoon blew in and had me in its grip for the next two days. I traveled from one side of the typhoon thru the eye of the storm and out the other side. On the 5th day one of our submarines accidentally crossed my path and pulled me aboard. I was aboard for a month, participated in the sinking of three enemy ships and was depth bombed three times. When the submarine picked me up I was about 75 miles from where I was shot down. After 60+ years I am still in touch with members of the submarine."

Col. JULIUS (BUCK) IRELAND
VMF-223   F4F Wildcat
5.33 Victories

AN ANONYMOUS SAVIOR

"In WW II I felt very confident when I encountered enemy aircraft because my F4U Corsair could dive faster and I had good armor in the cockpit for protection. It was well known that we could not out maneuver the enemy aircraft so it was best to get above and dive for the target. If we missed we kept diving until clear and then returned to the conflict for another opportunity. The most terrifying moment I had during my combat flying days was the time I was concentrating on firing at an enemy aircraft when I felt a hit on my plane from behind. I am sure that the pilot would have gotten me had a Navy F6F Hellcat not come from nowhere and shot it down. To this day I do not know who the pilot was but I probably owe him my life. After landing at my home base we discovered a large hole in the rear stabilizer and the heel of my boot had been shot off."

Lt Col. DONALD BRYAN
352 FG   P-51 Mustang
13.33 Victories

PINKS AND GREENS

"This is absolutely true and happened to me on 23 December 1944. To start with, it is important to remember that our crews were extremely proud of *THEIR* aircraft and cleaned and polished them so much that you could use them as a mirror. *The Battle of the Bulge* began around the 12th or 13th of December. The Germans were extremely lucky, or had real smart weather forecasters, because the weather closed in and stopped almost all 9th Air Corps ground support. It wasn't until around the 21st or 22nd that the weather opened up to allow support. About December 21st our group was informed that we were to deploy two squadrons to the Belgian air field A-29, at Asch, Belgium. The squadrons were the 487th and my 328th. Ground crews started deployment on the 22nd and the A/C deployed on the 23rd. It was a max effort for both squadrons. We were informed that the deployment was to be strictly that, we were to load up the aircraft with everything the A/C would need as well as things the crews and pilots needed for an extended deployment. The pilots were told to wear dress uniforms and that we should also take along our .45's. On the 23rd, the squadrons started deployment in two sections. Within a minute of starting engines we were re-ordered to fly a mission. We took off and formed up. Earl Abbott shook his wings and aborted. There went all the directions AND our 9th radar codes. We got over Belgium and called 9th radar. It went something like this:

9th radar this is ... Reply: 'Roger, Roger, Roger', then nothing. It went on and on like that until we gave up. To be honest we had no idea where Asch Air Field was, we had been told that the radar would give us directions. *WE WERE NOT ABOUT* to fly back home to Bodney. We milled around awhile until Hank White called, 'Yellow 1 you have two 190s closing from your 6 o'clock, I'll give you break.' Talk about nipping parachutes!!! I could not see a thing. All I could do was get ready. On *BREAK*, we did an 'in place', 180 degree turn. The first I saw of the FW-190 was in my windscreen, I kicked a bit of rudder and fired about five rounds from each gun. Hit in the belly, his canopy came off with the pilot right after it. I called, 'Where's the other one?' My number three said, 'I got him'. I called out, 'Form up'. We did another 180 and we were all in formation. The only problem was getting through the 487th formation's wing tanks that they dropped. We milled around over Belgium for another half hour or so and then lined up to land at an air field that had P-47 fighters parked on it. (It was Cheves, Belgium). After landing they parked me next to a P-47. (I don't think I have ever seen a dirtier one). I filled out the Form One, popped my Bancroft Flightier on and walked up to two 9th Air Force fighter pilots standing by their dirty JUG. They were in their OD's, with muddy boots. I said: HI, WHERE AM I? One of them looked at me, then at my polished P-51 *Little One III*, then at his buddy and then back at me and said: DAMMED 8th AIR CORPS! And walked away.

Talk about being ticked. It's not everyday you get to shoot down an enemy A/C. Then I realized what he was sore about. I never got the chance to tell him that 8th aircraft fighter pilots don't usually fly combat missions in *PINKS AND GREENS!*"

BGen. ROBINSON RISNER
4 FIW Korea   F-86 Sabre
8 Victories

THE BEST MiG PILOT

"My most memorable combat experience happened in Korea in the F-86 Sabre jet. We were flying against the MiG-15. One of the MiG pilots was the best I ever flew against. The MiG-15 flew down a dry river bed so low that he was kicking rocks up denting my plane. At times I was close enough to see the rivets on his airplane. He really gave me a run for my money. After fifteen or twenty minutes I finally shot the pilot down. It took about thirty minutes to reach friendly territory and my home base."

Lt. RICHARD BERTELSON
VF-29   F6F Hellcat
5 Victories

FLASH BACK TO MAUI

"A moment sticks in my mind. I was on CAP about 100 miles off Luzon and saw a Jill scout plane in the distance.

I must have had a faster plane than the rest of my squadron as I caught him first not far from the Philippines.

After the combat I realized I was alone and very low on fuel. I turned around with only my compass to guide me and eventually spotted something on the water far in the distance.

My mind flashed back to Maui practicing carrier landings with Captain Willard Eder, two-time Navy Cross winner and the best pilot I ever flew with. Captain Eder showed us a landing procedure that wasn't in the training manual. We practiced making straight in approaches that he said might save our lives someday.

I was nearly empty of fuel and saw dozens of our ships ahead of me spread out over twenty miles of ocean. It was the most beautiful sight in the world!

Luckily, my beloved USS Cabot (CVL 28) was the closest carrier. I knew I had but one chance to make a straight in approach or end up ditching. Somehow I remembered what we had been taught and made a successful landing."

Maj. EDWIN OLANDER
VMF-214   F4U Corsair
5 Victories

FRANK AND GREG

"My favorite book about the 'BLACK SHEEP' is *Once They Were Eagles* by Frank E. Walton. He was our squadron intelligence officer (and with our squadron medic one of only two non-pilots on the rooster). Actually Frank was the glue which kept the squadron together while Greg Boyington tried to teach us to fight".

Lt. EARLING ZAESKE
VF-2   F6F Hellcat
5 Victories

A VERY UNLUCKY ZERO

"A memory I'll never forget occurred over Iwo Jima. Seven of us (a flight was four planes), so we were two flights less one made up our group that day.

I remember meeting a Zero straight ahead and when all seven of our planes fired he blew up. I thought there would be no way I'd miss the debris, but I did."

MARTHA'S VINEYARD

"I joined VF-2 in mid 1943. We were stationed at Quonset Point in Rhode Island and went out to sea on a high altitude gunnery flight.

I checked my plane prior to takeoff and realized my radio transmitter didn't work.

I decided not to *down* my plane and proceeded to sea with the rest of our four plane flight.

After making several high side gunnery runs at 30,000 feet my engine quit.

I was at the bottom of my run and had no radio to tell my flight leader about my problem. No one saw me going down so I headed back toward land. There were several layers of thick clouds and 25,000 feet later I broke through the lowest layer and to my delight I spotted an island. I decided to ditch close to the island but soon discovered an air strip with a single runway.

I had plenty of altitude to make the runway even though a Hellcat glides slightly better than a rock. My glide plan was good and I touched down within the first quarter of the runway and rolled to a stop very close to the parking area for airplanes. I was told I was at Martha's Vineyard.

The plane mechanics tried to start the engine with a sling as they didn't have the large starting shells that were used on the F6F.

Finally our executive officer flew over from Quonset Point with the necessary shells to start the plane. After about an hour I was finally able to fly back to our home base on one magneto.

We had the early models of the Hellcat and some of the planes didn't have pressurized mags. I later found out that was the reason my engine had quit."

BGen. ROBERT L. SCOTT JR.
23 FG China   P-40 Warhawk
10 Victories

COMMENTS OF AN OLD FIGHTER PILOT

"These are comments of an old *Fighter Pilot* about the planes I have flown.

P-12 "It was yours, it belonged to you"

P-40 "When you got in, it always felt like you've been there before, it always felt the way it should be"

B-17 "A bigger P-40"

P-51 "Same way as the P-40"

Cdr. ROBERT (BOB) MAXWELL
VF-51   F6F Hellcat
7 Victories

SURVIVOR

"Getting into the cockpit of a Grumman F6F Hellcat brings back memories I will never forget.

As a youngster I always wanted to get into the Navy *(Join the Navy and see the world)*, I ended up getting my wish. (Although war was not part of the wish)!

I day dream about my experiences while flying *My Own* F4F and F6F fighter planes some 60 odd years ago.

Today when I see programs titled *SURVIVOR* I do not watch. But I sure know what the word means. I am a very lucky person."

1st Lt. DALE E. KARGER
52 FG   P-51 Mustang
6 Victories

THE BEST YEARS OF MY LIFE

"Our main mission was high altitude bomber escort to penetrate deep into the heart of Germany. I was fortunate to fly with such great guys as Pete Peterson, Bud Anderson, Kit Carson, Chuck Yeager and many other great fighter pilots. My first two shoot downs were FW 190s then I got two Me 109s on two other separate occasions. My crowning glory (becoming an ACE, one of the youngest in WW II), came when I chased and shot down a Me 262 jet propelled craft near Munich in 1945. After that, on different missions, I shot down one more 109 (shared with my flight leader), then on the day of the start of the Rhein crossing I got two more 109s. Also credited with four destroyed on the ground and did some strafing of trains and other misc. vehicles. I was awarded 10 Air Medals, 2 Presidential Unit Citations and the Distinguished Flying Cross. My favorite aircraft of all my flying was the P-51 Mustang.

When the war ended in Europe I had 65 missions completed (295 Combat hours) and was allowed to return to the U.S. with three other pilots from our fighter group. The rest of the group was dispatched to Germany as an occupation force. In spite of the danger involved and sometimes being reasonably scared out of my wits I considered this time as the best years of my life."

DANGLING MY WHEEL

"When taking off on a combat mission we would take off two aircraft at a time, this was called an element of two. We were always completely loaded with ammo and extra drop tanks of gasoline (2 tanks of 108 gallons each) which gave us a total of about 490 gallons.

On this particular mission after I became airborne I tried to raise the landing gear on my ship but only one wheel came up leaving the other one dangling! Not being able to continue with the group formation I proceeded out over the English Channel and dropped both my fuel tanks before returning for a landing. We were not advised to land with full wing tanks because the weight could possibly damage the wings if a hard landing would happen.

Well, I was feeling pretty good right now because I was going to get an extra day off from flying a mission and anyway they usually had a couple spares that would take off to fill in should anyone have a mechanical problem. So, I took my good old time landing and taxied into my parking spot. When I shut it down my crew chief advised that they had another plane ready and waiting for me so that I would not miss any of the day's excitement! There went my extra day off! We usually flew 10 days on and 3 off. I always thought that the guys in the infantry would like to have that kind of schedule.

About this time the whole fighter group was one half to three quarters of an hour ahead of me heading for Germany and my job was to catch them somewhere up around 30,000 feet and along the bomber stream which could be a couple of miles long. You find the long stream of heavy bombers and identify the group you were to escort and then look for your fighters. After I turned around about three or four times I finally passed a flight of four aircraft that was a real surprise. When I saw this flight zip on by with an enemy Me109 leading three P-51s. Not my squadron! Later this was thought to be three captured or repaired P-51s (by the Krauts), led by one of their 109s to mix in with us and observe our combat formation. I did find my squadron but missed the extra day off!"

Capt. THEODORE (HUGH) WINTERS
VF-19   F6F Hellcat
8 Victories

EXPLODING A KAMIKAZE

"The F4U (Corsair) was fast, tough, but hard to maintain (55% availability). The F4F (Wildcat), was inferior to the Zero. The F6F (Hellcat) was the ideal fighter and when we got them the war soon ended in the Pacific.

I mostly recall exploding a Kamikaze about 50 feet ahead of me and returning with chunks of it embedded in my right wing. It was very exciting and gratifying.

We were NOT heroes! We only did what we were thoroughly trained to do by the Navy and got pleasure doing it!"

Col. MORT MAGOFFIN
362 FG   P-47 Thunderbolt
5 Victories

ENEMY BANDITS

"I always flew with my men whenever possible. On April 24th 1944 when I did my 'pre-flight' I noticed my gun sight did not work. Not wanting to abort, I planned to change the globe on the way, which I did, but it still didn't work. I thought we wouldn't see anything anyhow and forgot it.

We completed our escort mission and on the way home some B-24 bombers called for help. They were being attacked by Me109s. I called to my men, 'Anyone who has 185 gallons or more and wants to, follow me.' Turk, my 2nd Cmdr. took the rest home.

Within a few minutes somebody yelled out: Enemy Bandits! Almost immediately several of them were diving through us. I got on the tail of two of them (to my glee), because they were diving towards the ground and nothing could out dive the P-47.

In a moment I switched on my gun sight (forgetting that it didn't work) and approached rapidly.

In my eagerness to catch up to them I dived too fast and overtook one. But I was without a gun sight! What a pickle! As I passed him I smiled and waved at him and he was so startled that he waved back! He steepened his dive and I skidded to avoid overtaking him. I was able to keep behind him and witnessed an unfortunate incident for the German pilot. As he was trying to avoid me he weaved his plane, lost his bearing and ran into a hill and exploded.

I called out to my comrades, 'We are 400 miles in Germany, let's beat it!' The Lord was with us and we could soon see the North Sea as we passed over Belgium. I called Air/Sea Rescue because we were running low on gas. In a little while we crossed the Channel and landed at an English base. They gave us some fuel and away we flew back home."

Capt. RICHARD E. (SNUFFY) SMITH
35 FG   P-38 Lightning
7 Victories

FLYING LOW AND SLOW

"I was always told: Fly low and slow and you won't get hurt. I don't believe it.

I started bumming plane rides when I was a teenager and finally learned to fly in 1941, before my time in the service.

I guess the biggest battle we had was the Bismarck Sea battle. It went on for three days and I was in the air all three days.

Some of the enemy pilots were real good in combat as we did lose some of our own pilots.

I would like to have flown a Zero sometime, it would have been fun. I went from fighters to bombers after I came back to the states. I flew B-24s, B-17s and B-29s, they were all fun to fly."

Maj. LESLIE C. SMITH
56 FG   P-47 Thunderbolt
7 Victories

GABBY

"I have your letter and beautiful photograph of Francis Gabby Gabreski's P-47D, with 28 German Swastikas painted on the side of its fuselage.

He was a fierce, aggressive combat pilot, whose combat film revealed that he didn't just damage an enemy plane and then claim a victory as did some of the pilots I knew. His strategy was whenever possible, to fly up into very close range behind the enemy plane and then, with zero deflection, blow it to pieces. He was the leading Ace in the European Theater during WW II and he certainly deserved that distinction. I was proud to have been his Operations Officer when he was C.O. of the 61st Fighter Squadron.

I was the Ops Officer of the 61st, as mentioned above, and was scheduled to replace Gabby as C.O. of the Squadron, after my first tour of combat, when I returned from a 30 day leave. Gabby ruined the prop on his plane while flying too low strafing an enemy airfield and had to belly land his P-47. He became a prisoner of war and was replaced as C.O. before I returned from my leave."

Cdr. HARRY E. HILL
VF-5   F6F Hellcat
7 Victories

A FOUR PLANE DIVISION

"My most memorable combat flight was at Palau Islands. We were middle cover for the bombers. They hit the target early and were being harassed by numerous Zeros. Our division encountered a four plane Japanese division (a first). My first run was a full deflection overhead one. He blew into a large fireball and quickly turned into a large black cloud.

Each of my division splashed a Zero and my number three man, Nelson, splashed a single as he recovered from his run. The division had nine aerial victories and five more destroyed by strafing at the field, a good score for the day."

Lt. TILMAN E. POOL
VF-17   F6F Hellcat
6 Victories

GIVING HIGH COVER

"We were on a strike mission against Japan's home fleet base when our planes were jumped over Hiroshima. All enemy planes were shot down except a single Frank. It was chased by four Hellcats on the deck. I gave high cover and used my altitude to gain a position to fire when the enemy pulled up at the end of a valley.

This was memorable because its one case where the enemy pilot survived."

Cdr. JOHN (TED) CROSBY
VF-18 and VF-17   F6F Hellcat
5.25 Victories

A LOT OF LUCK

"You needed a lot of luck to get thru the flak and ground fire in combat. No matter how well you could handle your aircraft, when your number was up, it was up. I lucked thru some pretty heavy stuff and made it home.

The Grumman F6F Hellcat was a great airplane. We called it the '*Grumman Iron Works.*' It could take a great beating and still get you home."

Capt. NORMAN BERREE
VF-15   F6F Hellcat
9 Victories

THE TURKEY SHOOT

"I flew most of the Grumman fighters during my career. (F4F, F6F, F7F, F8F and all the F9F series). I ended up my operational flying in the F4D Skyray.

The combat mission that stands out has to be with the initial fighter intercept of the Japs approaching the Marianas Islands-*the Turkey Shoot,* where I got three of my nine victories. The Hellcat's armor plate protection saved my butt."

Lt Col. DONALD S. LOPEZ
23 FG China   P-40 Warhawk
5 Victories

THAT'S WHAT I LOOK LIKE

"One of my biggest thrills in the war occurred almost daily when I took off and flew in formation with the other P-40s. When I watched them bobbing along next to me with the shark mouths I always said: That's what I look like!

We were well indoctrinated into General Chennault's tactics so we did well against enemy fighters.

Our training took place at Landhi Field where we were trained by pilots returning from combat. I instructed there on my way home also."

Capt. MICHAEL DIKOVITSKY
348 FG   P-47 Thunderbolt
5 Victories

CHARLES LINDBERG

"The #3 Thunderbolt assigned to me was flown by Charles Lindberg from Australia to New Guinea when he came to talk to us on how to increase the range of the *'BOLT'*.

What a thrill it was to sit in the same seat as Lindy.

I only flew my #3 on two missions before it was destroyed in a night bombing attack of our air strip. I had my helmet, leather jacket and gun in the cockpit also."

Cdr. JOHN WESOLOWSKI
VF-5   F6F Hellcat
7 Victories

DOUBLE DILBERT AWARD

"On one mission while based on the USS Yorktown in the South Pacific I took off and the winds were blowing in one direction and upon landing were blowing in the opposite direction. Consequently I got a little mixed up, I suppose, and landed on the WRONG carrier (The Ticonderoga), and was awarded a unique award for stupidity, the *'DOUBLE DILBERT'* by my commanding officer.

The whole stunt turned me into a hero with my shipmates however, as the USS Ticonderoga had whisky which the Yorktown did not, and I was able to transport some back with me."

Col. DAVID L. (TEX) HILL
AVG and 23 FG   P-40/P-51
18.25 Victories

CLAIRE CHENNAULT AND THE FLYING TIGERS

"I enjoyed flying both the P-40 and the P-51 very much. Each airplane had it's own strengths and weaknesses, but in the hand's of an experienced pilot most of the weaknesses were minimized.

The Japanese airplanes were generally lighter in construction but were worthy adversaries in a turning dogfight so we avoided this kind of engagement. Our airplanes were much studier, better armed, and could take more combat punishment than those of the Japanese.

Our favorite tactic in both the P-40 and the P-51 was to get higher than our opponents and use our diving speed to press our attack then get out of harm's way to repeat the attack. We developed these tactics based on General Claire Chennault's observations and combat experience in the Chinese Air Force several years before the American Volunteer Group (AVG)/Flying Tigers was organized in 1941. As the war progressed, we continued to use these tactics to great success. By the time the experienced Japanese pilots were slowly being eliminated, and their replacements were not of the same caliber, while our guys were gaining more and more combat experience. Nonetheless, the outcome of any aerial engagement is largely dependent on the individual skills of the pilot and his aggressiveness and situational awareness as much as the capabilities of his airplane. I know in my own personal experience that's what carried me through so many successful combat engagements during the war.

While a member of the Flying Tigers I received credit for 12.25 confirmed victories. Later, I would add six additional confirmed victories to my tally for a total of 18.25 during my two tours of duty in the 23rd Fighter Group. Initially I was Commander of the 75th Fighter Squadron and later was a Group Commander. I consider my time in China, Burma, India Theater as the hallmark of my military career and would gladly do it all over again if that were possible!"

Cdr. ALEXANDER (ALEX) VRACIU
VF-6 and VF-16   F6F Hellcat
19 Victories

SIX JUDYS IN EIGHT MINUTES

"As part of the American task force protecting the Saipan landings, we were expecting an attack by over 400 Japanese carrier planes on the morning of 19 June 1944. I was leader of the second division of a standby group of twelve Hellcats launched by the USS Lexington to supplement the combat air patrol already aloft. The full-power climb was too much for some of our tired engines, so I radioed our predicament to the FDO who ordered my group to orbit at 20,000 feet. A short while later we received a new vector of 265 degrees when the radar screens began to show another large force of enemy planes approaching. Taking that heading led us directly to a rambling mass of over 50 enemy planes 2,000 feet below, portside and closing. This was a fighter pilot's dream.

In the next eight minute tail chase, I was able to splash six Judy dive bombers, chasing the last two right into the task force's AA fire. As I looked around at that point only Hellcats seemed to be remaining in the sky."

NUMBER 19

"Your Hellcat photos are of my Number 19 and depicts nine Jap flags. It was actually my assigned aircraft. Seven of my first nine victories were obtained while in the cockpit of this very plane I flew off the USS Intrepid. (Three Betty's at Kwajalein and four Zeros at Truk).

Hellcat No. 19 is currently in the fighter collection at Duxford, England."

Col. HERSCHEL (HERKY) GREEN
325 FG   P-40/P-47/P-51
18 Victories

ALMOST SEVEN IN ONE DAY

"I liked the P-51D Mustang although the P-47 Thunderbolt was roomier.

The Mustang could turn tighter than the Luftwaffe planes which gave us an advantage in dogfight combat.

The P-47 couldn't turn inside the German fighters, but it went around its larger circle faster than the Germans went around their smaller circle, and therefore you could get far enough around the circle to tighten it for a few seconds, and take the proper lead for a shot.

I especially recall the mission on which I got six victories and turned down a chance for a seventh because I thought I was low on ammunition.

It was ironic because I was using Capt. Bunn Hearn's plane that day because mine was down for maintenance.

Normally I carried 50% of our maximum ammo supply to save weight.

Unknown to me, the plane I was flying had a full load of 800 rounds for each gun (two belts of 400 put together).

When I saw tracers (which normally indicated that our ammo was almost gone), I thought I only had a few rounds left.

After I landed I found out I had more ammunition left then I normally had when I would start a mission."

Cdr. ED (WENDY) WENDORF
VF-16   F6F Hellcat
5.5 Victories

MY ONE HANDED NO FLAP LANDING

"On December 4th 1943. I shot down three Zeros and one Betty bomber before being shot in my left temple. I was hit by four 40mm AA guns which made large holes and also had over 250 20mm shrapnel holes in my fuselage. My F6F Hellcat still brought me back safely.

The 40mm holes knocked out my tail hook rail, my hydraulic system and made me bleed severely. I had to hold my eye with my left hand so I could see the deck and make the approach. I landed using only my right hand. I claim to be the only U.S. Navy pilot to make a one-handed, no flap, no tail hook, no brakes, successful landing on a carrier. I rolled into a cable set up across the deck and nosed up as I stopped. I was happy to have survived.

Accordingly, I loved my Hellcat and think it was the greatest!"

Lt Cdr. ROBERT MURRAY
VF-29   F6F Hellcat
10.333 Victories

<u>MY CRAZY CHECK OUT</u>

"I went into the Navy in July 1942. I flew the F2F Buffalo to Miami Florida after earning my wings at Corpus Christi in September 1943. I then went to Daytona Beach for training in the SBD dive bomber. Orders were cut and I flew to Atlantic City flying the F6F Hellcat.

Before flying the F6F I was told to read the handbook, had a cockpit checkout and was told there's the runway.

Snow drifts were five feet high on each side of the runway. I survived that crazy check out and then went on to serve with VF-29 on board the USS Cabot.

On October 16th we had a good day. We were escorting a crippled cruiser from Formosa. I was one of eight Hellcats that were on Combat Air Patrol. We intercepted about 75 Jap planes. I shot down a twin engine bomber on my first pass, then did a Split-S because of Zeros coming up from behind. Upon coming out of the clouds I found nine Jill Torpedo Bombers on the water heading for a crippled cruiser. I shot one down, and had another one on fire about twenty feet off the water. The Jap pilot stood up in his cockpit and gave me a *Fist*. His plane then hit the water and exploded.

Climbing back for altitude a Zero made a run for me but was firing out of range. I just pulled up behind him and then 'BOOM', he exploded.

Our group of eight Hellcats shot down 26 of that bunch. One of our planes was shot down but the pilot was picked up and rescued."

Maj. RICHARD (DICK) BECKER
4 FIW Korea   F-86 Sabre
5 Victories

THE RIGHT PLACE AT THE RIGHT TIME

"When I joined the 4th FIW I had the pleasure of learning about combat flying from one of the greatest fighter pilots in the Air Force (Vermont Garrison). Gary taught me just about everything I know about flying fighters. He also was an Ace with 10 MiG victories toward the end of the Korean War.

In addition I learned to be aggressive from my Flight Commander Jim Jabara.(Our 1st Ace that finished his tour with 14 victories). I had been in his flight from May 1949 thru May of 1951 when he became an Ace and was sent home. I would never have become an Ace if it had not been for him. He recommended to my C.O. that I take over the flight after he left. This gave me the opportunity to be the leader and shooter instead of a wing man.

I flew on Jim's wing on three of his kills. In addition, during my tour I had great leaders such as Glenn Eagleston and John Meyer as well as Bruce Hinton. I was lucky to fly with this group of men and I always was at the '*right place at the right time*', and only did what I was trained to do. (No great deal), all it required was to be aggressive and have a bit of what I call GUTS. I believe this is what gives people glory and something I think all aces in all wars had."

Col. HAROLD (BUNNY) COMSTOCK
56 FG   P-47 Thunderbolt
5 Victories

MY INTRODUCTION TO CURTIS LeMAY

"This happened sometime in 1943 when the air battles were fairly intense. The 8th Air Force Bomber command under General Eaker was pushing the envelope and scheduled a bombing raid on Posen, Poland.

This was beyond the range of fighter escort. The 56th Group was scheduled to be the last fighter escort they would have and was to be the first fighter

escort to pick them up on their return. We could do this because we had suffi-
cient aircraft and pilots to split the Group. The part of the group that took
them in had the usual German fighter reaction. The second half of the Group
that picked them up coming back from Posen had a great number of Luftwaffe aircraft including FW 190s, Me 109s and Me 110s to deal with. I was in
the second Group that picked the bombers up on their return and subsequently shot down a Me 110 who had a rear gunner.

The battle raged for about a half hour at which time the bombers were
picked up by the other fighter groups that were assigned to escort them home.

Col. Zemke and I shared the same hardstand and after the mission he
stopped me and said there would be a debriefing of the mission the next day. I
attended the debriefing that was being held by a very irate Colonel. He turned
and said, 'where were the fighters?' and I who was a lowly Captain said, 'We
were there sir and we claimed 54.5 aircraft shot down' The Colonel said,
'From now on I want you right out front of the lead box of bombers where I
can see you.' I told the Colonel that we were useless at his airspeed and he
said, 'I don't care!'

Later I told Colonel Zemke that some Colonel named Curtis LeMay
wanted us to fly right in front of the lead bomber and that I had explained we
would be useless in this capacity. Col. Zemke sort of laughed and said, 'Okay
you have the job.'

I had to do this for four or five missions. It required that we weave back and
forth in front of the bombers at a low speed of around 170 mph.

The Germans used to gather all of their airplanes together in a circle out in
front and then they would peel off and hit the bombers head on. As soon as I
saw them peel off I moved my flight of four to the side and watched the German fighters go through.

After five missions like this Colonel Zemke let me off the hook. This was
my introduction to the future Chief Of Staff of the U.S. Air Force Curtis
LeMay. It was one introduction that I have never forgotten."

Lt Col. WILLIAM WESCOTT
51 FIW Korea   F-86 Sabre
5 Victories

THE FEMALE MiG PILOT

"Captain John Heard, Squadron Operations Officer, was given the job of 'wet nursing' me through a local checkout and ten combat missions. My first encounter with the enemy was observing two or three cannon balls going by my canopy while I was flying wing with John. There were two MiGs sitting on our tail at a range of about 600 feet. A hard *break* of about 10 G downward followed by a rolling pull-up shook the MiGs. They missed a great opportunity. It was obvious they didn't know gunnery.

In Korea, my F-86's guns were accurately harmonized with the gun sight, they never jammed or failed to fire. However, at high temperature, after a long burst of about 1.5 seconds, a *cook off* may happen. This will usually occur about five minutes after firing. It is caused by temperature build-up in the gun bay. This can cause the powder in the shell to explode/fire. Most likely the cook-off occurs in one of the two top guns, the one's closest to the pilot's head. The sharp sound of a cook-off, when unexpected, causes a physical reflex action on the part of the pilot.

Credit for one of the first two MiGs I destroyed must go to then Captain Bill Craig. We had served together at Nellis for several years. His flying skill and air discipline allowed me to gain advantage on the MiG and shoot it down.

We had just broken off from a successful attack when I observed a MiG closing on Bill. I told him to *break right*.' This resulted in both of them turning away from me. I stayed in a turn following them for a few seconds then told Bill to *break left*.' This put me in position to close on the enemy fighter and shoot it down. Bill Craig was one of the most dedicated and loyal Air Force officers and pilots I know.

During the engagements just mentioned I had the opportunity to fly alongside a MiG and observe the pilot. The pilot was either dead or seriously wounded, and unconscious. Slumped forward, I thought I could see long hair, such as could be worn by a female. The pilot wore a tan jacket, similar to a parka without a hood.

The dive characteristics of the F-86 were used to great advantage against the MiG since it could attain a higher Mach number than the MiG-15. Also, the MiG could not pull as much G force as the F-86 (about 5.5G). The dive characteristics of the F-86E provided the pilot confidence that he could dive away from a fight and leave the MiG unable to get him. This factor played a major part in the action which resulted in my 5th victory."

Capt. ROBERT C. COATS
VF-18 and VF-17   F6F
9.33 Victories

AFTER ONE MISSION YOU ARE A VETERAN

"In 1939 and 1940 I was like many other young men who wanted to fly for their country. The services provided good and careful training for every one of us before combat.

After one combat mission you are a veteran. Then you just accept it and get better with each mission."

Lt. EVERETT C. HARGREAVES
VF-2   F6F Hellcat
8.5 Victories

THE DAY I GOT FIVE

"I had eight months of combat flying protecting our bombers. I never saw a Jap plane in the air, although I had quite a number of Jap planes set on fire while on strafing runs.

Then on June 24th 1944 we were sent out on a fighter sweep up to Iwo Jima. We ran into an estimated 75 to 85 Jap planes. I shot down five but my gun camera only showed four of them.

I lucked out later in the same day when we had a quick 'scramble' of pilots for another mission. I was able to get one and a probable on this flight for my *ACE IN A DAY!*"

Col. BARRIE S. DAVIS
325 FG   P-51 Mustang
6 Victories

RUDDER LOCK

"Aces did what we were expected (and ordered) to do, plus maybe a little more. Most often the stories we tell are true, except when we are trying to outdo each other in story-telling just as we tried to outdo each other in the air.

Our fighter group first had the *B* and *C* model P-51 with the original style canopy and only four machine guns. The P-51D replaced those models, and we were happy to have six machine guns and a bubble canopy.

When the bubble canopy was placed on the D models, the plane sometimes would suffer a 'rudder lock' if flown in an uncoordinated manner. The P-47 Thunderbolt experienced this problem when it was fitted with the bubble canopy, and the added ventral fin solved that problem. The added fin also solved the 'rudder lock' problems on the Mustangs.

Flying in an uncoordinated manner caused a change in the airflow around the bubble canopy that caused the rudder to go into full left or right position. It was extremely difficult to regain control. Overcoming a rudder lock sometimes required both feet on one rudder pedal. I never experienced a rudder lock in either the Mustang or Thunderbolt, but those who did said it was a terrifying experience.

The WW II mission that is brightest in my mind is the one that earned me the Silver Star. My flight of four P-51 Mustangs had finished our assigned escort mission with plenty of fuel in our tanks, so we decided to protect some crippled bombers on their return trip home. We heard a call for help, looked behind us and saw swarms of German fighters attacking the straggling bombers. One B-24 and one German plane were shot down before we could fly back and go on the attack. In the melee that followed, I shot down two of the enemy fighters and the three others in my flight shot down three more. We lost no more bombers on that mission.

That night Axis Sal spoke on German radio telling how gallant German pilots had fought off swarms of American fighters. Actually, the air battle fought by my flight was the only one experienced by the 15th Air Force Fighter Command on that day."

Lt Col. CHARLES R. FISCHETTE
31 FG   Supermarine Spitfire
5 Victories

A MOST SURPRISED GERMAN PILOT

"The German fighters were no match against our Mk.VIII and Mk.IX Spitfires. To illustrate, I remember an incident related to me about a Me 109 pilot. While attacking a formation of Spitfires he was shot down while pulling up and away from our group. He bailed out and landed safely near our airdrome. During his interrogation he was told that he was shot down by a Spitfire. He answered: No way could a Spitfire Mk 5 shoot him down while climbing away at that altitude. This was his first encounter with a Mk 8 Spitfire. I don't know if he ever had another encounter, probably not, to his relief. The Spitfire Mk 8 was wonderful to fly and tops in air to air combat."

Col. CHARLES O'SULLIVAN
35 FG   P-38 Lightning
5 Victories

ALONE IN THE NEW GUINEA JUNGLE

"I survived for thirty days (alone), in the New Guinea jungle after being shot up by a Jap fighter on September 20, 1943. I made a good *crash* landing with both props feathered.

The good Lord and my guardian angel have been very good to me."

Maj. FRANK L. GAUNT (MD)
18 FG   P-40/P-38
8 Victories

THE ONE THAT DIDN'T COUNT

"After a rough fight over Munda Airport (while still in enemy hands), we found ourselves scattered all over. I found myself over the ocean trying to find any of our squadron on the way home. A single P-40 loomed up ahead so I pulled up beside him to see who it was. 'Doc' Wheadon tried in vain to transmit to me, but to no avail. He then made a gesture toward our rear with a desperate look on his face. He wanted to comment on the rough fight we had just had but I thought he meant some of our boys were in trouble back there. I immediately peeled off and went back to see if I could help. I saw no one anywhere so started to resume my long trip home.

I had began the relaxation movements of loosening seat belts and getting out some water and a cigarette when a lone Jap Zero came screaming down from above me. He put a few holes in my plane before I *'came to'*. We were *'one on one'* and he was no slouch. What followed was the longest and hardest time I ever spent in one battle. One of us had to die and I was determined it wouldn't be me. On a tight, almost stalling turn I raked him and set him on fire. I had to come out of that dangerous turn and dive for airspeed in the opposite direction. By the time I could turn around to take a *'picture'* with my gun cameras he had hit the ocean and was gone. I got a picture of a ripple in the water. He was just one more Zero that I had shot at that day. No fire showed up on the film, so no victory credit!

Unless the gun cameras showed fire, bale-out or a plane crashing, a kill had to be witnessed by another pilot. I felt pretty sure of fourteen but I'm happy to be credited with what I was given. Anyway, who's counting past the *five* needed for *ACE!*"

A "SCARED TO DEATH"
LITTLE COUNTRY KID

"I seldom write much more than my name to most of my 'fans', but your letter brought tears to my poor old eyes! You have to understand, I'm just recently revisiting the war years.

There was no time to think of anything but medical studies which began as soon as I returned from the war. No one ever asked what I did and I never told anyone what I did.

There was that kind of silence in my post-war years. As soon as I graduated medical school I was busy with a rough internship at L.A. County Hospital. This was followed by a successful and busy practice of Plastic and Cosmetic Surgery.

You just think you couldn't do what I did. If you were thrown into it like I was you would have done just as well. I was a *scared to death little country kid!*

A nephew of mine told me: I don't know what I would do if someone was shooting at me. I told him he would do the same thing I did: *SHOOT BACK!*"

Lt Col. JAMES MORRIS
20 FG   P-38 Lightning
7.33 Victories

THE FIERY WAVE

"I was leading the 77th Fighter Squadron on a mission of providing top cover for three combat wings of B-24's bombing the ME 410 Aircraft Assembly Factory.

My squadron consisted of four flights of P-38 aircraft, weaving over the bombers. About a minute after my flight had passed over the bombers from right to left, I spotted a large gaggle (no defined formation) of 40 to 50 ME 410s coming in a shallow descent at 10:00 o'clock to the bombers. They were escorted by numerous Me 109s and FW 190s.

I called for the squadron to drop their external fuel tanks and then did a right diving turn to get on the tail of the ME 410s. To my chagrin, there were three ME 410s providing rear protection for the main force. As I approached to within 100 yards of the first ME 410, who was on the left of the three, it began fishtailing (firing its rearward pointing waist guns from one side then the other). At that same moment I looked out to my left wing position to ensure that my wingman was with me. To my surprise a Me 109 was flying close formation with me. Since he was in no position to attack me, I began firing at the ME 410. Two good bursts of gunfire and the ME 410 went down in flames. At that time my right engine caught fire. I feathered it, compensated for the torque and moved over to my right, perhaps fifty feet to get on the tail of the second ME 410, who also began to fishtail. Two good bursts of gunfire got some fire and a lot of smoke and caused him to fall out of his position. Moving again to my right I got behind the third ME 410, giving it one long burst of gunfire and causing some damage. By that time I realized I had a serious problem. Not only was the right engine ablaze, but also the right internal wing fuel tank had been blown wide open.

Not being able to extinguish the fire, which was now in my cockpit, I blew my canopy, rolled over and exited the aircraft.

I made a free-fall from about 25,000 feet. My clothing was on fire so I spent the next couple of minutes beating out the fire. First my head and shoulders, then my body and last were my legs. As I fell through the void, I noticed the horizon would go one way and then the other. I finally realized that it was me who was tumbling as the result of flailing my arms and legs to extinguish the flames. At approximately 3,000 feet, assured that I was no longer on fire, I pulled the ripcord and minutes later I was on the ground and in the hands of the German army.

An anecdotal incident occurred in 1947, while on a cross-country flight. I landed at Barksdale, Louisiana and was preparing my flight plan to return home when a tall captain (Jim Flagg) came up to me, put his arms around me and kept repeating how brave I was when I bailed out. Finally after several more embraces, I asked him to explain. He said he followed me down, circling around me as I fell in a ball of fire. Every time he looked at me I would wave to him as I fell in flames. At 10,000 feet, he stated he had to break it off and go back up, but that I was still waving as he left. He was completely taken back when I explained to him that I was just beating out the fire and that I had not seen him as he circled, not even once."

Lt Cdr. JAMES D. BILLO
VF-10 and VF-18   F6F
6.25 Victories

SURVIVE AND GET HOME

"I got in the Navy in 1941 to improve my flight capacity. I had flown during school and had a private and a commercial license. To get more experience I enlisted and got into flight training in the summer of 1941. In November I received my wings, commission and a job on December 7th 1941. I was torpedo assigned and the lack of airplanes for required carrier qualification kept me from fleet duty until late in 1942. From then until mid 1944 I did two 9 month carrier tours in fighter squadrons. On each tour we lost about 1/3 of our squadron pilots to enemy fighters, anti-aircraft fire or operational accidents. No matter how it happened it was still a life lost.

Aboard ship we never thought of or discussed things like *get them bastards* or *run up your score*. The main topics for thought and discussion were *survival* and *get home*.

Carrier takeoffs and landings required constant attention but eased a bit with experience. However, accidents continued to happen. My division leader with years of experience was killed when his F4F prop went into high pitch as he was in final approach and he spun in and crashed.

Compared with spending time ashore on Guadalcanal, our carrier duty at least supplied clean drinking water and showers.

In 1946 I participated in an air group dress inspection . I got hauled into the commanding officer's office and given hell for not wearing my medals and decorations on my dress uniform. I explained that I *had no medals* and he was astonished. He knew my service record. As a result he dug thru the lost paperwork and eventually I was awarded a few medals while attending graduate school. Whoopie!

Later in the war medals were handed out for each five combat flights over shark infested water, etc."

Capt. HARRISON TORDOFF
353 FG   P-47/P-51
5 Victories

MY Me 262 JET KILL

"I flew about 85 missions, roughly two-thirds in P-47s and one third in P-51s while based in England and flying over the continent. In all, I was credited with five planes in the air, four Me 109s and one Me 262, and four and a half more on the ground. In summer and fall of 1944, we did lots of ground strafing, trucks and trains mostly in France and the Low Countries. I flew two tours, first from July 1, 1944 to December, 1944 and the second in March and April 1945. We switched from 47s to 51s around October 1, 1944, a quick transition with only a few hours in Mustangs. The switch was made easier by the fact that Mustangs were easy to fly, handling much like the AT-6, also made by North American Aviation.

Probably the most interesting encounter was with the Me 262, a jet. We were escorting bombers at about 24,000 feet over central Germany when I spotted two planes approaching us from the left and way below us. As soon as I saw that they were 262s, I dove vertically about 7,000 feet and leveled out behind them at about 500 yards and at about their airspeed. I saw I would get no closer so opened fire and burnt out my six guns in one long burst, getting a single strike on the left jet engine of one of the 262s. He gradually slowed down with fuel or smoke coming out. As I got closer, his undamaged buddy took off. My guy went to about 3,000 feet, burst into flames, pulled straight up and bailed out. I took lots of footage with my gun camera, but it failed on me and no record resulted. My wing man was behind me and confirmed the kill.

I had finished one tour of duty in a P-47 (named Anne) and a P-51 (named Upupa epops, the scientific name of a European bird noted for its bizarre plumage, weak flight, and untidy testing habits). Even then I was already headed for a career in ornithology.

In my first tour, I shot down three Me 109s and destroyed two more on the ground. When I started my second tour on March 1, 1945, I was assigned a new P-51. I flew it to the end of the war, shooting down an Me 262 and an Me 109, as well as destroying three more (one shared), on the ground. So I became an ace, just barely."

Capt. CLINTON BURDICK
356 FG   P-51 Mustang
5.5 Victories

TAIL-END CHARLIE

"When I arrived in England the 356th Fighter Group was flying the P-47. I had just finished gunnery school in P-47s so I was familiar with the A/C. However our Colonel required that all new pilots go through a series of aerial and ground gunnery tests, and practice formation flying with the squadron. The P-47s carried eight .50 caliber guns. Eventually I flew my first mission.

On a new pilot's first mission he is assigned to be the wingman of the last element. That makes him *'tail-end Charlie'*. At our briefing we were told to adhere to strict radio silence.

We formed up and nearing the Belgian coast at 12,000 feet my engine quit! Since I was the last man, nobody was watching me and I drifted down and behind the squadron. I checked everything to find the cause, but nothing was wrong. Fuel, ignition, etc. were all okay. I was starting to look for a place to land when all of a sudden the engine started again. I climbed to try to catch our squadron but at 12,500 feet my engine quit again. Now I knew what was wrong!!! Supercharger failure! I could fly below 12,000 feet but not any higher.

I took a look at the mission map and decided to go back home across the channel. It was getting late and dark when I got to England and I could not find an airfield. Everything was totally blacked out! I flew south towards London and hoped the British anti-aircraft guns wouldn't shoot me down!

It had been raining in England and I saw a long straight body of water. I hoped it was a wet runway and not a canal. I kept running my engine up and down hoping the noise would attract some attention from someone on the ground.

Fortunately I landed on a hard surface and when I came to a stop a jeep with a machine gun pointed at me pulled up alongside my plane. I was taken to the commanding officer and I explained my exploit of my first mission. The British put me up for the night and called my base for a plane to pick me up.

When I got back to my own base they were in the process of exchanging all our P-47s for P-51s. I flew the rest of my 53 missions in the P-51 Mustang."

Col. JAMES MOREHEAD
24 PG/49 FG and 1 FG
P-40 Warhawk/P-38 Lightning
8 Victories

THE HINGE OF FATE

"I think the most significant event that I participated in was at the stage of World War II that Winston Churchill termed '*The Hinge of Fate.*' This meant that the war was descending into a defeat for the Allies, with Germany closing in on the Baku oil fields of the Crimea, and about ready to cross the Nile and take the Suez Canal and Cairo as well as Egypt, Greece, Turkey and the Dardanelles.

Japan was in almost complete control of the Southwest Pacific having defeated the U.S. in the Philippines with a loss of 140,000 men, and Britain had lost Singapore and 150,000 men.

The U.S. was hanging on to Australia and the last of the Solomons by the skin of her teeth. Its loss would have been a disaster of monumental proportions.

Japan had conquered Indonesia and Timor on Australia's doorstep and had sent scores of raids to soften up Northern Australia. The port of Darwin had been completely evacuated in anticipation of invasion.

An invasion of Australia was a bit risky for Japan being 600 miles from their nearest base. It was difficult for them to maintain a patrolling force of protecting fighters over an invasion force.

Though inferior to the Japanese fighter, sixty five P-40s could devastate the invading ground forces if properly employed.

These left the commander, Admiral Yamamoto with the choice of invading Australia or Guadalcanal. At this point a big raid of 31 heavy bombers and 20 or so Zero fighters was made on Darwin, and I had the good fortune of leading a flight of eight P-40s against them.

We caught the Zeros on a wide swing away from their charges, moved in and shot down eleven. I claimed three bombers destroyed personally. This may have been the deciding factor in the Jap's decision to select the Solomons as their next effort. This decision ended in disaster for the Japanese.

A subsequent attack by my flight of two P-40s upon a flight of three Zeros where I killed a Japanese fighter group commander and another Zero with my wingman accounting for the other, all but terminated the effort against Australia.

This describes the most effective work that I consider I was able to perform for America and the Allies during WW II.

An amusing incident occurred once while leading a flight of four P-40s on a long cross country trip. I had partied heavily the night before and the warm sunlight beaming through the canopy on the long boring flight put me to sleep. I awoke diving straight for the ground. I jerked the plane up as my wingmen scattered in screaming dives trying to follow me. Later, on the ground, they complained rather vociferously."

Lt Col. WAYNE BLICKENSTAFF
353 FG   P-47/P-51
10 Victories

A MOST REMARKABLE LANDING

"From D-Day, it took only eight days to establish the Ninth Air Force solidly in Normandy. This allowed the Eighth fighters to roam farther inland. At the time we were still flying P-47s. Later the group switched to P-51s. I was leading a mission to destroy a bridge at Tours, south of the beachhead deep in France. The flak was intense and as we left, one of the pilots called to say he had been hit and was losing gas.

My wingman and I found him and he was all shot up with the side of his plane covered in oil. I talked him into staying with the plane as long as he could, hoping that we could make it to the beachhead and a friendly field.

He was scared, with good reason, but it helped that we were with him. Finally, with the gas almost gone, we saw an RAF field. We learned later it was the only one. He went right in, but just as he was landing the plane burst into flame. My wingman and I were horrified. Without thinking I dove for the runway telling my wingman to go home and that I was going to land.

As I neared the end of the runway I saw that it was narrow and covered with those metal, lattice-like things they could unroll quickly on any reasonably level surface. Reasonable was the key word. I rode it to the end like I was on a roller coaster, standing on the brakes most of the way. It was made for the short landing run of Spitfires. It had been an impulsive move, and when reality set in I wondered how I would ever get off again.

An English sergeant met me in a jeep and took me to a makeshift hospital a few miles away. Somehow our pilot got out of the burning plane and was okay, so I went back to my airplane.

I taxied out and positioned the plane as close to the end of the runway as I could, lowered the flaps all the way, and pushed the throttle all the way forward holding the brakes. Clouds of dust billowed out behind and the plane began to tremble and bounce around, straining like it knew it was supposed to be in the air and wondering why it wasn't. I held it as long as I could and then let it go. It leaped forward, bounding down the runway, up, down and from side to side like a jack rabbit. At the end of the runway it lifted, balancing precariously on the thin edge of a stall. I was thankful there was no fence.

On the way home I realized I had walked on French soil and that I was the first P-47 to land on and take off from the beachhead."

THE RELIEF TUBE

"The creative geniuses who designed our airplanes thought of everything. Today, however, they would have been crucified for being completely sexist. There was no possible way a female could have used the gadget they dreamed up for us…. *the relief tube.*

It was a long tube that, if you could find it, could be pulled up from somewhere down in the depths of the cockpit. It had a funnel-like end you could place in the proper position and pee into, replace, and continue on your merry way, happy as a clam. The only other requirement was to tell the crew chief that it had been used.

After a previous emotional and painful experience with cramped muscles trying to hold in my urge to go, I decided I would quit trying to play hero and use the tube the next time it became urgent to urinate. As usual, things are never quite as simple as they appear to the designers and engineers.

We were beginning to log six, six and a half, even seven hours on escort missions. That's a long time to be strapped into the small uncomfortable area of a cockpit. The tenseness of being under constant threat and the potential of becoming a statistic didn't help either. With the newer P-51s we could fly to Berlin, scout around for a half hour, and still get home without sweating the gas. I still carry the mental scars of being low on fuel, even in a car without the third dimension of altitude to contend with. On top of that there was the hungry-looking North Sea beneath me!

I was beginning to relax a bit on the way home when I felt the urge. Although still over land, I looked around and it seemed safe enough, so why not use the Tube and enjoy a more pleasant trip the rest of the way?

How naïve I was!

Okay, I thought. Let's make sure I get the plane trimmed. This venture has to be a two handed operation. The Mae West, seat belt and shoulder straps were first. No problem there. Absolute straight and level flight. I wasn't too worried about the flying anyway. I was by myself and a little erratic flying wouldn't matter much.

Not so easy with the G-suit, the flight suit and my regular pants. Who unzips in a sitting position anyway, with all the hills and valleys to overcome? With the concentration on that effort, I naturally sloughed off on the flying. I'd find myself in a dive and have to grab the stick to pull up, or in the opposite direction, I'd suddenly realize I was going up into a stall and have to dump the stick forward, sending me and everything else that was loose, including the map case, up to the top of the canopy. I had no seat belt on to hold me down and in that position I could barely reach the stick. I began to wonder if it was all worth it. It was truly a challenge!

The G-suit was a special problem in itself. It was devised to inflate on those areas around the waist, thighs, and calves according to the amount of G's. The more G's, the more inflation, and of course, any inflation made the zippers nearly impossible to operate. It was a necessity for me to keep the plane level.

But I did finally cope. All that was left was to get into my shorts and attempt to find the reason for going to all that effort to start with, which, as I now discovered, was all shriveled up with the cold.

I discovered too, along the way, that this whole procedure had to be done more or less blind. The oxygen mask and the bulky tube hanging from it kept me from looking down at the angle needed to see what I was doing.

With a big smile of anticipation I finally made what I thought was a workable connection between the two relief tubes and let it go. Once again, though, it was a two handed operation and I couldn't keep the plane level long enough to enjoy it. Any forward pressure on the stick sent me flying up, hitting my head against the canopy along with other debris that was knocked loose. Some picture I made! Squadron leader Blickenstaff stuck to the canopy, pants open, arms flailing about desperately trying to reach the stick and pissing upward all over everything including himself.

I was determined to succeed. Other people seemed to do this. Why couldn't I? It went on and on. Each time I would get everything all lined up and under control, the damn plane would either go into a dive or start climbing. Either way I had to grab the stick and lose my connection. I was constantly having to cut it off. This was worse than changing horses in mid stream. On top of that I had no feeling of relief whatsoever.

Finally I said to hell with it, sat back and let it all go.

After losing a great deal of altitude and being out over the English Channel, I was tempted to leave everything unzipped and unbuckled. I was naturally apprehensive and cautious about my survival in those icy waters so decided to put myself back in some kind of reasonable order. Easier said than done! A little like climbing a mountain—now that I made it up, how do I get down? Zippers were even harder to pull up and all my moving around had dislodged my straps so I had to hunt around to find them.

I finally made it home but I was not happy as a clam. My crew chief was good though. He never mentioned that he couldn't find anything after I told him I had used the Tube."

Lt. GEORGE KIRK
VF-8   F6F Hellcat
7 Victories

<u>TALLYHO</u>

"You have asked me to recall incidents that happened almost 60 years ago. That is not easy. As you get older your memory is less than perfect. In fact, as I think back to the images are like a bunch of photographs that were taken on a long trip and are not related to one another. But I do recall a day early in our campaign.

Fighting Eight was a part of Air Group Eight comprised of fighters, dive bombers, and torpedo bombers and was aboard the aircraft carrier USS Bunker Hill a part of, as I recall, the Seventh Fleet. The Fleet was proceeding towards the islands of Palau for the purpose of destroying the airfields and aircraft and whatever targets of opportunity were presented and to neutralize the island preparatory to landings in the Marianas.

It was late in the afternoon of March 30, 1944, the day before the start of attacks on Palau. Our division was flying Combat Air Patrol. A division was comprised of four aircraft, Division Leader Ron Hoel and his wingman Jack McGuire. I was the Section Leader with a wingman named Tom O'Boyle. At all times from dawn to dusk there were fighter planes circling the fleet to intercept any enemy intruders and to watch the horizons.

We had been in the air about an hour, just peacefully circling the fleet, when we received a call from the Ship's Flight Director that they had a *bogie* on the radar screen. They gave us a vector and directed us to intercept. It was a beautiful day without a cloud and the sky was light blue and the ocean a darker blue as we flew away from the sun. We had been on the vector for about fifteen minutes and about to give up when I spotted a tiny speck on the horizon just above the water. I called a 'tallyho' and the race was on. Each of us were trying to make the first interception. Ron dropped his external belly tank to gain speed and immediately we dropped ours to stay with him. As we raced line abreast we closed enough to identify an enemy bomber we called a 'Betty'. As we came nearer we could see flashes from the tail gunner firing at us. Although we were at extreme range we started lobbing shots at the plane and soon the flashes of return fire stopped. We flew right up to that Betty firing all the way but it kept right on flying just above the waves. As we overtook it, Ron and Jack on the left and Tom and I on the right, had a close up view of the enemy aircraft. The Betty was tan in color and had large red 'meatballs' painted on each wing and its tail. As we were watching the nose of the aircraft it seemed to touch a wave and then broke in half at the wings. A fiery crash resulted that spread debris across the water. As I circled the crash site the orange flames rising from the surface of the dark blue water against the purple sunset sky was a scene that I will never forget.

As we flew back toward the Fleet in the gathering darkness, Ron made the call to the Bunker Hill, 'Splash one Betty.' After many months of intense training, Fighting Squadron Eight had found the war."

Capt. GEORGE CHANDLER
347 FG   P-38 Lightning
5 Victories

A BELATED THANK YOU

"On November 8, 1943, our squadron commander, Hank Lawrence, led his four P-38s off Munda to be part of the aerial cover over Empress Augusta Bay on Bougainville where our troops were landing at the time. My flight of four was delayed by a breakdown of one of the fueling trucks.

I finally got fueled and was perhaps ten minutes behind Hank Lawrence and I could hear the radar fighter controller on the destroyer talking to him and vectoring his flight out to meet a big Japanese strike coming in from the ocean. I arrived at the intercept point a little after Hank had started his attack on a flight of 50 Betty bombers, 50 dive bombers and 150 Zeros.

It was a big rolling, boiling bunch of airplanes over Empress Augusta Bay and in a very short time I found that I was all alone and separated from my flight. I saw two Zeros with bombs hanging underneath, start diving towards our troop ships. I had lots of speed and could easily overtake the diving Zeros but I didn't want to run past and have them shooting at me. It was possible to get very close to the second Zero attack him and then fire at the lead Zero. Pieces of canopy from both enemy fighters were blown to pieces by my gunfire. It was fortunate that Tom Walker, element leader for Hank Lawrence saw both my shot up Zeros hit the water so I was able to get a confirmation.

About 1950, after moving to Pratt, Kansas and trying to get acquainted in business, I was at a country club stag and was seated across the table from a young man who was a life insurance salesman. At that age, the opening question to start a conversation was, 'Where were you in the war?' The life insurance salesman said he was part of the invasion force that invaded Bougainville at Empress Augusta Bay on November 8th 1943. Of course this had me quite interested and I asked him to tell me what he was doing that day. He said that there were two big infantry transports at anchor with maybe a thousand men on the deck of each one and they were climbing down the rope nets into the landing craft before going ashore.

He said he looked up and saw a big air battle overhead and saw two dive bombers headed straight for the two transport ships. 'He said he knew that if those Japanese planes hit their ships with a 500 pound bomb, they would all be dead'. Then he said, 'while I watched, I saw a P-38 come down *like a bat out of Hell*' and shoot both Zeros down. I was so thankful that I wish there would come a chance where I could shake that pilot's hand and thank him for saving my life'.

I responded as I stood up and stuck out my hand, 'You just met him because I was flying that P-38 Lightning!"

MY GOOD FRIEND, JACK ILFREY

"Jack was one of a flight of P-38s flying from England to North Africa with big belly tanks on the airplanes. While off the coast of Portugal one of his tanks came lose and fell off. He knew he did not have enough fuel on board to reach any of our air bases in North Africa.

He put the airplane down for a landing in Portugal and immediately had his plane blocked in. After the P-38 had been refueled, they asked Jack if he would show them how to start the airplane and give instructions on how to fly it.

Jack stayed in the cockpit and said he would be happy to help. The Portuguese Air Force officer sat down on the wing beside him and when the engines were started Jack went to full power and blew the officer off the wing. Jack hurriedly took off and flew back to North Africa.

The Portuguese were outraged at this turn of events and filed a formal complaint with General Eisenhower in England. After a period of time, General Eisenhower responded that he was unable to find the P-38 pilot and the matter was closed."

Capt. NIAL K. CASTLE
49 FG   P-38 Lightning
5 Victories

SHOT BETWEEN THE BOOMS

"There are perhaps a dozen of us 49ers remaining to sit around and tell stories. Our casualties were many and high. The bulk of them due to operational accidents and weather but many we lost in combat too. My survival is due to luck and my score not that impressive overall. During WW II there were about

1,000 Aces produced in the Air Force in all theaters of operations which were world wide. Our successes were of course due only to the devotion and skill of our ground crews who kept us flying. They are the heroes of all our stories.

I can go back to the day of my fist successful combat mission anytime I want. At night I wake up at 2-3 am for an hour or two and I amuse myself by reliving these events. It remains as vivid as if it had happened yesterday. Such searing events embed themselves in your mind. Of course we had our tragic loses. But those you carry as a distant and removed sorrow, but they are remembered too.

This particular day the Japs were landing troops from two destroyers that were beached at Ormac, west side of the Island of Leyte, Philippines. They were facing East on the beach. To the right of them were eight Zeros just circling around in a WW I Lufbery Circle, round and round and round in trailing fashion. They were no more than 200 feet off the water. I saw a P-38 place himself right in the circle with the Zeros. Shortly afterward his plane caught fire and he was forced to bail out. Why he did this is anyone's guess. He landed okay and I heard was later rescued by the Filipinos.

My guns failed and so I pulled up right next to the Japs in formation, very close. The gunners on the prow of the destroyers were shooting 20mm antiaircraft guns and I needed the protection of the Zero. We were only about 300 feet high as we passed just over the front of the Jap ship. As I passed I turned and climbed away from him. When I got out a little and up to about 700 feet the gunner really let loose on me. Looking back I could see the tracers passing right through the center section of the P-38, which has twin booms.

Earlier when I had shot down my first Jap plane, the pilot very bravely crawled out on the left wing and reached into the cockpit to guide his burning plane. He kept it level and heading towards land. I turned and passed over him. I came very close just above his head. He must have had a heck of a scare, thinking I was going to blast him. The thought passed through my mind, but only as a flash knowing that I could never do that. But I had him in my sights well enough. Just before I got to him he jumped off his airplane. Must have thought I was going to hit him again. By this time he was on fire and I did not need to waste any more bullets.

I was so scared that when I got back on the ground my knees were shaking. So much for bravery! I made it into the operations tent nearby but it took me a good half hour to calm down. At 24, which is what I was that day, I guess you just did what you saw needed to be done and what we were trained to do."

Col. ARTHUR FIEDLER JR.
325 FG   P-51 Mustang
8 Victories

IT HAS TO BE EXPERIENCED

"Thanks for the kind words but as I said before, the *'real'* heroes are those that gave their all. The rest of us tried to perform our duty as well as we could.

I recall several 'first' flights. The PT-17, the P-47, the P-51, the T-33, the F-94 and the C-130 all impressed me in one way or another.

In comparing the P-47 and the P-51, I felt that in the P-47, I was astride a spirited stallion. In the P-51, *I was the stallion!* On my first P-51 take-off, I was so immediately at ease with the aircraft that at the end of the runway, I made a steep turn around to my revetment at 50 feet and waved to my ground crew. Stupid, but I was age 20. In air-to-air combat, I would opt for the P-51. In strafing, I would very definitely prefer the P-47. But truthfully, I would prefer not to strafe. Flying through thousands of red and orange balls whipping around in front, behind and over you is not a pleasant experience, especially knowing that for every ball you see there are four you do not see.

All my victories were exhilarating, caused 'gallons' of adrenaline to flow, and resulted in a feeling of proud satisfaction that I had successfully destroyed an enemy aircraft. As a young lad, my heroes were WW I pilots and to emulate them had always been a secret hope of mine.

It is difficult to single out which of my combats; not necessarily a victory, stands out most in my mind. I vividly recall the time I attacked a German Group Commander and his wingman. We battled from about 24,000 feet to the ground where one of them made a mistake and paid the price. Or the time I blew up a Me-109 from 75 feet behind at 400 mph, ten feet above the ground. He attempted unsuccessfully to bail out. It was the first time I had witnessed a man actually die as a result of my action. Oil from the exploding 109 covered my aircraft, and my engine began sputtering. I remember my thoughts at that moment: 'I have just killed a man and the Lord is taking revenge.' But thank God, my engine kept running, and I returned safely to base some 450 miles away. Landing when one could see only out the sides of the canopy was also quite interesting.

I wish it were possible to put into words the range of emotions that one encounters and how rapidly they change during actual combat. As you can see from the above, it is just not possible to verbally explain them fully; it has to be experienced."

A MOST SURREAL SETTING

"There are few words that can adequately describe the pleasure of flying. There was one time when I was flying above an overcast that provided an experience I have never forgotten to this day. It was midnight or thereabouts and the moon was full. Apparently there was some instability in the clouds below and there were many places where weird cloud shapes rose several hundred feet above the overcast. I have never forgotten what a surreal setting this provided and always presumed that if another dimension actually exists, this could be what it might look like."

Maj. RALPH WANDRY
49 FG   P-38/P-47
6 Victories

I'LL COURT MARSHALL YOUR BUTT

"I was not happy to fly a single engine plane when we got the P-47 Thunderbolts. Richard Bong didn't want to fly one either, so he went to General Wurtsmith and told him he wanted to keep his P-38 Lightning. I went in with him. The General told Bong, 'Okay, I'll move you up to the 5th Fighter Command and you can keep your 38.' I stepped up and said, 'Sir, I don't want to fly one of them either!' General Paul 'Squeeze' Wurtsmith replied, 'Wandry, I'll court-marshal your butt if you don't!' (So that's why I had 60 missions in a P-47!)"

42 YEARS LATER

"On March 19, 1944 I led the 9th Squadron on a mission to escort B-24 heavy bombers to attack the Jap base at Wewak, New Guinea. It was a high level attack at 20,000 feet, and as the bombers were making their run on the target, I saw four or five Zeros just taking off before the bombs hit their airfield.

The B-24s finished their bomb run and headed back home. There were no Jap fighters around our altitude, so I radioed the alternate leader to escort the squadron back home while I went to see if I could catch a few of the Jap planes that had just taken off. I figured they would return to land because they thought our raid was over. I circled back to Wewak and flew along the coast to see if I could spot any enemy planes. I was still at 18,000 feet when I saw a flash of sunlight off glass about four miles away and below me.

I planned to dive on them, shoot and then run for home. I counted six planes flying in close formation. As I started down I saw two additional planes join up with them. I waited a few minutes as several more of them joined the flight, and when I counted fourteen in all, I decided that must be all of them and began my dive from out of the sun. They were all in a show echelon formation and very close together. Being alone I decided to see if I could join up with their group and try to fool them! I flew above and to the right behind the last man with my guns set to fire. I made a slow roll like I saw the rest had done and leveled out as if I was ready to join. The last man pulled out to his right and slid back into formation so I could join up with them!

I flew up and instead of dropping into formation I lined up all their cockpits in my sight and started firing from just ten feet away. Because all my guns were in the wings, the first four or five planes were safe. My bullets just went over them on both sides. However, they didn't dare to bank or turn or they would get hit. I ended up hitting the right wing off the 5th or 6th man down the line. I saw another on fire falling away to the left and I shot until I was almost out of ammunition. At this point I dove away and ran for home just above the treetops.

In 1986 an Australian historian told me he found some of the Jap records in the Imperial War Museum and that they lost eight planes and seven pilots that day!

I had gotten credit for only two probable, but later found out that I had become an ace with only fifteen seconds of firing. Our fighters ran out of ammo in that length of time!

My gun cameras only showed white and dark flashes as the film had gotten wet from rain the night before.

Unbelievably it had taken 42 years to find out I was a hero!"

THIS IS EASY

"The day finally came when I got a shot at a zero-and vice versa! We were high cover for a parachute drop mission and just when we were ready to head home someone called, 'Zeros at nine o'clock low-drop tanks!'

I pressed the button that released my tanks and looked around. It was a clear day, and there were plenty of zeros for everybody; in fact, it appeared there would be several left over!

I noticed a lone P-38 below me with three zeros on its tail. I dove to intercept the, and as I was coming from the side, I had to aim ahead of the P-38 to get a split-second shot at the zero closest to him. There was a satisfying flash as the zero burst into flame and plummeted downward. I gave the next one in line a burst and saw my bullets exploding on his engine and canopy. *This is easy'* I thought to myself as I gleefully lined up the third one. Suddenly I remembered to look around, and there at five o'clock high were four sleek zeros diving directly at me! They were almost within range, so all I could do was turn sharply toward them and climb with full power. This quick change of direction upset their calculations, and I hunched down in my armor plated seat as they hurtled past me and downward while I climbed. I peeked over my left shoulder and smiled to myself as I watched first one, then two and three zeros going farther and farther away! Then I remembered the fourth one; I snapped my head around so quickly that I nearly choked myself, and there, directly behind me and coming closer was number four!

I wriggled down a little further behind my armor plate and went to work. My instruments showed me I was 11,000 feet high and climbing 600 feet per minute at 230 mph; I retarded my throttle about 1/16th of an inch so my engines wouldn't blow up, and then I recalled that somewhere I had read that a P-38 could out climb any other plane at 150 miles per hour. Placing my trust in God and the Lockheed Company, I pulled the plane into a steeper climb, and exposing one eye above the armor plate, I saw the zero had begun to stall; its wings were shaking as its guns fired, and as it was quite close, I huddled back down in my seat and did some more thinking. I decided I could clear myself by lowering my flaps (which would cause the plane to rise suddenly), but as I reached for the flap lever there was a terrific explosion and the cockpit filled with smoke. I skidded the plane violently, and glancing over my shoulder, I saw the zero do a snap turn and dive away. I tested the controls, and as everything seemed to be working, headed north to Lae.

When I arrived over Lae I saw two P-38s circling, and we got into formation and returned home to Dobo. I happened to glance down at my right wing, and there, just outside the cockpit, I saw a jagged hole gaping at me! The more I looked at it, the bigger it seemed to get, so I finally forced myself to ignore it. After we landed I rolled down the window and without moving from my seat I could insert my fist into the hole! 'Chris' Christopherson, my crew chief discovered a hole in the right prop (which didn't cheer me any), and he dug several cannon shell fragments out of the wing while repairing it. He turned them over to the intelligence section, and when I tried to get one as a souvenir, they told me, 'That is the best specimen of Jap cannon shell we've obtained to date, so we sent it to Brisbane for them to analyze!"

SPOKESPERSON

"The Ninth was getting pilots transferred from the Seventh and Eighth squadrons in order to maintain pilot strength. These boys had been flying P-40s, and none of these transfers had twin-engine experience. They were checked out in 38s and only had a few hours' practice before we needed them on missions. They were usually assigned to fly number four plane in a flight, so one of them always ended up as 'Tail-end Charlie'-last man of the squadron with nobody to guard his tail. Three of these pilots were lost in combat in short order.

A group of us old wingmen discussed the problem, and we decided to ask Sid Woods, now C.O., to have the new men fly number two position in the flights. We felt this would give them a better chance to survive. I was elected spokesperson, and the next morning I walked into the operations tent and told Sid what we came up with. He leaned back in his chair, took his pipe out of his mouth and said, 'Young man when I want **your** opinion, I'll ask for it!'

'YES, SIR!' I replied, saluted and walked out. The next morning I was assigned Tail-end Charlie, a position which I flew for a great many missions. Eventually Sid must have decided I knew how to fly, because he made me 'his' wingman!"

Capt. ROBERT WINKS
357 FG   P-51 Mustang
5.5 Victories

SILENT ATTACK

"The following concerns my kill of a Me 262 jet fighter. The only reason I escaped from the German flak guns was that I had made the mistake of not turning the fuel selector switch onto the internal fuel tanks, and therefore had no screaming engine noise during my dive from 15,000 feet onto the Me 262, and also during my initial climb back to altitude. I had recovered good altitude by the time I switched onto my internal tanks. Now, I would like to take credit for that 'silent attack strategy', but do not wish to alienate 'He' who must have did it for me."

MEETING GUNTHER RALL

"I attended a breakfast meeting of the Old Bold Pilots at Denny's Restaurant in Oceanside, CA. in September 2004.

I was chosen to sit next to Gunther Rall the legendary German fighter Ace and later the Commander of the German Republic's NATO Air Force. I refused because I didn't feel that I had equal experience, etc., and would not make a good table mate. I was nevertheless pressured into it, and I sat thinking of what Gunther and I really had in common. What was I going to talk to him about? He was a high ranking officer in the Luftwaffe and a Commanding general in the Republic Of Germany's Air Force. I was a Captain in the 357th Fighter Squadron of the 8th USAAF, in England.

The only thing I could figure that we had in common was that both he and I were recognized by our respective Air Forces' as Fighter Aces! Gunther was credited with 275 victories and I was credited with 5.5. I never mentioned the war during that breakfast. In fact, I never mentioned flying either. Gunther Rall is a real gentleman … neither did he!"

Col. WALTER STARCK
352 FG   P-47/P-51
7 Victories

<u>A HAPPY PILOT</u>

"I was leading Crown Prince Blue Flight, a flight of four P-47 Thunderbolts. We had just completed escorting a formation of bombers and were returning to base.

At approximately 1100 hours in the vicinity of Arnheim, Belgium, we spotted a German Messerschmidt 109 attacking a P-47 Thunderbolt. Since we had adequate fuel on board, I decided to head toward the battle and maybe help our plane being attacked. We noted that another Me 109 was attacking a P-47 in the same area. While en-route to the battle scene, I saw the first P-47 catch fire and start to fall from the sky. The victorious German broke off combat and went after the second Thunderbolt.

It was then that I arrived on the scene. I decided to go after the German that had just shot down our aircraft. As I headed for the enemy the pilot broke off his second attack and turned to engage me. We entered a 'Lufbery'at about 25,000 feet. As I looked across the space between our aircraft, I got a strange feeling. Here I am, a young fighter pilot who has never engaged an enemy aircraft in combat, about to take on a most likely seasoned veteran. Am I an idiot? What chances have I in besting that pilot and destroying him? Strange thoughts for the moment. But they had merit.

What were the problems. The Me 109 was a seasoned fighter aircraft, with a very good turning radius. The P-47 was a larger, heavier bird with a more sluggish turning capability. A plus for the Me 109. However, we were at altitude and the P-47 performed far better there than at low altitude. My P-47 would be no match for the 109 when flying in a circle but if I could change our fight into an oval pattern, the P-47 would have a better chance.

If I in addition lowered flaps during the turn and reduced throttle, I would in effect turn square corners and thus reduce my turn radius. It had worked in training and now I would find out if it worked in combat. Such were the thoughts of this neophyte pilot. Around and around went and the textbook tactics taught in training flights paid off. Bit by bit I was able to turn inside the enemy aircraft and sprinkle a few shots onto his wings and fuselage. At one point the enemy aircraft entered into a high speed stall which let me get a bit more inside of him. Now shots were becoming more effective with hits all around his fuselage and wing roots. The 109 started pouring out smoke and white vapor. Soon he stopped evasive action altogether and entered into a steep dive which took him right down to Mother Earth.

I broke off the attack at about 14,000 feet and lost sight of him as I pulled up to rejoin my flight. We cruised on home at 25,000 feet.

Upon returning back to our home base, I found that many pieces of his canopy glass had lodged in my cooling fins and oil cooler of my engine. This was 'a happy pilot', one that had engaged in his first dogfight and claimed his first enemy aircraft destroyed."

Lt. PAUL E. OLSON
359 FG   P-51 Mustang
5 Victories

WHO SAID MIRACLES DON'T HAPPEN

"After D-Day we were primarily assigned to protect the bombers going to or from their target areas. Some times when the missions were fairly close to home, we would leave the bombers in the target area as other groups would escort them back home, and then we would drop down to low level and look for targets of opportunity such as freight trains, trucks, airfields, flak towers, etc. Other times our missions would be to dive bomb or strafe facilities such as pumping stations, ammunition dumps, truck convoys, trains, bridges and other targets that presented themselves.

One mission that was quite memorable was in the Hannover area in northern Germany. We had dropped our bombs on an airfield and some train cars being shuttled around a marshaling yard and pulled into the overcast that was at approximately 1,500 feet. We were all pretty much on our own as we lost track of each other. I dropped down below the clouds to get my bearings and right ahead of me was a truck convoy. I attacked them and got three to blow up. I then pulled back into the clouds to turn toward home while I still had some ammo to protect myself if necessary. As I was gaining some altitude I saw a shadow of a plane ahead and above me. I thought it was one from my squadron so I pulled up beside him with my wingtip almost in his canopy and was surprised to see my buddy was a Me109. I'll never forget the look on his face when he looked toward me with his mouth wide open. He readily flipped over and disappeared. I sort of chuckled thinking about his possible comments to his buddies when he got home. Most of us straggled back to base and mourned the two pilots that didn't make it back.

Another interesting mission was to protect bombers that were to drop supplies to the resistance in the Swiss Alps. The bombers would fly over a high meadow and push the supplies out the bomb doors. The area we were in permitted the bombers to fly close to the ground and drop the supplies and then they would be over a cliff with plenty of sky below them. We circled above them looking for German planes as they had a devastated a previous mission. On one of the passes a man fell out of the bomber to the meadow. My flight did a circle and we saw him slowly get up and move toward a rock formation where some people came out and helped him. *Who said miracles don't happen!*

There was a lot of celebrating when Paris was liberated. Shortly after, we had a mission that brought us close to Paris on our way home. I thought, can you imagine how much fun it would be to fly through the base of the Eiffel Tower? With a P-51 Mustang it's possible!"

GENERAL PATTON

"My last mission was quite special. On December 18 we were at a 32,000 foot altitude escorting the bombers to the Cologne area when I experienced problems controlling the ailerons on my ship. It took almost all my strength to stay with my element leader as we crisscrossed above the bombers. I finally called him and related my problem. He suggested we drop down to a lower altitude to see if the problem would clear up. When we got to about 10,000 feet I found that I could finally gain maneuverability of my P-51.

About five minutes later we found ourselves pulling up behind the biggest group of FW 190s imaginable. We couldn't do anything but aim and shoot like in a shooting gallery. All said and done, with three passes we both got our limit and had to get the hell out of there as the real pilots in that group started getting feisty.

Shortly after breaking off from the FWs we were being targeted by anti-aircraft guns. I took a direct hit. Quickly my cockpit filled with flames. I reached for my seatbelt latch with one hand and the canopy release lever with the other. I got the seatbelt released but before I could reach the canopy lever my plane exploded and ejected me. All of a sudden I found myself flying without an airplane and with my trousers on fire. I beat at the fire until I noticed

Mother Earth getting awfully big and pulled the ripcord. Thank God it opened and I got a good canopy before hitting the ground.

I was captured, patched up and taken to a POW camp until it was bombed by the RAF.

We were marched towards Munich by a few elderly German guards. Food was scarce for both us and our German guards. We woke up the second morning near the Mooseberg camp and noticed our German captures were nowhere to be found. At about 0900 that morning a loud motor noise and the clanking of tank treads got us all out of our makeshift shelters in time to see an American tank entering the camp with General Patton sitting on the front hatch. *AMEN!*"

Lt Cdr. ELVIN (LIN) LINDSAY
VF-19　　　F6F Hellcat
8 Victories

BRING ON YOUR BEST

"On 24 October 1944, I was 24 years old and a skilled Navy fighter pilot stationed on the USS Lexington, a large aircraft carrier. We were operating in the Pacific Ocean near Leyte Island in the Philippine Island group. A huge allied military force had just landed within the past week and the Japanese knew this could not be allowed to happen. They had formulated a special plan which called for four battle groups of battleships, heavy and light cruisers and destroyers to all arrive off Leyte Island at 0600 October 24th. Their goal was to blast the landing of troops and supplies and then completely throw the landing force out of the islands. They also had a carrier force of four attack carriers which included the large carrier Shikaku and the Chitose which had taken part in the attack on Pearl Harbor. The Japanese named this fantastic operation their SHO plan. It could be put into action using many different locations as their main target.

The enemy carriers had been sighted at over 100 miles northeast and Admiral Mitscher opened the throttle of our allied carriers and cruised at high speed all night to close the distance so that our planes could attack the enemy carriers early the next morning.

I had eighteen F6F Hellcat fighters loaded with 500 lb. bombs and a full load of .50 caliber ammunition. We took off at first light and joined up in loose formation on a northerly course. At least 60 other strike aircraft from other carriers took off at the same time heading north. We arrived at 18,000 feet and were surprised to see only three fighters assigned to guard duty for the large enemy battle group below us. The target coordinator assigned us to the Shikaku which by now was turning wildly to avoid the striking planes. Three bombs struck the flight deck and many near misses made the big carrier go dead in the water. The big ship sank in a matter of hours. After the bomb attack which sank three carriers was completed we stayed and strafed gun crews on other ships. This allowed our dive bombers and torpedo carrying aircraft to go about their devastating work. This action brought an end to the offensive actions of the Japanese naval force.

Parts of the SHO plan naval force arrived off Leyte on this same morning and laid down a withering storm of shells that sank a light cruiser, the USS Princeton and some smaller ships. Japanese navy officers misread the protecting navy force thinking it to be much stronger than it actually was. The rest of the SHO force turned around and headed back through the islands to a safer area."

SURPRISE FIGHT OVER CLARK FIELD

"On November 6th 1944 seven of us in F6F-5 Hellcats surprised a flight of fifteen Japs near Clark Field. Their leader tried to get away with his engine smoking badly. He finally bailed out at low altitude and smashed into the only tree in the area of our fight! He almost got me in an overhead full deflection shot. He missed when I skidded violently to spoil his aim. We shot down fourteen of the fifteen Jap fighters without losing a single Hellcat!"

1ˢᵗ Lt. CHARLES (CHICK) CLEVELAND
334 FIS and 4 FIW Korea   F-86 Sabre
5 Victories

<u>A CRACKERJACK PILOT</u>

"Major George Davis, 334ᵗʰ CO and double ace, was shot down by a MiG-15 just before I got there in February 1952. The squadron seemed in shock, the leaders had pulled their horns in, and the whole operation, if killing MiGs was the mission, appeared to be in a state of semi-paralysis. No kidding, we would set up our fighter sweeps along the Chongchon River, about 60 miles southeast of and parallel to the Yalu. Pilots from the other squadrons derisively called us 'The Chongchon Kids'. Boots Blesse, when he became our Operations Officer in May, changed all that. He got permission to stand the squadron down from combat, relieved some flight commanders, and made a couple of new ones. (I was one of the lucky ones). He flew with us personally to impact his skill, knowledge, and most importantly, his aggressive attitude, and directed us to fly training sorties with our flight members until they were ready for the big time. When we resumed combat flying, Boots almost immediately shot down his first MiG, and it electrified the entire squadron. At least it did me, and it validated everything we were doing.

With not much flying by the MiGs in June, about six weeks went by before I got into my first real scrap as a flight leader. On a Sunday late afternoon, after our schedule had been scrubbed all day due to reported bad weather in MiG Alley, I cajoled the Assistant Operations Officer into letting me take a wingman on a 'weather recon' to the Yalu. To my knowledge, we were the only two F-86s in the area. The weather around the river had broken, and there was a scattered to broken deck underneath us and a large thunderstorm just north of the Yalu. We were over the Mizou at about 35,000 feet when Dentist Charlie called a bandit heading southwest over Antung. We dropped our tanks, went 'Buster' and headed southwest. I sighted a lone MiG at about six to eight miles, dead ahead, at our altitude, on a reciprocal heading. Seconds later, we passed about 100 feet apart and turned for each other's tail.

I'll never forget the rush of adrenaline at the sight of that great high tail with the red star, and at the realization that this wasn't practice anymore. I must say I felt very confident as we joined the fight. It was high G, round and round, up and down, about five or six turns, with me gaining a little every time we passed. I finally settled into the six o'clock position, very close. We were down to probably 15,000 feet or so, and much slower than when we first started. Before I could fire, he bunted and throttled back, and I lost sight of him momentarily. I rolled on my back and he was practically underneath me, but with flaps and throttle I was able to get behind him again. He started a right climbing turn, and I pulled lead on him at about 400 to 500 feet range. The A1C gun sight worked to perfection. I put the pipper on his tailpipe and fired a long burst. Immediately strikes appeared along his tailpipe and along the right side of the fuselage up to the canopy area. He did a slow roll to the left and past 90 degrees. The nose went down and he started a leisurely descent, which I took to be a death throes maneuver. My wingman (who I remember as Lt. John Hager), did a great job of staying with me. We followed him down and he disappeared into the thunderstorm at about 3000-4000 feet. I'm positive he didn't make it, but I did not see him crash or bail out. The fight ended up probably five to ten miles north of the river. We found a hole and took a cursory look under the clouds and rain showers to no avail, and then headed home.

Major Dick Ayersman, 334th CO, met us and urged me to claim a kill, but I declined, due to lack of positive proof, and probably my own naivete.

With one confirmed victory in August (the pilot bailed out right in front of me, over the Yellow Sea), the MiG action started to heat up. September was a very busy month, and I got three more confirmed. I also had one probable, which some 48 years later, after a year-long investigation, was upgraded by The American Fighter Aces Association to confirmed status.

On a MiG hunting expedition, Lt. Don Pascoe (who was a crackerjack pilot), and I sighted two MiGs flying a westerly course at about 35,000 feet maybe 10-20 miles north of the Yalu River. We had already dropped our tanks and, after two turns, swung into the six o'clock position, about 1800-2000 feet back. In the ensuing tail chase, it did not appear at first that we were gaining on the MiGs. They did not take evasive action. I fired several bursts at the leader from long range, and Don and I observed hits on the right wing and engine area. There was a flash in his midsection and he started trailing a long stream of smoke, thin but persistent. A fire was burning, even at that altitude with precious little oxygen. We started to gain on him as he started to descend, but Don had alerted me to MiGs pursuing us from a higher altitude. The enemy fighters were gaining when he finally called 'break left'. We went south and down and were apparently not pursued any further.

Don urged me afterward to claim a kill and said he would report 'a big explosion' to confirm it. However, with no other visible evidence, no usable gun camera film, and another attack of the simples, I declined.

Without my knowledge, two members of the Aces Association (Dolph Overton and Boots Blesse), started an investigation in 1999. They identified Don Pascoe as my wingman on 21 September 1952. In response to a query from the Association, Don remembered the action clearly and confirmed, to the unanimous satisfaction of the Victory Confirmation Board, that it indeed was a kill. To say I was pleased is like saying the Lincoln Memorial is *'interesting'*."

MGen. DONALD STRAIT
356 FG   P-47/P-51
13.5 Victories

<u>MERRY CHRISTMAS</u>

"As we at Martlesham were about to greet Kris Kringle for the second year, our thoughts wander back to the snow covered trees and white streets of Montclair, Waterbury, Cumberland, Cranford, Tunkhamock and Brooklyn.

Although we were thousands of miles away from home we all had the Christmas spirit and decorated the Ready Room for the yuletide season. Ed Faison, Bill Hurley, Epley and Hook went out with the jeep and brought back a beautiful Christmas tree, a mile of holly and pine and several very fine holly wreaths. After Bill Hurley constructed a stand for the tree, it was placed in the corner of the Ready Room. Ed Faison, Ray, Campbell, Cope and Baskin were busy placing the holly and the pine along the rafters and over the maps. Holly wreaths were placed in the windows and on the door, and the outside of the building was also trimmed with holly and pine. Some of the boys went to the Red Cross and Helen Meninger graciously gave them colored paper, crepe and a couple of red Christmas bells. The fellows then went to work with the scissors and before long the tree was covered with paper chains and a maze of colors. Toby, Whitson, Wallace, Burdick, Jett, Burden, and Morgan enthusiastically strung the colored crepe paper from rafter to rafter, trimmed the tree, and put the finishing touches to the room. Blackie brought over some chaff and Dock contributed some cotton which Bowers and Carwile scattered on the Christmas tree. Campbell constructed an ingenious candelabra, which, notwithstanding the fact that the candles were empty .50 caliber shells, gave a convincing effect when placed in the Ready Room window. The halos for the candles were made by Ray. Sgt. Forrester and Cope painted ping pong balls and made other novel Christmas ornaments out of whatever scraps they could find. Considering the 'ersatz' nature of the decorations, excepting the greens, they were remarkable for their originality and ingenuity. A table decoration of holly and pine by Cope was a masterpiece of floral arrangement that would have done credit to any professional.

We were called immediately and a teletype was read. We were called again at 0400 hours in the morning, when the field order for a Christmas mission came in. It was a little after 0500 when the crews started to get our planes ready. It was a cold night and it would take some time to get the frost off the ships. At 0530 hours the pilots were awakened and told to wear their 'long johns' and their warm flying togs and to be at the officer's mess by 6 o'clock. After breakfast the pilots were told to get two blankets, their mess kits, canteens and cups, flashlights, some cigarettes and their 45s. At briefing the pilots received K-rations for two days. Our emergency airfield in France designated for the mission was CAMBRAI/NIERGRIES, No. A-74. We had the prospects of spending a very dull Christmas.

Our pilots returned from the mission at 1340 hours and the party started promptly at 1600 hours. Everyone came, the beer flowed freely, the food was enjoyed, traditional Christmas greetings were exchanged, and despite our absence from home and the deprivations of war, it was indeed a *Merry Christmas for all*."

Lt Col. STANLEY ANDREWS
35 FG   P-38 Lightning
6 Victories

FIRST AIR COMBAT OVER NEW GUINEA

"I have had so many combat experiences that are still vivid in my mind that to pick one requires a lot of thought.

My first air combat took place over New Guinea and took place on 27 December 1942. Incidentally, it is this same fight that Dick Bong (leading

American Ace of World War II), got his first two kills. However, he was not in the same flight that I was in that day. He was attached to the 39th Fighter Squadron, 35th Fighter Group; the same squadron that I was in.

On this day I was tail-end Charlie in a flight of four P-38's lead by Lt. Eason. (He was killed a few months later in the Bismarck Sea Battle). We were flying a patrol over Buna, New Guinea. My radio was out so I was just staying with the flight and keeping my eyes open. There were broken clouds over the area at about 15,000 feet. We were cruising in and out of the clouds and underneath them from time to time. I noticed the leader started down through them all of a sudden but since I didn't have a radio that was functioning, I didn't know what was taking place. When I broke out of the clouds, I was looking head-on at a Zero coming at me with a lot of little lights blinking on the wings.

Needless to say, I suddenly got very busy turning on gun switches, pushing the throttles and prop pitches full forward and taking evasive action. I was scanning the sky at this point, clearing my tail, underneath and above, etc. All of those fly specks on my windshield and canopy were turning into Zeros in a hurry.

At this point, I can't remember seeing another P-38. I felt that I was a huge target, very slow and very vulnerable. Time seemed to slow down. After a few unsuccessful passes at an infinite number of Zeros, I got on the tail of one diving toward the water just off the coat of Buna. I had the impression that he never saw me. I gave him a long burst with no apparent damage until I noticed that the stabilizer and rudder were coming apart. I was shooting behind him and almost missed the plane. About that moment, he seemed to lose control and shortly afterward crashed into the sea between the reefs and the shoreline. By this time, I was so far away from the original fight that I couldn't see any planes, ours or theirs! I finally found some other P-38s and joined forces with them for the trip back to home base. I don't think that any of us ever forget our first aerial combat."

Lt Cdr. WILLIAM (PAUL) THAYER
VF-26   F4F Wildcat
6.5 Victories

MY LUCKY RING

"We were flying out of the Russell Islands and down to Australia for some R & R. 54 of us flew back in one big air wing and landed at an emergency field at Munda. There wasn't anything flyable on the field except one brand spanking new F4F Wildcat. It didn't have a pilot and nobody remembered how it got there. I just climbed in and flew it back to the Russell Islands. That abandoned brand new F4F Wildcat will be a mystery that will probably go on without being solved.

The story about my 'lucky ring' has a superstitious character to it. We were asked to help escort a carrier down into the war zone to the south of Guadalcanal. About eight of us flew out to the carrier for about a week. During that time we got into a friendly scuffling match in the ship's ready room like we had a habit of doing. I caught my fraternity ring on one of the chairs and cut a little gash in my ring finger. I took the ring off and put it on my little finger. About that time they hollered 'man your aircraft'. We ran out jumped in our Wildcats and took off. I was leading a division of four planes.

I had a habit of twisting my ring finger around the throttle as we would get into our formation. I started to twist the ring around my finger and realized it wasn't there. It wasn't on my little finger either. We ended up flying back to the Russell Islands and operated out of there for a couple of months. Of our original 54 Wildcats only six had survived. Some were lost in enemy action but most were destroyed due to operational accidents. Fortunately I had one of the surviving airplanes.

When I got shot up in combat I was in another F4F and not my own. We got back to Espiritu Santo and I was standing there in the officer's club when a crew chief came up and said, 'Hey, is this yours?' It was my ring. He had dug it out of the bowels of my Wildcat. I decided that was an omen. My good luck charm. I have worn it ever since that day and I never take it off!"

SINKING A JAPANESE DESTROYER

"I had shot down a Dewoitine D 520 on the Algerian peninsula and never got credit for it. However, I finally got enough victories to become an ace.

During the Philippine invasion we were assigned to the middle carrier group totaling eighteen flattops. There were six carriers in each group. When the Japanese fleet turned around and went back through the Straits I was airborne leading five aircraft. (That was an unusual number to have). On a fighter sweep we ran across a Japanese destroyer and actually sank it. I led our group on a strafing run and raked the entire top deck from the stern to the bow. We killed everything that was on the deck. We made about three runs apiece right at the waterline and when we left it was listing. By the time we got back to our carrier it was reported sunk. We had six .50 caliber machine guns each and they put out a hell of a dense wall of lead. They just demolished almost everything they came up against."

Lt(jg) JOHN STOKES
VF-14   F6F Hellcat
6.5 Victories

FLYING ON INSTRUMENTS

"The Japanese attack on Pearl Harbor was something we had never even thought about. We were a bunch of innocent kids in college. How could Japan do this without first accusing us of being unfair with them! They stirred up a hornet's nest big time!

We were young and tough and proud we were being called upon to save our country!

Before finishing our advanced training flying in the F6F Hellcat, each one of us had to fly on instruments for a final check ride. We used the SNJ airplane, which was equipped with a canvas cockpit sliding cover for the rear seat. The checkout instructor flew in the front seat to observe and prevent any crashes with other aircraft. This was my day under the canvas hood and I had to fly totally by dashboard instruments. I had an altimeter and a speedometer. I also had an instrument to show what the plane was doing. This showed whether you were in a turn, skid or dive. I flew until the instructor told me I did well enough to come out from under my hood. At this point I wanted him to fly us back to the base so I 'wagged' the wings, which meant for him to take over. He apparently thought an updraft shook the plane. I found out later he thought I was flying. The SNJ was trimmed nicely and it was flying all by itself. A plane like this will gradually turn slightly and lose a little altitude and then get into a graveyard spiral. The spiral will wind up tighter, pick up speed and eventually crash. I thought my instructor was viewing the everglades and he thought I was doing the same. When we were within ten feet of the ground, Ensign Bienvenu, my check pilot, grabbed the stick and said, 'Damn it Stokes, you succeeded in scaring the hell out of me!' I came back with the statement, 'I gave the controls to you!' Bienvenu said, 'Oh my God, we could have been killed, *please*, take me back and land this crate!'

This taught us both to double check our communications from that day on."

I CUT THE ZERO IN TWO PIECES

"In combat, I never did have to engage an enemy fighter in a typical contested dogfight. There are several reasons for this. First and foremost we had radar on all our aircraft carriers, so incoming enemy planes were picked up quite a distance from our forces. This gave our pilots an altitude advantage. Most of the time our engagements with the enemy planes were short; we got in the first shot and the fight ended. When there were large numbers of enemy fighter planes, they were escorting their dive-bombers and torpedo bombers and that gave our fighters an additional advantage. A good example of this was the June 19th 'Turkey Shoot' of 1944.

The one time when I thought I might be engaged in a one-on-one dogfight with a Zero fighter was on the first day of General McArthur's Leyte Gulf Invasion. The USS Wasp was in the vicinity of Palau. My Air Group Fourteen was supposed to be replaced by another as we were scheduled to be sent back to the United States on a six-month furlough of rest and recuperation. The Japanese High Command had other plans, so our air group was called back to battle stations.

On October 20th, I was sent out alone to Leyte Gulf to make an aerial photographic mosaic of our invasion forces. Since the invasion covered an area of some ten square miles, I started my runs at the southern beachhead and went out over the gulf winding back and forth, moving north at each turn. After some twenty or thirty minutes I saw a Japanese Zero starting a reconnaissance run where I had begun my first pass. We both were at 11,000 feet, going toward the beach at the same speed. I immediately turned south to challenge the enemy, and could not believe he didn't turn north to meet me. I suppose the Japanese pilot was busy radioing information to his headquarters on the number of our ships, boats and landing craft, for he never turned toward my Hellcat.

When I was at the proper distance I opened fire and instantly cut the Zero into two pieces. The Zero's front sections with the propeller still at full speed, and the pilot still in the canopy, headed straight down, while the tail-end fuselage momentarily stood on its tail and then started down.

A dogfight possibly would have not occurred even if the pilot had turned into my Hellcat. There also existed a chance that we would have shot each other down, but luckily it ended in my favor. After this, I circled back to my original location as best as possible and continued my 'strip' photography. During my time over the landing forces there were no other airplanes around to protect our forces. Had I not been there, I suspect the Zero pilot would have strafed our troop ships after he had finished reporting."

Lt Col. DONALD CUMMINGS
27 FG and 55 FG   A-36/P-51
6.5 Victories

TWO GERMAN JETS IN ONE DAY

"The aerial combat I experienced was late in the war in Europe when I flew out of England. Our combat was usually over quickly. When I was dive bombing and strafing we seldom ran into any enemy aircraft.

I was fortunate to fly many of the fighter planes of World War II. I flew the P-40 and later switched to the A-36 (a P-51A with dive brakes in the wings and two .50 caliber machine guns in the nose). You had to pull handles in the cockpit to load them. They fired through the propeller like on World War I fighters.

With the brakes out you dove straight down at full throttle. A most effective aircraft. We had 150 of them and lost them all too accurate German Ack-Ack in about ten months.

I flew the P-47 Thunderbolt in gunnery training and went to England as a P-47 pilot. Later we transferred to P-51s (A,B,C and finally the D models). We spent the first months of the war escorting B-17 and B-24 bombers over Germany.

Combat was an experience with long periods of routine flying mixed with short episodes of actual aerial combat.

My first contact with a German fighter was over Sicily. We were on a dive-bombing mission and I saw tracers fly by followed by a Me-109. He was so close I could almost reach out and touch the pilot's square shaped goggles! I ended up going around and around with four or five Me-109s until I finally managed to escape.

I missed a chance for a victory or two, but we were supposed to drop bombs not shoot down aircraft.

My only noteworthy action was when I shot down two ME 262 jets on the same day. I used the proper procedure we had been taught on the first one. I caught him trying to land with his wheels and flaps down. The second was a mistake. I saw a 262 leaving the area and took off after him. Being much faster he could have escaped. Instead he made the mistake of turning back toward his base. I was able to quickly turn into him and fire. The jet fighter caught fire and crashed.

Near the end of the war the British invented a fuel additive that increased our engine power and enabled us to use a much higher cylinder head pressure. We went from 62 to 95 inches. This gave us additional speed but also caused a varnish deposit on the fine parts in our engines and often caused them to fail. I lost power at 25,000 feet once over Germany and headed west to try and get to our lines. I was ready to jump when the engine started again.

They cleaned out my Packard-Merlin and gave it to another pilot to fly a mission.

The young, inexperienced pilot who flew my plane also had the engine quit and then later mysteriously re-start. He was so *shook up* that upon landing back at our base, hit the tail on the runway, nosed over and completely destroyed my aircraft."

Lt Col. SAMMY PIERCE
49 FG   P-40/P-38
7 Victories

AUSSIE DOG TAGS

"The day after I joined the 8th Fighter Squadron we were assigned flights ever day before light in the early morning until dark. We flew what ever mission was needed including area defense, escort and cover for bombers, strafing and dive or glide bombing and support for our ground troops.

In the middle of 1943 we were scrambled to intercept a formation of Jap twin engine bombers. Our flight shot down or damaged over half of them and scattered the rest of the formation so that their attack was not possible.

On May 14th my flight intercepted another formation of 24 'Betty' bombers. I was personally credited with one fighter and one bomber destroyed with two more as probable.

On September 16th I was flying in support of a special PT boat operation. We were caught in very bad weather and as my P-40N was not equipped with the necessary instruments to fly in those conditions, I was forced to eventually bail out.

I was near the Aussie ground forces and also the Japanese. I had a very hard time coping with the eight to ten foot Coonia grass where I landed. Every time I moved I would make a noise, and every time I made a noise I was shot at.

After six days I reached a native village and found two recent graves with Aussie dog tags on them.

Eventually I reached a beachhead where I knew the Aussies had control. Though weak, I was at least finally safe. My recovery took many months and surgery to correct my injuries.

Our Fighter Group, the 49th was the highest scoring group in the Pacific and is still active and has flown in every scrap since World War II. In addition to being the highest scoring group we also had the top two scoring pilots, Dick Bong with forty and Tom McGuire with 38.

The last plane I shot down McGuire was also trying to get. I didn't know he was close to catching Dick Bong until much later. When we got back Tom gave me a dissertation on my heritage. Finally he got up close to me and said, 'Sammy Pierce, its yours you little bastard, but it was a good shot!' Tom was killed not more than a month later trying to get his 39th victory. Tom McGuire helped start the 475th Fighter Group when it split from the 49th. However, Tom was always a 49er!"

Capt. STANLEY (SWEDE) VEJTASA
VF-5 and VF-10   SBD/F4F
10.25 Victories

TERRIFIC LADS

"I am thankful to have had a part in our aviation history and survived the odds. In something over 33 years of service in three wars I can recall some very busy times.

Interestingly, Korea was the tough one. We operated from our carriers during typhoons. It was bitter cold with ice and also high winds. I often think of our boys on the open flight deck under such pressure. They were terrific lads!

During the many meetings I am invited to, World War II action is the item of interest and I am pleased to be able to contribute a bit. The action is vivid and real, especially the air action. Aviation was relatively new and the aircraft carrier was still in question as a weapon of war. We were so fortunate to have a few such vessels. We had the Lexington and Saratoga (converted battle cruisers), the Ranger, which was our first carrier from the keel up. We also had the Yorktown and Enterprise which represented our most modern developments. I was fortunate to spend my early days in the fleet on all these vessels flying dive bombers and fighters.

My wartime action was mostly on the USS Yorktown (CV-5), USS Enterprise (CV-6), the USS Essex (CV-9), and the USS Wasp.

The Yorktown was lost at Midway and the Wasp was torpedoed and sunk in the South Pacific."

Lt Col. ROY W. EVANS
4 & 359 FG   Spit./P-47/P-51
6 Victories

BELLY TANKS CHANGED THE WAR

"The first P-47 Thunderbolt's we used had four .50 caliber machine guns in each wing. The 4th FG left the two outboard guns off so we could carry more ammunition. When we started using 'belly tanks' we had more escort time and found ourselves running out of ammo. That's the reason we left the two outboard guns off so we could carry more ammunition per gun.

With the eight guns we carried 250 rounds per gun. This was about twenty seconds of fire power. With six guns we carried 300 rounds per gun and that made about 25 to 30 seconds of firing time.

Ammo was so critical that I had the tracers removed from the front end of each belt. Only the last 25 shots had the tracers left in. When the tracers showed up while we were shooting I would stop. This allowed me a little more ammunition for self protection on my way home from deep in Germany.

Our crew chiefs used to gather on the revetment to watch our returning planes. When the guns are fired the patches over the barrels are blown off. Then the guns make a peculiar whistling sound. This made for much jubilation and sorrow among the crew chiefs.

The 4th Fighter Group was the first fighters to use 'belly tanks' in the E.T.O. during World War II. I was the first pilot to install these tanks and to put in a report about their use. The tanks were carried on bomb shackles. This was quite a story in its self as until this time the Germans paid very little attention to our fighters.

After a rest in the United States I returned to England and was made Deputy C.O. of the 359th FG.

I was leading the 359th when I went down while leading a mission to Dresden. When I was a P.O.W. all my time was spent in a German hospital. I was finally released by one of General George Patton's reconnaissance spear heads."

Capt. DONALD (FLASH) GORDON
VF-10   F4F Wildcat/F6F Hellcat
5 Victories

REAL-REAL AIRCRAFT

"I got into interested in flying in 1940 while attending a community college in Kansas.

The government was interested in more pilots so we were allowed up to sixty hours of free flying time. I soloed in a thirty horsepower Piper Cub.

In July 1941 I moved in with the Navy at Jacksonville Florida for more controlled training in the N3N, OS2U and PT 12.

We were now ready for the 'real-real' aircraft! I had my start on the SNJ (I wished I had one), F3F-2 and the Brewster Buffalo.

When I received my wings in March 1942 it was not an impressive change to transition to the F4F Wildcat. Our ego in the Wildcat was deflated by the enormous buildup about the attributes of the Zero.

With six guns, a reliable engine and survivable airframe I was comfortable in the F4F. Of course, I never engaged a Zero during my deployment of August 1942 to May 1943.

In July 1943 we received new Hellcats at Sand Point in Seattle Washington. Still, I was only impressed because I wasn't in the Wildcat. I hardly noticed that the Hellcat was quieter, much faster, more agile and a better gun platform. The F6F also climbed higher.

Our transition from one plane to another was not too noteworthy because we gradually stepped up into higher performance.

It will not show up in the 'kill' records but I shot down three Kates and two Bettys. (I didn't get credit for the Bettys).

I think if I had been in the F6F Hellcat at that time I would have had three Kates and several more Bettys.

I had to chase five Kates so long in my Wildcat that three survived to sink the USS Hornet on October 26, 1942. It took so long to close the range on eleven Bettys with my F4F that five survived to sink the USS Chicago on January 29, 1943.

After the war I was really ready to fly the F8F Bearcat. It was the best propeller driven plane to fly!"

Cdr. LeROY (ROBBY) ROBINSON
VF-2   F6F Hellcat
5 Victories

SIX-GUNS AND THE TEXAS LASSO KID

"The six shot .38 caliber revolver was worn under the throttle arm of 1944 U.S. Navy carrier pilots.

Pilots were told not to be captured. They sat on their parachutes and their backpacks contained all manor of survival gear including food, morphine, and believe it or not, a lasso! The purpose of the lasso was to throw over the periscope of a possible rescue submarine.

The submarine could and often did operate at periscope depth. Our fighter pilots thought the lasso idea was frivolous. However, it was definitely a good idea!

Ensign Red Brandt was knocked down by a 'five inch' anti-aircraft burst over Guam. He parachuted from his Hellcat at about 11,000 feet over the island and luckily drifted off shore but still within range of spastic gun fire. He was being shot at when fellow pilots dropped him a raft. He had been in a Mae West jacket up to this time but at least he was in fairly deep water.

A circling Hellcat helped divert enemy attention when a submarine came to him at periscope depth. He lassoed the periscope and was pulled out far enough so the sub could safely surface and pick him up!!!

As was the custom, Red gave the sub commander his .38 caliber six gun. Brandt of course was forever known as the *'Texas Lasso Kid'*.

The sub commander had a nice collection of six-guns. Red met several pilot friends aboard but his arrival was the only cowboy style rescue! The six-gun was a token price for a boat ride.

I carry a lariat in my pick-up truck today just in case I get shot down!"

W/Man JOHN (DICK) ROSSI
AVG "Flying Tigers"   P-40
6 Victories

BANDITS

"Since our group of pilots were the last to arrive, we were way behind the first arrivals. They had already had months of lectures from Chennault and many hours of indoctrination in the P-40, plus gunnery, formation and dog fighting practice.

Many things happened before our arrival including a couple of fatal accidents, resignations, and various training accidents, resulting in the loss of quite a few of our P-40s. The first few of our group to get P-40 flight time managed to have a couple more accidents. Chennault was upset about this and cancelled P-40 checkouts for new arrivals until they had an indoctrination flight in our BT-9.

Our P-40 cockpit checkout and instructions came from an ex-Navy pilot, Edgar Goyette. One of my main motivations for joining the AVG was to get into combat type planes. The P-40 definitely fulfilled that desire. It required full attention to keep it under control.

The RAF squadrons at Mingaladon Airdrome in Rangoon had Brewster Buffalo aircraft. Many of our Navy types thought these would perform better that the P-40 Tomahawks. Chennault thought differently and so arranged for the RAF to send up a pilot in a Buffalo and have him dogfight with one of our P-40s. RAF Squadron Leader Brandt flew the Buffalo. He was an Ace from the Battle of Britain and we were quite in awe of him. Erik Schilling flew our Tomahawk and soundly defeated the Buffalo. That was a real morale booster for us.

The Sunday edition of the *'Times of India'* carried a color photo in its magazine section of an RAF plane in North Africa with the shark mouth painted on it. It was an instantaneous hit with our whole group and within days all our planes were adorned with it. It fit the P-40 perfectly."

ENS. DONALD McPHERSON
VF-83   F6F Hellcat
5 Victories

FLYING COVER FOR BATTLESHIP MISSOURI OVER TOKYO BAY

"On December 18, 1944 we were put aboard a seaplane tender bound for Pearl Harbor. On arrival we were housed in a barracks on Christmas Eve on Ford Island for the night. The next morning we could look out the bunk room window and see Battleship USS Arizona, whose superstructure was sticking out of the water where she had been sunk.

In March 1945 our Air Group #83 boarded what would be our home until the end of the war, the first of the large carriers built during World War II, USS Essex. On the first evening aboard, two Japanese bombers made a Kamikaze run on the fleet as it lay at anchor. One of the planes overshot his approach and clipped the radar mast of our ship and crashed on the island nearby. The other bomber crashed into the carrier USS Hancock.

Our first combat tour of duty began with support missions on Iwo Jima. We dive bombed, strafed and made rocket attacks on the many islands around Okinawa. The next eight months would find us on sorties over the Philippines, Okinawa, and all of the Japanese home islands. We also supported the invasion of Okinawa.

After flying combat air patrol over the fleet to furnish a protection umbrella for the ships, my first taste of attacking the enemy happened on March 19, 1945 as we departed before dawn on a 300 mile mission to hit Nittigahara airdrome at daybreak.

Most of the fighters were carrying high-velocity aerial rockets. We also were carrying belly tanks to have enough fuel for the long round trip.

When we approached the Japanese airfield we were positioned to make diving attacks from inland toward the ocean. Air born aircraft were our primary concern, but seeing none, we proceeded to destroy parked aircraft and hangers. As I entered my diving attack, I spotted a large twin engine bomber that I lined up on strafed and destroyed with machine gun fire and rockets. I saw it explode and started to climb when my engine quit! In the excitement of my first combat mission, I had neglected to switch to a wing tank and the fuel pump could not pump enough fuel to the engine against the G-forces.

I was able to start the engine and could see tracer bullets impacting my Hellcat. Fumes from the engine stalling had filled the cockpit so I rolled the hatch back to clear the air and had my flight helmet and radio earphones fly outside.

On the return to the carrier my Hellcat didn't perform normally but by making trim tab adjustments I was able to land back aboard the Essex. We found that an anti-aircraft shell had gone through the fuselage about a foot behind my back and had severed a cable that controlled part of the tail surface.

From March through June our air group flew 6,500 sorties from the deck of the Essex, totaling more than 24,000 hours in the air. We often flew four missions per day. Our fighter group alone was credited with destroying 220 Japanese planes in the air and many on the ground. We were also responsible for destroying much of the Navy fleet the Japanese had left.

The biggest day of aerial combat was April 6, 1945 as the air group fighters shot down 69 planes that were sent on a kamikaze effort to counter the invasion of Okinawa. VF-83 alone accounted for 38 of those aerial victories.

My first opportunity happened on that day as 'Wonder-5' division was assigned the duty to attack an airfield on the island of Kikai Shima, off a distance from Okinawa. After doing great damage to the Japanese airfield with our rockets, we were proceeding back toward our aircraft carrier at about 1,200 feet when I spotted two Aichi D3A 'Val' dive bombers approaching on a converging course low over the ocean. I was fortunate that I still had my machine guns off safety as I only had time to nose my plane down and get in one burst on the lead plane. I saw the pilot slump in the cockpit and his plane dove into the ocean. I immediately did a wing over to see what happened to the second 'Val' and it was racing toward the island air strip to land. I applied full power to my Hellcat and was just about ready to pull the trigger when my division leader said to break off our attack as we were being shot at from the ground. As I was already in the act of shooting I strafed the 'Val' until I saw it catch fire. I had to do some violent maneuvering to get away from there in one piece!

On May 5, 1945 the Japanese were planning an all-out raid on the invasion fleet in a last ditch attempt to stop our invasion. They sent a vast amount of planes as suicide aircraft and our fighters shot down over 100 of them in an hour's frantic attack.

I reached 'Ace' status that day by shooting down three Kawanishi E7K float planes.

The remaining months of the war were spent on supporting the ground troops on Okinawa and attacking air fields, ship yards, factories and trains.

After the U.S. dropped the Atomic bombs we had a cease fire. We were ordered to fly low level flights over some of the cities in Japan where prisoner-of—war camps were located. We were to chart them so the allied prisoners could be quickly found and released. We dropped parachute packets to them with candy, cigarettes, snacks, etc. plus leaflets informing them that the signing of the armistice would take place very soon and they would be set free.

Our last flights were to fly cover for the signing of the surrender papers aboard the Battleship USS Missouri in Tokyo Bay!!!"

Col. PERRY J. DAHL
475 FG   P-38 Lightning
9 Victories

THE ZERO WILL HAVE YOU FOR LUNCH

"The year was 1943 on a beautiful November day and WWII was in full swing. As a Second Lieutenant with only a few combat missions under my belt I was assigned as tail end Charlie for a mission to Lae, New Guinea .The mission was led by the 432nd Fighter Squadron commander code named *Clover*.

Upon reaching our target area you could see the build up of cumulus clouds that seemed to inevitably form over the land areas. Somebody in the flight of 18 aircraft sighted bogies and called them out to Clover red leader and he began an immediate climb trading airspeed for altitude. This was a truly bad decision when you are amongst Japanese Zeros. If you get caught in a P-38 by a Zero when you are below 200 knots or so *'he will have you for lunch'*. No way you can turn with them and your only salvation is to dive and hope you can generate enough airspeed to separate yourself from him and then come back at him from an angle of your choosing.

As tail end Charlie I was down to just about stalling speed when bandits were sighted and lead called 'drop tanks'. Due to my inexperience I failed to select internal tanks before hitting the jettison tank button and as the tanks separated from my aircraft, both engines quit. It took but a micro second to realize my error, switch to internal tanks and get both engines going again. I had to dive sharply to prevent stalling and I became separated from the flight. I called Clover Red Leader and told him I had experienced troubles and though I was now okay, I had lost sight of the formation. He advised me to head for home. Along the way I spotted a flight of 'Betty' bombers about to make a pass on the runway at Lae. I started towards them and was so concentrated on watching them that I failed to see a Zero diving down at my 3 o'clock. The flashing of his guns were caught in my peripheral vision. I mean this guy was all but in the cockpit with me. The only action I could take was to roll the aircraft and dive for the deck. He poured a lot of rounds into my right engine, but better that than me. Many coolant lines were severed and as I looked up into the rear view mirror all I could see was what appeared to be white smoke trailing behind my P-38. Actually it was the hot coolant leaking out. I was able to out run the Zero with both engines still running.

Eventually I had to shut down my shot up right engine because it was overheating from lack of coolant. So here I was flying serenely homeward with one engine out but otherwise certainly sound enough. Unless I was jumped again I had little chance of not making it home. There were no Japanese bases along the journey home and another Lightning pulled up on my right wing as an escort.

Finally I called Buna tower for a DF steer, gave them a long count and received a new heading towards our field. I made a long approach, threw down my landing gear and greased my wounded machine down onto the PSP runway. It was important to make a single engine landing on the first try. To attempt a go around on one engine for another approach was definitely not recommended. I could fly straight and level and even climb a little, but with my speed down and wheels extended, a badly judged landing would result in buying the 'proverbial farm'. We already had a burned spot on the side of a hill just off the runway where somebody had already tried that maneuver. I wasn't about to make that mistake. This experience was another tribute to the twin engine P-38. If I had been flying a single engine bird all of those slugs would have gone into the cockpit rather than the engine. It was a nice feeling to know you have those two mills and that one could always bring you home if needed."

Lt Col. RICHARD ASBURY
363 & 354 FG   P-51 Mustang
5 Victories

FIGHTER SWEEP MISSION JULY 18, 1944

"As I lifted off the grass runway at Maupertus near Cherbourg around 0900 July 18, 1944, I was closing in on 200 hours of combat flying time and this was my 51st mission.

The bulk of the previous missions were bomber escort. Our Group and Squadron leaders ruled with an iron hand and demanded that we stay with the bombers at all costs. I had seen enemy aircraft on numerous occasions but could not engage because of the *'stay with the bombers'* theory. I had been in a couple of scrapes, but only had half of a kill, (shared with Jimmy Jabara), to my credit. Most of my other missions were dive bombing attacks.

It was a rather a dreary morning with fairly low broken overcast layered above with a promise of better weather as we traveled East.

I was always in 'D' flight even on my second tour with the 354th Fighter Group. Our flight of four planes proceeded southwest and climbed to approximately 7,500 to 8,500 feet before leveling off. On the way up we encountered some P-47 Thunderbolts to the north of us. Very soon after leveling off came an excited call of *'Break'* by one of our pilots.

At this time I saw perhaps twelve or more Me109s close behind us and starting to attack. They were close enough for me to see puffs of smoke coming off their guns. I broke to the left with my wingman. A melee followed with everyone going around and around, up and down and then repeating these maneuvers over and over. Everyone, friend and foe alike, had an enemy on his tail. More enemy aircraft joined the fight from somewhere. I don't know how many this totaled but it was a lot. 109s crossed my nose numerous times and I fired at each of them with short bursts. I hit at least two that I know of, but was unable to follow up because there was a 109 on my tail that I was unable to shake. Finally I pulled the circle as tight as I could, spinning if I had to, and pushed the prop speed full forward. My P-51s nose was brought up so I could bleed off a little speed. Simultaneously I rolled to the left and dropped some flaps. The German fighter could not stay with me and I was immediately on his tail. Flaps could be used this way momentarily, and I was fairly proficient at using them to help turn the tables on an enemy fighter.

I had a lot of confidence in my airplane and knew that you must fly the airplane and not let it fly you. As long as you kept the air flowing over the wings you were in no trouble. The P-51 Mustang was a great airplane.

The Me 109 dove away with me following close behind. I pulled the trigger and lo and behold, only one of my four guns would fire. Only the machine gun outboard in my right wing would fire. All the others had jammed due to the high G forces I inflicted on them. Our .50 calibers had a habit of doing this since all our guns were mounted on an angle in the wings.

I moved my gun sight to the 109s left wingtip and fired. The recoil of the gun would kick my airplane to the right and I was able to obtain hits from wingtip to wingtip. I did this twice and on the third time the 109s engine erupted with black smoke and appeared to stop. We were at low altitude and the pilot headed to a little field and crash landed. He plowed a furrow and the German fighter burned. I did not see the pilot get out of his airplane. After making a couple of passes at the spot I headed back to the air battle.

On the way I encountered more Me109s and saw a P-51 mixing it up with them. The Mustang pilot was able to shoot down both of his attackers.

All of a sudden it was over. The enemy had totally disappeared! I was wet with sweat but also relieved. It seemed like I had been fighting all morning but the battle had really only lasted a very short time. Thank God I had survived!

We had destroyed ten of the enemy plus some probable. We felt good about this because this was truly a great air battle. Even though we had been greatly out numbered we had fared well. The mission we had just completed was to give me my greatest excitement and apprehension of the war. Our intelligence officer called it a *'classic'* and

It truly was!"

Capt. RICHARD FLEISCHER
348 FG   P-47 Thunderbolt
6 Victories

GARDENIA

"On June 3rd, 1944 our squadron was patrolling northwest of New Guinea to provide cover for our troops landing in the Philippine Islands.

PBY Catalina's were also patrolling in the area to provide air-sea rescue for our planes. The Catalina's code name was 'Gardenia'.

We received a call form 'Gardenia' saying they were under attack by four Japanese fighters.

I was leading our last flight of four P-47s and proceeded to cover the ten to fifteen mile distance separating us. We practically ran into an equal number of Japanese 'Oscars' and engaged them with head on passes.

We went in high and shook them loose from the PBYs. When I fired, only my guns on the left wing would work. All four machine guns on my right wing were silent. I had to use hard rudder to avoid swinging off target every time I fired due to the recoil from only having my left wing guns operatable.

The Oscar I shot at headed into the clouds with me in hot pursuit. At about 3,000 feet I lost him in the thin, wispy cloud cover and decided to throttle back, change my direction and come back down through the clouds hoping to spot my adversary again.

Things were happening a lot faster then it takes to talk about them. The Oscar came around just in front of me at an angle and I fired. He pulled up and stalled on his left wing at about 1,000 feet. At that point he was finished.

Our P-47s shot down three of the four Japanese fighters we were up against.

It was fortunate that my adversary pulled up at an angle to my plane. Firing from straight behind was always harder because you had a much smaller target to aim at. The more of an enemy I could see, the better I liked it.

When I returned I asked our armament officer why my right wing guns failed to operate. He never did tell me if they were loaded incorrectly or if there was an electrical or mechanical failure."

FREEZING

"We knew enough to never go around in circles with the Japanese fighters. It was important to keep as much altitude as possible and never be caught under 250 mph. High and fast was the rule we lived by!

I think many of our combat losses were due to pilots just 'freezing'. It was hard not to think about what is going on and just instantly react when encountering the quick and agile Japanese aircraft. If you took time to 'think', you were dead. After a few combat situations you lose any 'fear' you might have had. I was constantly searching the sky for the enemy and as long as I could see them I was okay. My only fear was if I couldn't find them.

The first time I engaged the enemy was when sixteen of us were jumped by a large group of enemy fighters. During this part of the war the Japanese pilots were very 'cocky' and very aggressive. I was leading the last flight of four P-47s when I saw red balls of cannon fire go past both wings. I pushed the stick straight forward and dove nose down. Our Thunderbolts were untouchable in a dive and once again we had victories.

We had released our belly tanks earlier but mine hung up and wouldn't drop. I used up as much fuel as possible and came in to land. As soon as I hit the ground the tank let loose and released on its own.

This was my first encounter with the enemy and I mentioned to our 'doc' how dry my throat had been during our combat. I was unable to even swallow. Luckily I was still able to function and do what I was trained for.

My only goal during my combat career was to shoot down an enemy plane so all my expensive training wouldn't be wasted."

Col. CECIL G. FOSTER
51 FIW   F-86 Sabre
9 Victories

THE DOUGHNUT SHAPED RING OF SMOKE

"As we reached the vicinity of the Sui-ho Dam we paralleled the Yalu River in an elongated pattern. We spotted a flight of eight MiGs coming towards us in a head-on approach.

I was able to cut off the last man in the flight of MiGs. The closest thing I can compare this maneuver to is a cowboy cutting off a cow from the herd by riding in and forcing one to turn away from it herd.

I forced him to leave his position, and as he swung out wide he appeared to be confused as what to do. As I lined up on him, he started heading directly into the sun. This was an old World War II trick. But I had a radar computing gun sight, and when I put it on him I could tell it was locked on. I gave him a long burst, and my airplane slowed, we were at around 42,000 feet and headed up in a climb.

I could see that I was hitting his engine. Every time I hit him, a doughnut shaped ring of smoke would come floating back. I actually was able to fly right thru the doughnut shaped cloud. We continued in this way for what seemed like a very long time. I was flying through his jet wash, which caused my airplane to wobble around. I dove to increase my speed, closed on the MiG, pulled up behind him again, put my gun sight on him, shot, nearly stalled and dropped my nose again. This maneuver was repeated seven or eight times until we were over the Yalu River.

We finally headed for home and landed at K-13. During the debriefing a Major Visscher stated that he had seen my combat. The MiG finally burst into flames and the pilot ejected. I now had a confirmation on my 4th victory."

Cdr. HAMILTON McWHORTER III
VF-9 and VF-12   F6F Hellcat
12 Victories

MR. GRUMMAN

"I was airborne as part of a strike force against Yap on March 21st. As we approached the island I couldn't make out anything that warranted our attention. The airfield appeared to be in ruins-hangers and other buildings were bombed-out hulks, and the rest of the installations were a shambles as well. As we came in range the enemy gunners started putting out anti-aircraft fire. From my position ahead of the bombers, I pushed over into a dive to strafe one of the anti-aircraft positions. Through my gun sight, I saw dirt and debris kicked into the air by the impact of my machine-gun rounds. The Japanese gunners had disappeared, gone to ground in an effort to escape the hail of thumb-sized bullets I was spraying down on them. As I pulled out of my dive at about fifty feet, I heard and felt a thump, and a sudden flash on my right wing caught my attention.

Not all enemy gunners had gone to ground! About four feet from the cockpit, my right wing was engulfed in flames that reached all the way back past my tail. Thinking that the wing was about to depart the rest of the airplane, I felt I had to get out. My body reacted more quickly than my mind; before I had time to even think about it, my hands had thrown back the canopy and released my shoulder and lap harness.

As I stood up to bail out over the island I was surprised at the force of the slipstream, which pushed me back into the cockpit. At that moment, common sense began to prevail over panic. First of all, I noted that my airplane was still flying and gaining altitude. Second, though the midsection of the wing was still on fire, the portion of the wing that joined the fuselage was still very sound. If I bailed out over the island, I was certain to be captured by a very angry and cruel enemy whom I had just finished strafing. My chances of survival then would be slim to none.

I settled back into the seat and continued to climb my airplane out over the water. In a minute or so-it seemed like forever-the fire burned itself out. Soon after that I was joined by my wingman, Jay Finley. He looked my plane over and reported that he saw no damage other than a hole burned through the top of my right wing.

I stayed with the strike formation for the rest of the trip back to Falalop, but off to the side with Finley. I was still flying unstrapped and with the canopy open. If the wing fell off, I wanted to be sure that I wouldn't run into any other planes and that I'd be able to make a quick exit.

Thanks to 'Mr. Grumman' and his trademark practice of over-engineering everything he built, the wing stayed attached. When I got back, we discovered that an enemy round had penetrated the gun boxes and ammunition trays. It had also ruptured the gun-charging lines, igniting the flammable hydraulic fluid. The burning hydraulic fluid had in turn cooked off the ammunition in the gun trays. Fortunately, most of the fire had burned aft of the load-bearing main spar.

Ensign Delbert 'Snuffy' Martin, who had scored the squadron's first aerial victory during the first strike at Tokyo, had not been so lucky. He was seen to crash straight into the ground, probably killed in flight by anti-aircraft fire.

Privately, I questioned the wisdom of these strikes on an island that posed so little danger to our fleet. We had paid for this one with Snuffy Martin's life-and nearly my own. It didn't seem like a fair trade."

Lt Col. ROBERT J. GOEBEL
31 FG   P-51 Mustang
11 Victories

HE MUST HAVE REALLY PUCKERED

"On July 3rd 1944 we were to provide escort for the 304th Bomb Wing's B-24's, which were going to have a go at the Malaxia Locomotive Works and the Titan Oil Refinery there.

The rendezvous was made 40 miles east of Craiova on time at 1141. After rendezvous, the R/T traffic began to pick up with a steady stream of bogie call-outs, so I called for my flight to drop tanks. About fifteen miles northwest of the target, a gaggle of fifteen Me-109s approached the bombers in small groups from the direction of Bucharest, at 26,000 feet. I spotted the two Me-109s above at about one o'clock, I think the leader saw my flight about the same time. He had balls. I'll say that for him. The two Germans started down to attack either the bombers below or the four of us; it was a rash act indeed. Perhaps he had recently come from the Eastern Front and had no fear of Russian fighters, but we were not the Yaks or MiGs he was used to fooling with.

We broke into them. In thirty seconds he had discovered his mistake. As soon as we broke, he pulled straight up into a loop. Then, as he got over the top and started down, he rolled out, doing a sort of half Cuban eight. He lost his friends in this maneuver; the wingman continued diving, and I'm not sure anyone picked him up. I tried to follow my man, but I didn't have enough speed. In military-emergency power, I just managed to stagger over the top of the loop. But once I got my nose down, I accelerated rapidly. He had opened quite a lot of sky between us, but I had kept him in sight. Now I began to close the distance. We were in a long shallow dive. His wingman gradually grew within the bright orange circle of my sight. A quick glance down at the gun switch verified that my guns were hot. I stayed slightly low in his blind spot. He may have mistaken my wingman who was quite far back, for me, because the German continued in his descending, high speed run. Although my wingman was way back, he was well out to the side, and my number three and four were wide on the other side. We had the poor bugger boxed in.

Now the 109 almost filled my sight; I had to be in range now! Surely I was no more than 200 yards away. I had the pipper low in the center of his fuselage when I squeezed off the first short burst. No strikes. Thank God our group did not put tracers in the normal load, or they would have given me away. I didn't like tracers anyway; they tended to draw the eyes away from the sight. The pilot invariably wound up holding the trigger down, trying to steer the tracers onto the target-a nearly impossible task. Quickly raising the pipper almost to the tip of his tail, I fired again and was rewarded this time with strikes quick-flashing around the fuselage and wing roots. Then his prop wash threw me off him momentarily.

Before I could get the sight back on him for another burst, the pilot left his airplane. The 109's nose dipped suddenly, catapulting him out. His chute blossomed. I could plainly see him suspended beneath it, a dark, toy-like figure, swaying gently as he floated down. Putting my gun switch in the Camera Only position, I made a pass at him, being careful to break off so my slipstream would not collapse his chute canopy. As I passed to the side of him, I raised my gloved hand in a half wave-half salute and then re-formed my flight.

It occurred to me as we started for home that he may have thought I was going to shoot him out of his harness when I lined up on him. Poor bastard; he must have really puckered up. I don't think we would have tolerated anyone who would shoot Germans in their parachutes. Leaving chutes alone was not a written policy, just an application of the Golden Rule-no one knew when his turn to bail out was coming."

Col. CLARENCE (BUD) ANDERSON
357 FG   P-51 Mustang
16.25 Victories

<u>10 FEET TALL</u>

"We were all 10 feet tall. We swaggered along like John Wayne and talked tough like Bogart. And when it came to the ladies, we thought of ourselves as Clark Gable carrying Vivien Leigh up the staircase in *Gone With The Wind.*

We were fighter pilots, flying the damnedest, fastest, most lethal airplanes anyone had ever dreamed up, the forward line in defense of the entire free world. We were 22 years old, give or take one or two years, and carrying the entire war on our shoulders-and doing a pretty good job of it, too, to judge by what the newspapers told us. We were winning the fight, and developing egos that would make Mussolini look humble.

We weren't like other people, at least not in our own minds. We were bolder, braver, smarter, more spirited ... better. Our eyesight was keener, our reflexes quicker. We were risk-takers who worked and played hard. We were confident, self-reliant, able to stand on our own and proud of it.

Most of all, we were motivated, aggressive. Only the fittest and most competitive survived the training, and then the deadly winnowing out imposed by our last and best teacher, the German Air Force. I was no fighter by nature, at least not with my fists; I can count the fights of my youth on one hand. But I enjoyed competing; and racing cars, or dueling with airplanes, it was a way of compensating for my slender build and testing myself against anyone. I enjoyed combat, which is not quite the same thing as saying that I enjoyed killing. Combat was exciting, addictive, a test of our mettle and manhood-a crucible in which men became a cut above the ordinary.

We were never afraid. Most of us, anyway. I truly believe that. Scared sometimes. You would have to be stupid not to be. Concerned. Respectful. But never *'afraid'* the way a little kid is afraid of the dark, or the way you might fear some dark alley knowing something is there, waiting for you. We were so young, I suppose we just didn't know any better."

G-SUITS

"We were wearing G-suits by then-contraptions you would fill with water, or air, designed to help prevent blackouts. The Mustang, generally speaking, could take harder turns than the people who flew them. Long before the wings flew off, the pilot would simply lose consciousness, the blood drained from his head by centrifugal force, which was measured in 'G's. Five Gs and you might 'gray out', but be able to function. Six or so, and you could 'black out', lose consciousness. The form-fitting suits simply inflated as the airplane pulled Gs, hugging you, preventing your blood from running from your brain all at once.

They were strictly experimental, which is why we had two different kinds. The water suits were like overalls. The crew chief filled them up at the top with a funnel and a pitcher, and when the mission was done you would sit on the wing and open two little drains at your ankles, and the water would empty in two silver streams. The problem with the water suits was that they were cold, and I only wore one a couple of times. We tried filling them with warm water, but six miles up and they cooled quickly. The air suits, attached to a G-sensing valve, drew air through a line that ran from the pressure side of the engine's vacuum pump. These wrapped around your abdomen, thighs, and calves in three attached sections that looked like a cowboy's chaps, and they inflated automatically. Those worked much better.

With the G-suits, we could fly a little harder, turn a little bit tighter. We could pull maybe one extra G now, which gave us an edge. There was no resistance to wearing them. Not at all. We understood what they meant right away. Wearing the G-suit was the same as making the airplane fly better."

Col. STEVE N. PISANOS
4 FG   Spitfire/P-47
10 Victories

RHUBARB MISSIONS

"As a fighter pilot, flying out of England in WW II, before and after the 8th Air Force arrived in the United Kingdom, I was confronted by taking part in numerous operational tasks, namely standby alert, convoy patrols, fighter sweeps, escorting light and heavy bombers and strafing targets on the ground or at sea.

Standby alerts were of two types. One sitting at the dispersal hut and waiting for telephone call to scramble, the other was the type where you sat in the cockpit of your Spitfire and waited for the signal for you to scramble. Normally a smoke flare was fired as the signal for takeoff. The intent of both was for the pilots to become airborne and be vectored to incoming enemy aircraft.

Convoy patrols were normally conducted by two aircraft flying over a convoy of ships in the English Channel or North Sea.

Fighter sweeps were primarily conducted by one or two squadrons flying at altitude over enemy territory and looking for trouble!

The art of escorting was to accompany the bombers, after the fighters had rendezvoused with them, all the way to the target. If the target was close to the enemy coast the fighters would normally stay with the bombers all the way to the target. If the target was deep in enemy territory, we would have to turn back to base. The bombers would then proceed to their targets without fighter escort, an unacceptable situation.

Strafing ground targets were also known to fighter pilots as Rhubarb Missions. This type of mission was actually an adventure flown at very low level over the sea with the plan of sneaking into enemy territory undetected. We would then strafe either an aerodrome, train, military convoy or other targets of opportunity.

My favorite missions were the fighter sweeps, escorting bombers and rhubarb missions. On sweeps and escorting bombers, you had the chance to meet adversaries with a possibility of getting into a fight. On Rhubarb Missions, the pilot was king! We had great satisfaction when we could fire a stream of bullets at a steam driven locomotive and see it blow up.

When you are chasing a foe thousands of feet above the surface of the earth and trying desperately to maneuver your aircraft for position, you are actually in a different world. If the adversary you are after is unaware that you are on his tail, the kill was a piece of cake.

But if the enemy happened to be an experienced aerial warrior and spotted you as you were approaching, he would attempt to go into the most violent maneuvers possible to try and shake you off his tail. If you were also an old-timer in the game, it wouldn't make any difference what he did in front of you.

The events in an aerial duel with the enemy is happening so fast you don't have the time to worry or think about other matters than concentrating on getting as close to him as possible while watching your own tail.

As you are closing in and getting ready to pull the trigger, your heart begins to pound faster than normal. Your feet begin to shake and your muscles become tense and you feel the dryness of your mouth. All this happens as you quickly glance behind, left and right and up and down to make certain that no one is on your tail.

When you pull the trigger you begin to tremble and you feel the sweat dripping on your face and down your spine because you are going to end the life of another human being. The enemy in front of you begins to smoke and be engulfed in flames. You are still trembling as you pull away and look desperately for some of your friends.

Strafing ground targets was one of the most dangerous tasks for fighter pilots in World War II. Rhubarb missions were actually more precarious than dueling against a foe in the sky.

The targets we strafed on the ground were of two categories; fixed and mobile.

My agile Spitfire with its two 20 mm cannons could cause heavy damage on most targets.

Rhubarb missions were normally conducted by two aircraft flying very low and at high speeds. Not only were these missions dangerous but they were also very challenging for a pilot. It was very demanding to be constantly alert and aggressive while trying to navigate your fighter on the deck over enemy territory.

We would proceed directly along the French coast closest to our target area. A spot was normally picked where enemy radar did not overlap. Once you had penetrated into occupied France we would fly until we found railroad tracks. You could always tell the approach of a train by the coal smoke it produced. We would attack the locomotive from the most advantages position using only our 20 mm cannon.

After the engine was blown to pieces we would get away by skimming just over the treetops and head for home. On the way back we would strafe any other target we would encounter such as aircraft parked at an aerodrome or a military convoy on a highway. This was the manner we conducted rhubarb missions during World War II in both the RAF and the 4th Fighter Group.

When the B-17s and B-24s began to arrive in England in large numbers, the 4th Fighter Group was taken off the Rhubarb business and shifted to escort duty. For those of us that had served in the RAF, strafing was always on our minds. Luckily for us, the game of strafing targets in enemy territory appeared again while we were involved with escorting heavy bombers deep inside Germany.

After we had escorted the B-17s into Germany and had to turn back toward England, some of us would get permission to break away from the formation and hit the deck for some strafing. With our powerful Thunderbolts, we would attack parked aircraft on aerodromes, rolling stock on highways and barges on the Rhine River. Intelligence indicated that many of the barges were used by the Germans to store aviation petrol.

It is interesting to note that many of our pilots had the guts to make a second pass on well defended aerodromes. These pilots, I regret to say, became targets for the aerodrome defense gunners. When they came around the second time many never made it back home."

LtGen. GORDON GRAHAM
355 FG   P-51 Mustang
7 Victories

A RATHER SPIRITED LIFE

"Flying combat as I did in three wars was a rather spirited life. I was shot up, shot down, bailed out, bellied in and always made it back. But, I must tell you- I had someone looking after me, otherwise, I wouldn't be able to write this!!"

Cdr. PHILIP KIRKWOOD
VF-10   F6F/F4U
12 Victories

THE INFAMOUS JAPANESE ZERO

"I was fortunate to be in the first Navy Squadron to receive new F6Fs in Squadron VF-10 in Sand Point Naval Air Station, Seattle Washington. They were much improved over the F4F Wildcat fighters with which we had just won the successful Battles of the Coral Sea and the Battle of Midway. This was the turning point in the Navy's Pacific War in retaliation for the dastardly and infamous attack on our forces at Pearl Harbor Naval Base in Hawaii!

The Hellcat was much more powerful and well built with its huge radial engine, and large propeller, plus self-sealing gas tanks with longer range. It had a thick sheet of armor plating mounted behind the pilot for his protection. They also had six .50 caliber machine guns. This made it faster, more powerful, and much better protected and longer range than the main competitor, the infamous Japanese Zero!

However, with all these advantages, it was also heavier than the Zero fighter, and as such was less maneuverable, which was overcome by our tactics. We always stayed together in no less than two plane sections, which doubled our firepower, and we never tried to intentionally 'dogfight' with them, as they could easily out turn us.

We therefore, used our superior speed to gain altitude advantage whenever possible, and climbed to attack, then speeded in a slashing firing run, and fast climbing recovery, to again slash at them rapidly. We never attempted to turn with them, because we knew too well that being so much lighter, with less protection, they could get on our tail in less than two turns or loops.

Our advantage was great and proved so, when our six .50 caliber guns hit them, they invariably blew up in a terrible explosion of their gas tanks. There would be nothing left of them, as all of their planes were far more lightweight, and so much weaker aircraft, in comparison with ours.

Later our F4U-4 Corsair fighters (which I also flew), were even more powerful with two banks of R-2800 cylinders. They were considerably faster than the F6F Hellcats, with all of the same protection and a longer range.

You should know however, that the F6F Hellcat was a more steady gun platform, and would stall (with lack of flying speed), by mushing down more controllably straight, whereas the Corsair would at that point, enter a wing-tip stall, which would flip it off into an uncontrollable spin and if at low altitudes, like during carrier landings, resulted in many crashes at sea. Many pilots unknowingly got too slow during approaches, and spun in. All pilots were of course much aware of this characteristic, but when involved with the intensity of carrier landings, some inadvertently became too slow. Even with the immediate application of power, the plane could not pull out, but contra-rotated around the propeller forcing an unavoidable and usually fatal spin! That was only a small part of the challenge of carrier flying. Operational losses were always more of a threat than the vaunted enemy pilots!"

Col. JERRY D. COLLINSWORTH
31 FG   Supermarine Spitfire
5 Victories

MY WARPED SPITFIRE

"We were flying a mission out of North Africa and after battling the enemy, I found myself at about 4,000 feet, alone and out of ammunition.

All of a sudden bullets started flying by my right window. What saved me was the peculiar way in which my Spitfire flew.

Earlier, I had been sent down with a few others to Gibraltar to uncrate and test fly the new Spitfires that had come in. They arrived in three wooden crates per plane and the Spitfire I ended up with had a warped fuselage. When

I flew, it looked like I was in a skid heading west when I was actually flying south.

Two FW-190s came up behind me and began firing. They were very close and the German pilots aimed to where I should have been, but I wasn't there! It was one of the luckiest days I ever had in combat!"

MY GOOD FRIEND, WOODY

"They sent four of us out flying in a box formation and the cloud cover was at about 700 feet. I looked down and ahead of us and saw a German tank firing straight up in the air. We should have had a clue to what his firing meant, but at the time we didn't. Actually he was firing a warning to his FW-190 buddies that were hiding up in the clouds ahead of us.

I was the number three man in our box and my wingman who flying behind me was my good friend Woody Tomlinson.

Our flight leader started a left hand turn to avoid the tank ahead. I hesitated my turn so I wouldn't end up over the Panzer and Woody shot passed me. We had now traded positions with me on the outside and Woody as the number three man. Woody was a very competent flyer and I had no problem with him in the lead position. However, Woody was accustomed to flying in the number four slot, so he again crossed over me and back to his original position. That unfortunately put him directly over the German tank. His final maneuver saved my life and cost Woody his.

The next thing I saw was his plane take a direct hit, roll over and plunge to the ground."

A STRANGE MANEUVER

"I couldn't fly well on instruments so after following a German FW-190 into a cloud bank, I decided to come back down.

The German pilot must have thought I had left the area and he also came back down through the clouds. I ended up right behind him!

I accelerated to a position very close behind his plane. Finally, the German pilot spotted me and though we were already flying very low, dove straight for the deck. He skimmed along the ground at about 25 feet and 350 mph.

I fired and saw him do what I thought to be a 'Split S'. A strange maneuver to try at a low altitude and one impossible to accomplish at 25 feet! A moment later he crashed into the ground and exploded.

No other aircraft was in sight and being totally lost, I turned to the west with the hopes that my ninety minutes of remaining fuel would get me safely home.

Beneath me I saw an in-lined engine fighter going 90 degrees from my left to right.

As I got closer I noticed it was a 109. One of my cannon had jammed during the earlier combat and that left me with but one 20mm and my four .303 machine guns. (The .303 caliber guns are about as effective in bringing down a German fighter as a pistol would be).

I was about to open fire when I remembered what a British flight instructor had told us, 'Chaps, where there is one German fighter, you are probably going to find two!' Sure enough, I did a 180 degree and saw his partner. I barely escaped the trap that had been set for me.

Feeling fortunate to be alive, I again headed toward home traveling due west. I've always seemed to have a knack of remembering land marks and this paid off in a big way during this mission.

Nearly out of fuel I looked to my left and spotted a familiar looking hill. I turned and flew in that new direction and it brought me straight back over our airfield."

THE HOT JULY SUN

"One of the strangest things I experienced occurred while I was in Sicily.

It was July and the grass was real tall and very dry. Somehow a fire got started and two of us decided to try and put it out before it reached our parked Spitfires.

A moment later there was an explosion, something hit my stomach and knocked me down on my back.

The doc was afraid to come down and look at me due to the fire and explosions. Our squadron commander came over to me and started yelling that he was going to 'court marshal' our surgeon if he didn't find the courage to help me. They continued arguing with me laying there in the July heat.

Finally, I told them to stop their fighting and get me out of the damn sun!

I was taken down to Tunisia for treatment and put on board a hospital ship, given a much needed bath and an operation.

When I woke up the next day, a nurse was standing over me. She tried to give me the two inch piece of metal they had removed from my stomach for a memento. Like a damn fool, I said no. I told her I've already had that hunk of metal once, why would I want it again.

Today I wish I still had it. It was stupid of me to turn down that souvenir."

Cdr. RICHARD (DICK) MAY
VF-32   F6F Hellcat
5 Victories

OUR GRANDMOTHERS COULD HAVE SHOT THEM DOWN

"The first part of the war the F4F was up against the superior Zero, flown by well trained fighter pilots. During this part of the war we were pretty even in victories and losses.

During the middle of the war the Hellcat entered the fight … it was superior to the Zero and our pilots were better trained. We destroyed nearly all their good pilots.

The last third of the war had the Japanese fighters flown by inexperienced and poorly trained pilots. It was possible that our grandmothers could have shot them down.

During the war the Jap tactics were lacking and lousy. For instance, at the February raid on Truk, eight of us attacked 44 enemy fighters, consisting mostly of their new Tony's with self-sealing tanks, Zeros and Oscars (the army version of the Zero). The 44 consisted of eleven divisions of four each climbing through 13,000 feet over Truk. Smart tactics would have been having each division climb on a different heading. As it was, we blew up eight Zeros on our very first attack. When we finished we had 21 confirmed, 6 probable and one damaged. During this fight I received a victory confirmation when I sliced through the tail of an Oscar. When I landed I had the Oscar's fighter colors on the blades of my propeller.

99 % of fighter against fighter victories occur in a turn, flying upwards or downwards. The Hellcat sloped down over the top of the engine nacelle from the bottom of the gun sight and windshield, enough so in a turn the Hellcat allowed its pilot to keep the gun sight mil ring with the proper lead. A P-51,

Corsair or P-47 all had straight, not sloped cowlings that caused the pilot to lose sight of his target while turning.

The Hellcat's six guns were adjustable. If the Zeros had .50 caliber machine guns they would have won the war against the Wildcat. The .50 caliber machine gun is lethal. On strafing flights we had the guns arranged in a vertical pattern. In air-to-air fighter sweeps the guns were arranged in a horizontal pattern. All the planes in my division were armed with the first shell on the belt in the breech, but only four guns were hot. (Pull the trigger and the guns fired). We fired only in one second and two second bursts. Each gun held 400 rounds. Four guns fired around 100 shells in a one second burst.

During three hour strafing flights the four guns may be fired a number of times. If strafing targets are plentiful, you don't know how many rounds remain in the belts. So, you turn off the four gun switches and activate the two inside guns. Now you know you have 400 rounds available for each gun.

My last kill was made using only my two inside guns.

Our Hellcats were steady and solid gun platforms to fight with. Our normal load of ammunition was tracer, armor piercing and incendiary.

During night launches or during missions that would begin during the early morning darkness we would have the tracer ammunition removed from our belts. Tracer brightness destroys the pilot's night vision."

Lt Col. DAVID THWAITES
356 FG   P-47 Thunderbolt
6 Victories

<u>6 JUNE 1944</u>

"62 years ago 6 June 1944, all our planes were marked for the invasion. I flew two missions that day, the first one in the dark!

I was very lucky to have finished my tour in September without going down during my combat missions. I was hit by flak twelve times and by enemy aircraft two times!"

Lt Col. BROOKS (PAPPY) LILES
55 FG and 4 FIW   P-51/F-86
5 Victories

52 LOCOMOTIVES

"I became a flying instructor pilot for the P-51, P-47 and P-40 until July 1944 when I was assigned to a combat unit in England. I flew the P-51D until March 1945. During that period I had my first 'kill', shooting down a FW-190 and was credited with destroying 52 locomotives.

I was shot down on March 3, 1945 on my 70th mission. After capture, I was held in German POW camps and released in May 1945 near the end of the war.

After several assignments to different bases flying P-51, P-47, F-80 and F-86s, I was assigned to the 4th Fighter Wing in Kimpo, Korea in November 1951. During my seven month tour in Korea, I flew the F-86A and F-86E for 100 missions. I obtained four MiG-15 'kills', two probable and two damaged."

Adm NOEL A. GAYLOR
VF-3 & VF-2   F4F Wildcat
5 Victories

JUST OPEN THE THROTTLE

"The Grumman F4F Wildcat fought the war in Asia. The F6F Hellcat was my 'baby' and the F8F Bearcat, a copy (almost), of the German FW-190. The Germans put in 1,600 Horsepower in her and we put well over 2,000.

You didn't have to fly the Bearcat, just point where you wanted to go and open the throttle!"

Capt. KENNETH LAKE
VF-2   F6F Hellcat
6 Victories

PUSHED OVER THE SIDE

"The F6F was heavier than the Japanese aircraft we faced. However, we had self-sealing fuel tanks and armor plate behind the pilot. I was trapped with a Zero on my tail during the Mariannas Turkey Shoot. Unable to shake my enemy I hid behind the armor plate and took all of the .30 caliber and 20 mm cannon shells he had. Upon my return to the USS Hornet the aircraft was considered non-repairable and pushed over the side.

The F6F Hellcat was remarkable for its rugged construction."

LtGen. GEORGE LOVING
31 FG   P-51 Mustang
5 Victories

AN ADVANTAGE

"Fighter aviation enthusiasts always want to know how a particular fighter stacked up against its best opponents in a one on one show down. That situation didn't occur all that often. Most air encounters began with one side or the other having an advantage. The advantage might be in altitude, positioning or numbers. Surprise played a role as well. In the case of the P-51 Mustang versus the Me109, the Mustang had an edge in dive speed, and was marginally superior in turning. More often than not, the deciding factors were starting positions, pilot aggressiveness and pilot experience.

But what made the Mustang a star was its range. It had a capability to fly out 500 miles, fight over the enemy's airdrome and then fly home. This remarkable capability made possible the great strategic air offensive against German oil, transportation and armament. Without the protection of the Mustang, such bomber operations would not have been feasible."

Maj. JAMES (DAD) LOW
4 FIW Korea   F-86 Sabre
9 Victories

LIKE SITTING IN A ROCKING CHAIR

"I have flown some mighty nice aircraft while in the USAF. I started in the T-6 Texan, F-51 (260 hours), and upgraded to the F-80 and F-86 in Korean combat. I have also flown the F-104 (Project Test Pilot), and the F-4 in Vietnam.

In Korea, the MiG-15 was a better flying machine while the F-86 was a better fighting machine. The MiG had a service ceiling of 55,000 feet, the F-86F had 47,500. The MiG had problems near Mach 1, the F-86 did not. Our gun sight was also better.

When the aces returned from Korea, they met with the then Chief Of Staff, Hoyt Vandenburg and the F-104 Starfighter was born. Like sitting in a rocking chair. All switches were easily reachable. I made over 200 loops at military power and really knew the aircraft. The F-4 Phantom was much more cumbersome.

The F-86F was tops in 1952. I once pulled 9 ½ Gs and had no structural damage. It had railroad tracks for wings.

My most memorable flight was in June 1952. Several MiGs were at 55,000 feet and we were at 45,000. They had to come down and I was fortunate enough to shoot two down. This was a tuff fight, but I prevailed using a tight barrel-roll around the MiG-15 to lose headway and stay on his tail.

I should have been dead a 100 times, but the good Lord has always looked out for this poor old soldier."

Lt(jg) FRANKLIN (TROOPER) TROUP
VF-29   F6F Hellcat
7 Victories

HE SHOOK HIS FIST AT ME

Over Tokyo a Jap 'Tojo' came in from 12 o'clock and I never saw him till I had a cannon shot explode under my seat. He turned away from me to fire on another plane. I banked and wasn't on fire, so I went after him and finally set him on fire. He bailed out but got caught on his plane's tail and ploughed into a haystack on the beach.

Another time I got a 'Jill' burning bad. I went along side him and he just stood up in the cockpit and shook his fist at me as he hit the water."

Capt. ROBERT SUTCLIFFE
348 FG   P-47 Thunderbolt
5 Victories

COLD BEERS

"The P-47s could out dive any plane in the whole air force. To utilize this strength P-47 pilots always flew higher than the enemy in order to facilitate a surprise attack diving down quickly.

The only disadvantage the P-47 had was it left a white trail behind, but even so we could still out fly most anyone due to the tremendous speed of this plane.

The only comparable plane was the P-51, their strength was they could fly straight and level for a longer period of time so they took over longer flights for the P-47s.

Our crew chief was excellent. He and the five or six men that worked on our planes did an excellent job. Our success and safety directly resulted from their good work.

Several times while on the ground with time off we were like most regular servicemen and wanted to enjoy some cold beers. However, there wasn't much cold in New Guinea so we would elect one of the youngest pilots to unload the ammunition in the P-47, load in the beer and fly it at an altitude in order to chill it! There is nothing like a cold beer on a hot day and that method worked like a charm.

Some folks know of a couple of rascals who while finishing up a training flight spotted an aircraft carrier on the way back to the base. I won't mention any names but one pilot asked the other to follow him and both proceeded to conduct a 'touch and go' on this aircraft carrier in Boston Harbor. As they approached the runway back at Bedford lots of company were awaiting their landing!

Another story was a flight taking them under a bridge-I believe it was the George Washington! Not sure there were any repercussions from that one!

There was also a story about a mission into a canyon one day. The weather began to deteriorate rapidly and the squadron leader told the pilots, 'You are on your own to get out.' They lost a young replacement pilot that day, Bill Desilets, from Worcester Maine. For fifty years he had been missing in action. A fellow looking for a lost relative found Bill's wreck in 2000 and he was eventually brought home to Worcester where he received a beautiful funeral. Bill had been the only boy in a family of eight children."

SCARED

"I was scared maybe once during the war. We ran out of coffee, pilots can't be without coffee so we flipped a coin as to which pilot would fly to Australia to get coffee. I won the toss and flew from New Guinea to Australia, a very long flight. I would have to say I was scared then because I wasn't flying with all my buddies."

Lt(jg) BEN AMSDEN
VF-22   F6F Hellcat
5 Victories

TASK FORCE 30.3

"I flew wingman on my division leader and it was my responsibility to protect his tail from enemy aircraft. As such, I did not get the opportunity to initiate many aerial attacks.

However, one memorable incident on October 15, 1944 remains very clear in my mind. Our Task Group 38.1 was under the command of Admiral John S. McCain. Our carrier, USS Cowpens, along with another carrier, the USS Cabot and five destroyers were assigned to escort two cruisers that had been hit by Jap torpedoes back to Ulithi for repairs.

Our small Task Force, known as Task Group 30.3 began to come under constant attack from the enemy.

On that day our division was led by Lt. R.A. Richardson, intercepted seven Jap planes, (four Betty bombers and three Zekes), a few miles from the Cowpens. We shot down all seven of the Japanese planes.

It was for this encounter that I was awarded the Distinguished Flying Cross."

BGen. BRUCE MATHESON
VMF-214   F4U Corsair
3 Victories

CHECKING MY SIX O'CLOCK

"During my time flying Corsairs in the Solomons we very seldom saw an Army Air Corps P-39. I honestly don't recall ever being on a mission with one, but I do remember both the P-38 and the P-40. We used to call the former aluminum fox holes since they were capable of extremely high flight and in our opinion, didn't come down to our level (enough), to engage the Japs. As for the P-40s, they were the exact opposite. They had no altitude capability so were seldom in harm's way. I do recall one fighter escort mission where the New Zealand pilots flew their P-40s in dive bomber formation (sections of three instead of the normal fighter fours), and pretended to be dive bombers en route to the target. I don't think we fooled anybody but at least none of them got shot down.

My most memorable mission, which I can relive to this day, came in October of 1943 during a fighter sweep to Bougainville. Previously I had not been successful in shooting down a Jap plane although I had hit three but had to score them as probable.

On this day I was determined! As luck would have it we found a number of Japs willing to tangle and I picked one out and gave chase. It took me a long time to get him smoking, and then flaming, and in my determination and tunnel vision I neglected to pay attention to anything other than my own little two plane battle. After seeing the 'Hap' Zero go down in flames, I turned to see if I could find another Corsair and in my turn I heard a sound which was sort of like hailstones rattling off a tin roof.

I thought that rather strange, since the weather was clear. At the time I felt that the sound had lasted for several minutes. I realize now that it really was only a matter of a second or two. A big thump on the starboard wing got my attention; it was a cannon shell exploding there.

Obviously the 'hail' was a Zero sighting in on me with its machine guns and then firing its cannon to finish me off. Needless to say I immediately put the Corsair into a very tight right hand spiraling dive. This was the tactic that we had been promised could not be followed by the Zero.

Thank God it worked. I was alone and definitely out of the fight. I made my way back over a hundred miles or so of open-ocean to our base at Munda and executed a gingerly approach and landing. I then learned that I had also taken a cannon hit in the elevator. After I shut down, my plane captain counted two 20mm cannon hits plus 105 more holes from the Jap 7.7mm machine guns.

From that moment forward (through the rest of World War II and combat in both Korea and Vietnam), I never again failed to routinely and constantly check my six o'clock."

1st Lt. ALDEN P. RIGBY
352 FG   P-51 Mustang
5 Victories

FIRING AS MY WHEELS RETRACTED

"My first victory came on November 27, 1944 over a Me-109 that did not put up much of a fight. The most exciting thirty minutes of the war came on January 1, 1945, when we were caught on the ground at Y-29 by some 50-60 German aircraft. This day has been published as the 'most devastating air-ground attack in the history of World War II'.

Twelve of our 487th Fighter Squadron Mustangs were sitting on the runway when attacked. The score was 24-0 under the most difficult odds of any encounter in the ETO. I was in the #4 slot and was firing as my wheels retracted. Three of us with four kills each, accounted for twelve of the twenty four victories. We were the only individual Fighter Squadron to ever receive the Presidential Citation. It was in this battle that I won my Silver Star.

I should add that three of my four victories came after my gun sight failed. Two of the victories came by shooting down a Me-109 and a FW-190.

I flew some 76 missions of mostly escort, with some dive-bombing and strafing included. This came to some 300 hours of combat before my tour was completed in April of 1945."

WORLD WAR II CARRIER OPERATIONS

I have always been fascinated and somewhat in awe of pilots that attempted, accomplished and survived wartime carrier flight operations. The following naval fighter aces were kind enough to discuss what it was like to make take-offs and landings on an aircraft carrier during combat conditions.

Lt Cdr. PAUL THAYER
VF-26   USS Sangamon/USS Santee
F4F Wildcat

"Strangely enough after you have made 25 to 30 carrier landings in normal sea conditions and normal light, I would just as soon land on a carrier as on a run-way. However, on a heaving deck the stern of the ship is bouncing up and down through an arc of about fifty feet. That gets a little ticklish. The real tough carrier landings that I did quite a few of was during so called dusk patrols. We take off as the sun was going down and come back when it was pitch black. The carrier is not lit, from above you can't see it. You can't see the wake, you can see some fluorescence in the wake. You can see if you parallel along the starboard side and then you're able to peel off on the downward leg until you pick up the only light you can see, fluorescence lighting along the port side of the ship.

There are 300' to 400' feet of florescent lighting that you can see. That's all you can see. Then the signal officer is holding lighted wands that are about five foot long. You get your landing signals by watching those wands. It was really an intense experience and I never got used to them. I would tighten up as would all the other pilots. If you follow the signal officer's signals you're going to be okay. Your life was in their hands. It was a welcome feeling when you finally made it. It never seemed comfortable like a normal daytime landing. You don't really relax until you get on deck and hit the wire."

Lt Cdr. C.E. (BILLY) WATTS
VF-18, VF-17　　　　　USS Bunker Hill/USS Hornet
F6F-3/5 Hellcat

"Weather and night operations had a definite influence on carrier landings. When the seas were rough the CV would rise and fall quite a bit. If the LSO gave a cut and you caught the deck when it was rising you could expect to blow a couple of tires. Take offs and landings at night were more difficult. Trying to get groups of planes together on a dark morning when three carriers are operating together could be difficult. You could wind up chasing a star thinking it was a plane. You can imagine 70-80 planes in a dark sky would create problems-mid air collisions occurred all the time.

Night landings could be classified as controlled crashes. Only shrouded lights on each side of the deck, only a dim outline of the ship. At best it was quite an experience."

Capt. WALTER A. LUNDIN
VF-15,　　　USS Essex
F6F Hellcat

"Carrier landings and takeoffs, day and night, required 100% concentration and were never considered routine. To relax, even momentarily, could result in a most unusual ending. They were taken seriously."

Cdr. CLARENCE (SPIKE) BORLEY
VF-15,   USS Essex
F6F-5 Hellcat

"I have a couple of personal recollections which may be of help picturing the life of a pilot aboard ship. It should be emphasized though that the camaraderie and willingness to engage the enemy under any circumstance outweighed any personal hardship we may have suffered.

Operational losses (accidents in shipboard operations that were not necessarily enemy related) were always hard to bear. In one instance we were loaded with depth charges for an anti-submarine patrol and none of us fighter pilots had any experience with them. We didn't anticipate any trouble dropping them since it would be a simple glide bombing run if we spotted a submarine, but we had little information on the danger of carrying this weapon. Sure enough, the 4th Hellcat to be catapulted with a depth charge aboard got a 'cold catapult' shot; that is, the cat malfunctioned and the fighter got only about half the impulse it needed to become airborne. He settled right off the bow and hit the water a couple of seconds later. It was a good water landing, the plane was still in one piece, and the pilot climbed out on the wing as the Hellcat started to sink. We all thought he'd get a little wet swimming, but would be picked up in a few minutes by the destroyer which was always in position to the rear of the carrier during flight operations. However, when the plane had sunk to about 25 feet below the surface, the hydrostatic pressure exploded the depth charge. Needless to say, the pilot disappeared in the tremendous eruption of water.

Keeping the crew supplied with adequate food was not normally a problem as we could add to our stock with underway replenishment when necessary in normal circumstances. But occasionally we could not replenish because of combat conditions, when flight operations were almost constant or when the fast carriers had got too far beyond the replenishment fleet. Then the meals got pretty bad. In one case, weevils had invaded our flour supply and all other stocks were almost non-existent. In addition to bread filled with weevils, we had only canned asparagus, canned beets, dehydrated eggs, and weak onion soup. A day or two of this diet would have been okay, but during the initial air operations in the Philippines this was our fare day in and day out."

Cdr. ALEX VRACIU
VF-6, VF-16   USS Intrepid/USS Lexington
F6F-3 Hellcat

"Carrier landings, day or night, were considered far more challenging on the straight decks of World War II carriers than on the angle deck carriers of today for the obvious reason, on a poor landing, of not being able to 'wave off' before hitting the barrier, planes and or personal forward of the barrier."

Lt. JOHN D. STOKES
VF-14,   USS Wasp
F6F-3/5 Hellcat

"I have a lot of memories of take offs and landings on our aircraft carriers. All but one take off was smooth-the exception was ugly! I didn't have flight speed and went off the deck into the drink! No problem, I was put back in the cockpit of another plane and joined my flight. I also had a tail-hook that wouldn't come down. I climbed to 10,000 feet and did every kind of maneuver to shake the tail hook loose. Nothing worked! So I was ordered to make a water landing up close to the ship and climb back on board. That's what ropes are for I was told."

Lt. JAMES L. PEARCE
VF-18, VF-17   USS Bunker Hill/USS Hornet
F6F-3/5 Hellcat

"We did have to fly in some miserable weather. I vividly recall the morning of the first raid on the Tokyo area. It was sleeting and snowing. We were up on deck with engines running at about 4 AM preparing for take off into the overcast night sky. The radio and radar masts of the Hornet were in the clouds. Suddenly there was a big explosion just above us in the overcast where two of our aircraft collided and fell into the water beside the ship. Regardless, we launched, rendezvoused and proceeded to our designated target area south of Tokyo where at dawn we found our airbase target under low ceilings and snowed in, the Japs apparently still in bed. So, no air to air action, only shooting up of snow covered, parked aircraft and the sinking of a few small cargo boats proceeding along the shoreline. Through some goofy circumstances at takeoff, our flight leader, in the overcast, got joined up with fighters from another carrier which had a different target than ours, flew off with them and I ended up leading the now 48 plane flight. In those days only the night fighters were exposed to night carrier landings on a regular basis. And those guys had received special training to perform these landings. However, circumstances sometimes led to the rest of us, having pursued an air born target away from *home* late in the day, not returning to the ship until after dark, so most of us experienced an occasional night landing. It was spooky. I had only four during my carrier tours.

As to your question about recollections of unusual carrier take offs or landings, I could mention my experience, rare in the history of Naval Aviation, of having been catapulted out of the side of the Hornet's hanger deck while she was steaming forward at about 30 knots and launching aircraft from the flight deck, again in the pre-dawn darkness. The ship only did this to me and my section leader before deciding maybe it was too dangerous. The hanger deck catapult was 30 feet closer to the water than the flight deck, far shorter than the flight deck catapults and, thus, required a heavier kick in the ass to get an aircraft launched in the short distance. Plus I was being shot into a 35 to 40 knot crosswind. Just climbing into the Hellcat was treacherous. The tail was sticking out over the water on the catapult and I had to climb into the cockpit over the front of the wing (not the designed way to do this) and if I had slipped I would have slid directly into the sea next to the port side of the racing ship. I think the real reason the Hornet only did this goofy thing once was that the hearing of the hanger deck crew was probably permanently disabled by the decibels bellowing out from the 2,000 horsepower engine and thirteen foot diameter prop of the Hellcat at full power all within the confines of the hanger deck *garage*.

Col. Steve Pisanos

Top: MGen. Frederick "Boots" Blesse Bottom: Col. C.E. "Bud" Anderson

Capt. Fred Gutt

F4F Wildcats in flight autographed by:
Capt. Stanley "Swede" Vejtasa and Col. John Maas, Jr.

P-39 Airacobras in flight autographed by
MGen. Charles "Sandy" McCorkle and Lt Col. Robert Goebel

Col. David L. "Tex" Hill

Supermarine Spitfire in flight autographed by : Col. Steve Pisanos and Col. Jerry Collinsworth

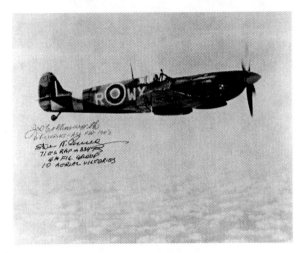

Maj. George Carpenter

Top: Lt Col. Donald Bryan Bottom: Lt. James Pearce

Cdr. LeRoy "Robby" Robinson

F6F Hellcats in flight autographed by 27 Navy aces

Col. Arthur Fiedler, Jr.

P-38 Lightnings in
flight autographed by:

Capt. Paul Murphey
Maj. Nial Castle
Maj. Ralph Wandry
Capt. George Chandler
Lt Col. Bill Harris

Lt. Vincent Rieger

Col. Jerry Collinsworth

VMF-214 F4U Corsair autographed by"Black Sheep" aces :
Capt. Ed Olander, Lt. Chris Magee, Capt. Robert McClurg, Capt. John
Bolt, Lt. Don Fisher

Carrier Operations F6F Hellcats autographed by aces attending 2006 convention in San Antonio.

Rare personal portrait autographed by BGen. Robert L. Scott, Jr.

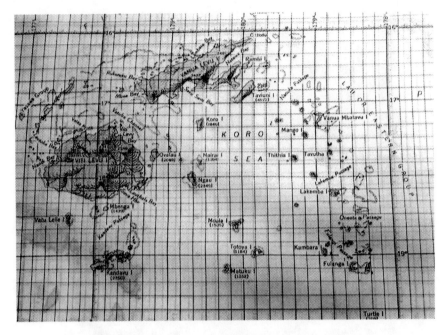

Silk Naval aviators map of Fiji and Tonga Islands
from Cdr. Robert H. Davis

Test pilot Scott Crossfield

PART II
AIRCRAFT OF THE ACES

INTRODUCTION

The second segment of this book deals with the aircraft flown by the American fighter aces and the enemy fighter aircraft they fought against.

Fourteen legendary fighter aircraft of World War II will be discussed as to the positive and negative combat abilities and general flight and handling characteristics. Following the information for each plane will be 'first-hand' accounts from American fighter aces. Each pilot will give his personal thoughts and views on the aircraft he flew or fought against.

It is of interest to note that fighter pilots were usually very loyal and expressed deep fondness for *one* particular type of fighter over all the others they have flown. This is only natural as a pilot's life was directly and ultimately dependent on his aircraft. Regardless of what particular plane he flew, if a pilot succeeded in consistently obtaining victories and coming back alive, he would quite naturally develop an affinity and close-knit bond with his fighter. Only the devotion, trust and friendship of his fellow pilots and maintenance crew could approach this level of loyalty.

A brief look from a statistical stand point of an aircraft's handling and fighting abilities should point to a *single* fighter being judged superior to all others. I've been around enough heated discussions between fighter pilots to know this is not necessarily true.

The truly gifted flyer could turn whatever plane he was assigned into a competent and lethal killing machine. A skilled pilot could amplify an aircrafts attributes and minimize its short comings, thus producing significant results in air-to-air combat.

Legendary AVG Flying Tiger pilots bear this out. Though flying the much less maneuverable Curtiss P-40 Tomahawk against the more agile fighter aircraft of Japan, they were still able to establish spectacular scoring records. Claire Chennault and his pilots scored decisive victories time and time again by adopting tactics that would neutralize the Zero fighter's strengths. The AVG flew in pairs, and always started their combat at the highest altitude possible. The P-40s would dive to attack, make a quick pass and then break off combat by out diving their opponent's lighter and less sturdy aircraft.

The P-39 was deemed totally unacceptable by both Great Britain and many early Army Air Corps units that were forced to use it. Only one American ace, 1st Lt. William Fiedler, achieved this status while flying the Airacobra. However, even the often maligned and unorthodox mid-engine Bell fighter could emerge victorious if flown by an aggressive, competent aviator that knew how to best utilize the strengths and minimize the weaknesses of his aircraft. Actually, in the case of the Airacobra, a good measure of luck didn't hurt either!

In the hands of the hard-pressed Russians, the P-39 became a low-level and ground support aircraft of unrivaled value. Most Russian pilots revered this cast-off American fighter and 180 became aces while flying it.

American pilots were awestruck by the infamous Mitsubishi Zero until they learned of it's inherit weaknesses. Japanese pilots favored maneuverability above all else. When the lack of armor and fuel tank protection was finally addressed, combat veterans were nearly unanimous in their disapproval. Japanese aviators viewed these modifications as an unnecessary nuisance and a burden on their ability to fight affectively.

The F4F and P-40s produced by America early in the war could never hope to compete in a classic dogfight scenario against a skilled Japanese opponent. To survive it was necessary to utilize the Wildcat's and Warhawk's rugged construction, heavier fire power and better dive performance.

The best naval fighters of World War II were the Grumman F6F Hellcat and Vought F4U Corsair. These two aircraft achieved everlasting fame and true greatness during their combat careers. The rugged construction, durability, speed and fire power allowed the U.S. Navy and Marine Corps pilots to totally dominate air combat in the Pacific.

Many aviation experts consider the North American P-51 Mustang as the premier fighter aircraft of its day. The superb Packard-Merlin engine, great range, maneuverability and high ceiling capabilities were all excellent, but a single well placed enemy bullet into the coolant system could quickly spell disaster.

The huge, robust, Republic P-47 Thunderbolt never won a beauty contest and could never be mistaken for the elegant Spitfire or the sleek P-51 Mustang. It should be noted that beauty does not always equal greatness in the combat arena. Many P-47 pilots owe their lives to its massive fire power, sturdy and forgiving structural strength, reliable radial engine and unequaled dive qualities.

The legendary Lockheed P-38 Lightning combined many attributes of other great American fighters and was popular with its pilots for its dual-engine reliability and powerful nose mounted armament.

In Europe the most impressive and best remembered fighter aircraft were the British Supermarine Spitfire and the German Messerschmitt 109.

Each time one country would produce a better aircraft variant with a technological advantage, the other would counter and regain air superiority.

The small, sleek and aerodynamic Focke Wulf 190 also ranks as one of the Second World War's classic fighter aircraft. It was a nimble, deadly interceptor and fighter bomber that was both simple to produce and structurally strong.

The Korean War saw the advent of the 'jet' as the primary fighter aircraft used by both sides during the conflict. The principal U.S. fighter was the F-86 and for Korea the MiG-15 was introduced with great effectiveness.

Other Allied aircraft were indeed utilized, including the USAF F-82 Twin-Mustang, F-51D, F4U-4 Corsair, F-80 Shooting Star, F-84 Thunderjet, F-94 Starfire and the Navy's F9F Panther and Great Britain's Gloster Meteor.

North Korea used many different World War II vintage Russian Yak, Lavochkin and MiG fighters with a limited degree of success.

However, the U.S. North American F-86 Sabre and Russian Mikoyan-Gurevich MiG-15, were the most widely used and acclaimed aircraft of the Korea War.

Both the United States and the Soviet Union relied heavily on the German 'swept-wing' design studies of World War II. The F-86 and MiG-15 each had their own distinct strengths and weaknesses that will be explored later in the book.

My hope is that the reader will gain an insight from the following pages as to the reasons so many accomplished fighter pilots favored one individual aircraft over another.

BELL P-39 AIRACOBRA

The P-39 was perhaps the most unconventional widely used fighter of World War II.

The Allison V-1710 liquid cooled engine was mounted mid-fuselage, behind the pilot and drove a long, extended shaft to the propeller. It was hoped that this would lead to a fighter with weight finely balanced for superb maneuverability. This would also allow a large cannon to be mounted in the normal forward engine area to fire through the propeller hub.

Originally designed with a supercharger to allow power at altitude, it was unfortunately produced without one. This severely hampered its effectiveness as an interceptor. Though it never fulfilled its originally intended role, the Airacobra proved to be an excellent low-level fighter and ground attack plane. The Russians especially found favor with the P-39 and many of their top aces flew it exclusively throughout the war.

FLIGHT AND HANDLING CHARACTERISTICS

The cockpit was hard to enter with a car like door and a low, non-moveable cockpit roof. Only small pilots were comfortable in the cockpit as there was inadequate headroom for anyone else. Cockpit visibility was good except to the front where the armored wind screen and metal cabin frame met.

Elevator and rudder controls were light and smooth but steep movements of the ailerons were heavy and sluggish at speeds over 300 mph. Flaps were electrically operated and easy to use. However, pilots were never happy or comfortable with the lack of manual backup controls if power was lost.

Though there were few undesirable handling characteristics, some pilots had trouble keeping the plane from porpoiseing up and down. A pilot entering a spin knew this could be deadly and it was obviously avoided at all costs.

The Airacobra was the fastest of America's early fighters but was always held back from its intended role as an interceptor by its lack luster engine performance that could only reach 13,000 feet under full throttle.

The P-39 was hard to repair and took a very long time to rearm its cannon and machine guns.

The tricycle landing gear was well liked by seasoned pilots but could cause errors of judgment during landings. This caused many an unwary novice pilot to suffer the consequences.

My very good friend and mentor Tony 'Denver' Porter flew Airacobras in World War II and echoed what many other P-39 pilots have voiced. "The P-39 is a wonderful airplane to fly if you aren't in combat!"

Maj. William H. Allen
55 FG   5 Victories

"I was 6'2" when I flew the P-39 and instead of getting in I put it on. Not the most comfortable airplane I ever flew."

Col. Jerry D. Collinsworth
31 FG   6 Victories

"When a flight instructor proudly told us that the P-39 had a tricycle landing gear, I told him that we don't fight combat on tricycles!"

Lt Col. Donald S. Bryan
352 FG   13.3 Victories

"The P-39 was the worst aircraft I ever flew. We were sure lucky the stupid Russians liked them."

Lt Col. Donald McGee
8 FG   6 Victories

"I flew the P-39s and P-400s with the 8th Fighter Group. I was credited with three air to air victories in my P-39 Airacobra."

Col. Charles O'Sullivan
35 FG   5 Victories

"I flew the Bell P-39 Airacobra and the Bell-400 (British model), June-July 1942 in New Guinea. The P-39 was a 'dud' for combat and didn't have enough altitude capability. During my time with the 39th Fighter Squadron we had nine shot down. Luckily, all the pilots came back. The 40th Fighter Squadron had twelve P-39s shot down and only four of their pilots made it back."

Capt. William O'Brien
357 FG   5.5 Victories

"Never could understand their failure to replace that no good Allison engine with a Merlin! I logged over 700 hours in P-39s."

Maj. Robert C. Curtis
52 FG   14 Victories

"I had 70 hours in the P-39 at Hamilton in California and had no trouble with it. I never tried to spin it because of what I had heard about its tendency to spin flat, i.e. nose level instead of down. This was because the engine was in the middle of the plane giving it an unusual weight distribution.

A high school classmate of mine, Gerald Demming, was a test pilot for Bell and he told me that when a P-39 spun, its nose would gradually come down and that a normal spin recovery would occur. Pilots were scared by the initial flatness and tended to panic.

When I first did a loop in a P-39 the plane stalled at the top and rolled over very smoothly, turning my loop into an Immelman turn.

I used to lift the plane off the ground as soon as it reached flying speed and I did this once with a tow-target attached. When the target lifted, the plane stalled but recovered nicely without the nose dropping as would have happened in any other fighter."

1st Lt. Paul E. Olson
359 FG   5 Victories

"The P-39 was the most difficult plane to do maneuvers and aerial gunnery. With the engine behind the pilot, pulling a tight turn to lead the target could have you in a flat spin which is rather 'iffy' to get out of. Well, we did okay on the assignment with only one target-tow plane landing with holes in his rudder and aft fuselage. However, we did cut the tow line on two of the targets."

Capt. Paul Murphy Jr.
8 FG   6 Victories

"Anyone that ever flew a P-39 Airacobra in combat is lucky to be alive."

<u>Capt. Thomas Maloney</u>
1 FG   8 Victories

"The P-39 was to me one of the best looking single engine fighters of World War II. Unfortunately, having the engine behind the pilot loosed up the weight and balance. This left the plane with several unsolvable problems.

PS= I'm probably the only fighter pilot you will ever encounter who stepped on a land mine while I was 75 miles behind enemy lines."

GRUMMAN F4F WILDCAT

The Wildcat was the U.S. Navy's first and most important monoplane fighter at the beginning of World War II. F4F's were never able to match the Japanese Zero in speed or maneuverability but its greater firepower, armor and studier structure compensated for its other deficiencies.

Despite its short comings, the Wildcat was available when it was needed and many Navy and U.S.M.C. Medal Of Honor winners flew the plane with great success.

Initially, the main criticism's of the F4F were faulty ammo feeding during high stress maneuvers, cockpits with high carbon monoxide levels, bad cabin venting, high cylinder temperatures, vibrations in the cockpit and weak tail wheels. Nearly all of these problems were corrected by the time the F4F-4 was introduced.

General Motors also produced a version of the Wildcat known as the FM-1 and FM-2.

Nearly 8,000 Wildcats were produced during World War II with 5,927 built by General Motors.

FLIGHT AND HANDLING CHARACTERISTICS

The F4F's cockpit gave the pilot very good visibility and when the vibration problems were resolved, the Wildcat's cockpit was very quiet.

Controls on the small Grumman fighter were easy to find, use, and were very firm. Engine boost was not automatic and had to be constantly regulated, especially in high speed dives. However, regardless of the maneuvers attempted, controls stayed effective and easy to use up to 350 mph. The ailerons were especially light and responsive. Dives of up to 400 mph could easily be controlled as long as the pilot compensated for a tendency to yaw to the right.

The ability to taxi the aircraft was above average and upon takeoff the archaic hand cranked manual landing gear was at least smooth and easy to operate.

Takeoffs required full right rudder and still produced a tendency to swing towards the left.

Capt. Stanley (Swede) Vejtasa
VS-5/VF-10   10.25 Victories

"The Grumman F4F-3 had four good .50 caliber machine guns but did not have folding wings. These planes had even better performance than the F4F-4s as they were lighter. Of course with the folding wings we could get more aboard the carrier.

I had so much time in this craft in combat and found it rugged and trustworthy. The armor plate, self sealing tanks and .50 caliber guns were great and the engine was so reliable. We used a lot of armor piercing and incendiary ammo which provided quick results."

Lt Cdr. William (Paul) Thayer
VF-26   6.5 Victories

"The F4F Wildcat was a neat little fighter for its time. It had rugged characteristics that were always welcome in the war zone. I had one punctured with quite a few holes and it still flew. One shell was even logged in the engine."

Cdr. Richard H. May
VF-32   5 Victories

"The F4F was a sweet flying little fighter but under-powered. A half inch steel plate aft of the pilot saved all our Guadalcanal and early carrier pilots from the Zero's machine guns. The bullets just bounced off.

Our defensive fighter division tactics saved the day. Joe Foss, a friend of mine, was at the Canal. He had three Wildcats shot-up so badly that he had to bail out. On one landing at Henderson Field Joe had a Zero on his tail shooting the hell out of him. He landed safely and the Zero flew on out and away."

LOCKHEED P-38 LIGHTNING

The P-38 Lightning was responsible for shooting down more Japanese planes than any other aircraft. To the Germans it was known as 'Der Gabelschwanz-teufel' (the devil with the cleft tail).

The Lightning was built by Lockheed Corporation from 1940-1945 and nearly 10,000 were produced. The Lightning served in every battle zone and was successful in a multitude of roles. The P-38 excelled as a high altitude interceptor and in photo reconnaissance work. It was a superb night fighter, fighter bomber, and was the only U.S. fighter aircraft to carry and successfully deploy torpedoes.

America's top two leading aces, Major Richard Bong and Major Thomas McGuire flew the legendary P-38 twin engine fighter. The Lightning became an instant icon when it was used to find and shoot down Admiral Yamamoto's transport plane in April 1943 after an extremely long range flight.

H.L. Hibbard and Clarence "Kelly" Johnson designed the unique twin-boom fighter for Lockheed Corporation in 1937 and it became America's first long range fighter.

The P-38 Lightning ended its illustrious World War II career by being the first USAAF aircraft to land in defeated Japan.

FLIGHT AND HANDLING CHARACTERISTICS

Compressibility had been a chronic problem with early P-38 variants. This in turn affected the entire tail assembly. Modifications including a small electrically operated dive-flap under each wing cured the troublesome problem on later models.

In 1944 Colonel Benjamin Kelsey passed 550 mph in a dive. (700 mph was actually shown on the air speed indicator). Regardless of what the Lightning's true dive speed actually was, the P-38 enjoyed a rugged high strength airframe that could handle very heavy aerodynamic loading and high speed maneuvers. The Lightning utilized modified Fowler type flaps and on later variants had an indicator that projected above the wing whenever flaps were not fully raised. Luckily for pilots, the later P-38 models were equipped with hydraulically boosted ailerons.

Spins were to be avoided in the P-38. The Lightning had a tendency to flatten out after two or three rotations necessitating increased engine power to put the plane back in the pilot's control.

Though the Lightning was quite docile for a twin-engine fighter, pilots were cautioned to avoid:

A. Extending the landing gear except when necessary for landing.

B. Wing flaps should not be extended at speeds over 150 mph.

C. A pilot has only one chance of landing if you have gear down, flaps fully extended and you are below 500 feet altitude.

D. Opening the cockpit side windows will cause buffeting of the tail surfaces.

E. The Lightning was able to fly well on one engine and could actually climb to over 26,000 feet. A level speed of 255 mph could easily be achieved at 20,000 feet.

F. Pilot operating instructions restricted snap rolls and intentional spins or continuous inverted flight.

Pilots were also warned not to do any aerobatic maneuvers where downward recovery was attempted below 10,000 feet.

If the Lightning was flown in a tail heavy condition, full down elevator was required to prevent stalling if flying with flaps down and the gear up. Extending the landing gear would cure this problem.

The P-38 taxied easily and forward visibility with its tricycle landing gear was very good. The aircraft was in no danger of nosing over or ground looping even when turning sharply or applying full brake pressure.

Manifold pressure was to be held at no more than 45 lbs at 3,000 engine rpm to allow straight forward flight with normal rudder pressure being used.

The Lightning was stable at all normal speeds and with its counter rotating propellers there were no torque problems.

Pilots were told that they should not ditch into anything but smooth water and that baling out offered the greatest chance for survival. The P-38 had a tendency to sink immediately after a water landing.

P-38 pilots were often apprehensive about bailing out. Many young flyers had heard of pilots striking the horizontal tail surface and never looked forward to an emergency jump. If forced to bail out, the pilot was told to pull the emergency hatch that would release the canopy top and then to push or crank down the side window, crawl out on the wing and slide off head first.

If one engine failed during takeoff a pilot was told to close both throttles and raise the landing gear and crash land in as near a straight in approach as possible.

The contra-rotating propellers allowed the pilot torque free takeoffs and landings. In fact, the P-38s twin engines allowed for increased maneuverability and dog fighting abilities. Though the Lightning was not at its best below 250 mph, its turning ability could be greatly enhanced by powering up one engine and decreasing the power to the other. The result was often a rude shock for enemy pilots.

The P-38 was very docile in the stall and could do rolls and loops effortlessly. It was a credit to the P-38s design that maneuvers could be safely completed with only one engine operating and nearly the same cruising speed could be maintained as having both motors in operation.

New pilots transferring from single engine fighters to the Lightning were often perplexed by the placement of the plane's instruments and flight controls. There was only a finite amount of room available in the cockpit and instruments were placed wherever they would fit.

Once airborne the twin Allison engines would block a pilot's view downward and to either side. In a combat area it was necessary to keep rocking and moving the P-38 to get views of the blocked out and obscured viewing area.

Col. Darrell G. Welch
1 FG   5 Victories

"I had the good fortune of being assigned to the 27th Fighter Squadron of the First Pursuit Group in May 1941 when I graduated from advanced flying school. I had seen one or both of the YP-38s while in primary flight school in Glendale California. Burbank was right next door. I hoped that one day I would fly that plane.

The 27th was the oldest squadron (and still is), and was the first to be equipped with the new P-38s. We got our first in July and went on maneuvers in Texas, Louisiana, Georgia and North Carolina.

The P-38 was a great airplane!"

Maj. Ralph H. Wandry
49 FG   6 Victories

"I never had to return on one engine in my P-38. I had a crew chief who was very good and I was only shot up once (on my first combat!), after which I never let an enemy plane get behind me. I flew 161 combat missions in the P-38 Lightning, and only had to abort one when a canvas cover fell out of my right boom and wrapped around the elevator.

Actually, I did come home on one engine 60 times, but that was when I had to fly a P-47 Thunderbolt after they took our P-38s away. I did manage to score kills in the P-47, but never liked it as much as the P-38; I felt safer flying over shark infested waters with two engines rather than one.

The E, F and G models of the P-38 all had manual controls that took over a minute to set before you were ready for combat. The fifty caliber machine guns had a separate button from the cannon; and all guns were bore sighted to hit a 12" circle at 300 yards. The cannon carried further than the 50's, and I always shot that first on any head on pass. I flew a few missions with Richard Bong when the two of us made early morning flights."

Lt Col. James C. Ince
8/475 FG   6 Victories

"The Lightning was such a wonderful plane to fly. I flew my wonderful P-38 about six to seven months. I'll never forget it!"

Lt Col. Frank Hurlbut
82 FG   9 Victories

"The P-38 was an outstanding fighter that could bring you home on one engine if you had one damaged or shot out. It did this for me in North Africa for over 400 miles.

The Lightning could outrun any enemy fighter that I personally fought with. Because of its unique counter rotating props there was NO torque and with its low stalling speed and stability it was a real champion.

The four .50 caliber machine guns and single 20 mm cannon fired straight ahead with a cone of fire that could sink a naval ship as well as destroy any enemy fighter or bomber it was after.

I loved the P-38 as did every fighter pilot who ever flew it in combat."

Maj. Robert Aschenbrener
49 FG   10 Victories

"I loved the P-38. It was my favorite of all the fighters I flew, although I destroyed one after being shot down by ground fire at Clark Field on Christmas Day 1944.

I was lucky to have survived."

Capt. Paul Murphy Jr.
8 FG   6 Victories

"I flew most of the fighter planes of the World War II era. None could compare with the speed and ease of handling of the P-38. The P-51 was certainly a little faster than the P-38 but it did not fly any better.

The Lightning was one of the fastest fighters ever built. The P-51 is the only one I know of that was faster."

Col. Joseph H. Griffin
23/367 FG   7 Victories

"In combat I flew the P-38, P-40, P-43, and the P-47. After the war I flew the P-51 several hundred hours. I have also flown the P-80, QF-80, T-33, F-84, F-86 and F-89. I have also checked out and flown about 30 other types of airplanes, from the B-17 to the Cub. In combat I would select the P-38, P-51, P-47, P-40 and the P-43 in that order.

I believe that the P-38, with the Fowler flaps could turn inside of the others in a dog fight. The firepower in the P-38 was far more intense because of the location of the guns. All of the bullets would be hitting in a very small area, regardless of the range.

A major advantage of the P-38 over the others was the extra engine. I brought my P-38 back across the channel, from a strafing mission, with over four hundred bullet holes. The right engine was shot out and the upper half of the right vertical stabilizer was gone. The P-38 was faster on the deck than either the FW-190 or the Me-109."

Capt. George Chandler
347 FG   5 Victories

"The Zero fighter could easily turn inside of a P-38 at low altitudes. However, at 32,000 feet or above, the P-38 could still generate full power in both engines because of the turbo-superchargers and, at this altitude, the Zero was not able to develop full power from its engine. The result was that at or above 32,000 feet, a P-38 pilot could successfully engage a Zero pilot in a turning dogfight. I did it once and won.

The type of mission that the P-38s were assigned to fly were sometimes almost impossible to carry out without taking horrendous losses. As an example, when we were flying cover over the B-25s that were strafing and frag bombing Rabaul, our orders were that we were to be no more than 1,000 feet above our bombers. The B-25s were right on the deck and we suffered grievous losses because the Zeros were able to attack us from above. In a turning fight at only 1,500 feet above sea level, the Zero's performance was much, much better than the P-38.

In the Pacific war, the P-38 had unusual capabilities that made it particularly effective in that war.

First of all, the P-38 had two engines and, in combat, you could have one engine shot out and still return to base. A single engine airplane like the P-40 would be down in the water and the pilot would probably never be rescued.

The P-38 carrying the big belly tanks were able to fly great distances. Bill Harris mentioned that he came home from a mission with one engine shot out and his P-38 brought him safely back nearly 1,000 miles.

The P-38 armament of four .50 caliber machine guns and one 20 mm cannon, all firing exactly straight ahead, gave the Lightning a tremendous advantage in a head-on confrontation with a Zero or enemy bombers. In a head-on attack, if the closing speed of the two airplanes was 500 mph, the closure speed was about 750 feet per second. The P-38, with straight forward firing guns, could start firing at 3,000 feet and could fire a two or three second burst of bullets before making a break to avoid collision.

The Zero pilot, with his guns converging from the wing-mounts could not deliver effective head-on fire until much, much closer. So, in a head-on engagement of P-38s and Zeros, the P-38 had the significant advantage.

And finally, the P-38 had armor plate back, bottom and front of the pilot's compartment and the Zero had no such protection."

Capt. Marlow Leikness
14 FG   5 Victories

"I remember when a Navy Corsair pilot was bragging about his plane. I replied, oh yeah, we used to feather one of our props and dogfight you guys-and still win!"

REPUBLIC P-47 THUNDERBOLT

The P-47 became a superb combat fighter and ground attack weapon. It was the largest and heaviest single engine, one seat aircraft built during World War II.

Nearly 15,000 Thunderbolts were produced in several prominent versions. Fondly referred to by pilots and ground personal as the 'T-Bolt' or 'Jug', the P-47 began service in 1943 and soldiered on in modified forms until the cessation of hostilities in 1945. The P-47 was flown by more countries then any other Allied fighter of WW II.

Alexander Kartveli, the P-43 Lancer designer had his original in line powered fighter concept rejected by the USAAF. What they wanted was a more powerful fighter. What they received was the 2,000 horse power P-47 Thunderbolt!

The P-47's most enduring qualities were its massive fire power and extremely rugged and strong airframe. Many pilots safely returned home with battle damage that would have destroyed any lesser aircraft.

One aspect of the P-47 that needed to be addressed was the restricted vision of the 'razorback' models. The late 'D' model provided a vastly improved clear bubble canopy.

Though it is hard to believe that anyone could mistake the huge radial engine 'T-Bolt' for the sleek FW-190, white identification bands were painted on the fighter's nose to avoid confusion. Most fighter aircraft built for use in the European Theatre during World War II had inline, water cooled engines and a slim fuselage design. Early in the war only the USAAF Thunderbolt and the German FW-190 broke with this tradition.

Increased ground clearance was needed for the massive four bladed propeller of the P-47. Republic developed a unique telescoping landing gear to accomplish this. The novel gear retraction system was a full nine inches shorter when up then when fully deployed and locked down.

Late model P-47s were built with even more powerful engines to help catch and counter the V-1 flying bomb menace.

During its illustrious World War II career the P-47 Thunderbolt dropped 132,000 tons of bombs, fired 135 million rounds of .50 caliber ammunition and fired over 60,000 rockets. Pilots flew 1,934,000 hours in combat and used 204,505,000 gallons of hi-octane fuel.

After V-J Day many Thunderbolts were transferred to the Pacific Theatre for use as long range escort fighters. At low and medium altitudes the P-47 had no chance of staying with Japanese fighters in dogfights and turning maneuvers. Fortunately by 1945 few first line enemy fighters were available or air worthy.

FLIGHT AND HANDLING CHARACTERISTICS

The original P-47 had numerous 'teething' problems. This was to be expected in such a huge and novel fighter design. Above altitudes of 30,000 feet the ailerons 'snatched' and often froze up. Also experienced were very heavy control loads and a sticking cockpit canopy. Unique and specially built ailerons, control surfaces of all metal construction and a canopy that could be jettisoned, solved these problems.

The Army Air Force had very heavy armament in mind for the P-47, (eight .50 caliber machine guns), and to accomplish this and to safely control the massive fire power required a rugged, large and sturdy airframe and wing system.

The Thunderbolt was a very good high altitude fighter with quite good dog fighting capabilities. P-47s were also excellent low altitude attack aircraft. Pilots enjoyed its ability to absorb great amounts of enemy ground fire and the ability to return fire with a hail of bullets that would cut enemy targets to shreds in seconds. The P-47 would quickly and easily obtain dramatic speeds in a dive and to counter the destructive tendency of sharp shock waves and locked up control surfaces when compressibility was encountered, new ailerons and electric dive recovery flaps were developed.

Final production models of the Thunderbolt had excellent control harmony and its rate of roll was equal or better than any other fighter of its day. Pilots were favorably impressed with the lightness of the controls on the massive P-47. The ailerons were actually superior to those of the renowned Spitfire and P-51 Mustang.

It was critical to properly line up for landings and to make no turning movements below 130 mph. Upon landing it was necessary to have a very long runway available for the heavy Thunderbolt. This was needed to reduce the P-47s speed so minimal braking would be necessary. It was very easy to burn-out or lock up the brakes if applied at to high of speed.

Col. Joseph H. Griffin
23/367 FG   7 Victories

"In my opinion the P-47 was heavier than either the P-51 or the P-38 but it had more firepower than the P-51. It had a larger turning radius in a dogfight than the other two. The P-47 could sustain more extensive damage than either the Mustang or Lightning and still bring its pilot home. The P-47 was the slower of the three talked about fighters."

Col. Frank Klibbe
56 FG   7 Victories

"Other fighters had in varying degree some of the inherent qualities of the total P-47 design package, but none could equal the P-47 performance, capabilities or combat record. Let's review the specifics behind the Thunderbolts superiority;

1. Eighteen cylinder radial engine: Capable of absorbing sever engine damage and continue to operate while damaged.

2. Engine air cooled: Operate damaged without being dependent on a complete liquid coolant system for cooling.

3. Aircraft rugged construction could absorb sever battle damage without falter, as well as forced landings with minimum damage.

4. Turbocharger provided increased engine horsepower and enabled the Thunderbolt to fly over 40,000 feet, unlike most other fighters.

5. R-2800 Pratt & Whitney engine generated nearly twice the horsepower of other fighters and was water injected.

6. The P-47 was equipped with eight .50 caliber machine guns, four located in each wing root. It had more fire power than just about any other fighter.

7. The P-47 weighing 7.5 tons loaded could out dive any other conventional fighter of the war. It could reach 700 mph at the point of compressibility and was considered dangerous to reach such speeds for lack of the pilots control.

8. Engine equipped with the four bladed 'paddle propeller' increased rate of climb and turning radius and was superior at 30,000 feet and above.

9. The Jugs record during the war was tops. The ratio of kills to losses was remarkable. The Thunderbolt pilots destroyed a total of 11,874 enemy aircraft, over 9000 trains, And 160,000 vehicles."

Lt Gen. George Loving Jr.
31 FG   5 Victories

"The P-47 was a workhorse in Europe during WW II, serving as an escort fighter and as a fighter-bomber, chalking up sterling records in both roles. With its air-cooled engine, and its rugged design, it could take a lot of punishment from ground fire, and excelled in the fighter-bomber role. I flew the P-47 for many months as an instructor training new pilots in how to effectively employ the Thunderbolt as a weapon. This included strafing, dive and skip bombing, air to air gunnery and air to air combat tactics.

The P-47 Thunderbolt was big and hefty. I found it to be an exceptionally fine airplane for the fighter-bomber role, and a pleasure to fly."

Col. Edward Roddy
348 FG   8 Victories

"Although I have flown the P-51 for many, many hours and consider it a great aircraft, the P-47 Thunderbolt is my favorite. My Form 5 (Flight Record) shows that I have flown 232 combat missions."

Lt Col. Donald S. Bryan
352 FG   13.33 Victories

"Up until the A-10 'Warthog', the toughest aircraft flying was the P-47. It was the best performing high altitude aircraft ever built until the jets came along. Not to good in dogfights below 20,000 feet. Their eight .50 caliber machine guns made a lot of noise. You could get knocked out by compressibility real fast and the cockpit was rather cold above 25,000 feet."

Col. Barrie S. Davis
325 FG   6 Victories

"The P-47-M was terrific. It looked almost the same as the 'D' model Thunderbolt, but it was a different airplane with lighter weight, larger wing, and much greater endurance. It was built for long-range escort in the Pacific and actually had an auto-pilot. My last assignment of World War II was instructing in this plane at Wilmington, North Carolina. We taught rocketry and ground gunnery. Very little of our flying was at altitude, where the Thunderbolt performed at its best."

Lt Col. Charles Fischette
31 FG   5 Victories

"The P-47 Thunderbolt was the best air to ground aircraft. It had tremendous fire power, eight .50 caliber guns and two 1,000 lb. bombs. It was very rugged, could absorb a lot of damage and get you home. The P-47 had the long range capacity needed for long range bomber escort. It was a god sent for our ground forces with its great ground support capability. It could also hold its own in air to air combat. During my second combat tour, I commanded a P-47 squadron (494th Fighter), doing mostly air to ground attacks while supporting our ground forces.

This aircraft was rated by some foremost authorities as the best fighter considering its all around capabilities."

GRUMMAN F6F HELLCAT

The Hellcat started out to be a larger and more powerful design extension of the F4F Wildcat.

The F6F was not a thoroughbred like the Vought F4U Corsair, but was nonetheless the backbone of the U.S. Navy's carrier air arm from 1943 to 1945. Over 12,000 Hellcats were produced in three years and were dramatic and effective improvements over their earlier siblings the F4F Wildcat.

Hellcats were extremely rugged and though they could not match the fabled Zero in maneuverability, it possessed far better protection, armament, reliability and dive performance. F6Fs excelled in the role of night fighter, interceptor and fighter bomber.

The Hellcat was so domineering over its Japanese opposition that it laid claim to a 19 to 1 kill ratio, the best of any fighter aircraft. In fact, there were more F6F aces produced during World War II than from any other American fighter.

In order to keep its wing loading within acceptable bounds, the Hellcat was produced with the largest wing area of any single engine World War II fighter.

Several unique design features helped make the Hellcat the superb performer it was destined to be. The wings were attached with the minimum angle of incidence possible to help alleviate drag. However, a very large angle of attack was needed so a negative thrust line was incorporated into the mounting of the powerful 2,000 horse power engine. This created a tail-low flying attitude. A high mounted cockpit enabled the F6F pilot to have excellent all around visibility during flight.

All these features forced the overall design to provide function over beauty and though the Hellcat could never be called aesthetically appealing, its overall form allowed plenty of room for armor and internal bracing. Pilots swore by its reliability and its ability to be shot up and still survive became legendary.

Even the Hellcats' production records were amazing. Grumman turned out the rugged fighter faster than any other aircraft, with a record setting 600 being built in one month!

When comparing the Hellcat to the Zero it is interesting to note that the Hellcat held a 45 mph speed advantage at 10,000 feet and a 75 mph advantage at 25,000 feet.

When compared to the F4U Corsair the Hellcat was approximately equal at altitudes up to 10,000 feet, then at a disadvantage up to 30,000 feet. Though the F4U Corsair was certainly flashier and got better press, the fact remained that the Hellcat was the major factor and the key ingredient that caused the eventual collapse of Japanese air power.

FLIGHT AND HANDLING CHARACTERISTICS

Early Hellcats had longitudinal stability problems and needed constant trimming to maintain proper flight attitude. The later models of the Hellcat could dogfight on a nearly equal footing with the legendary Zero fighter. The only area of deficiency was in trying to do a tight loop. Not a smart move when flying against the light weight Japanese fighters.

Japan's warplanes did not stand up well or last long when being hit by the bullets of six .50 caliber Browning machine guns from American fighters like the F6F. High speed dives caused considerable vibration and tail flutter in the Hellcat, but this only occurred at speeds approaching 500 mph.

Though very powerful and reliable, the massive radial engine produced severe vibrations at 1,500-1,900 rpm and was very noisy in the cockpit at around 2,200 rpm.

The front of the canopy was very thick and produced bad distortions as it curved to the side panels. Dirt and moisture was able to seep between the glazing and was not able to be cleaned for better visibility. In bad weather conditions the canopy had to be opened to help with visibility problems.

It was necessary to use the fuel booster pump at altitudes above 15,000 feet to allow for proper fuel pressure to be maintained. Trim tabs often froze when flying above 20,000 feet. Special oil was developed (DTD 539) that cured the problem. Elevators were responsive at most speeds but ailerons became hard to use when the plane exceeded 350 mph. Ailerons were also deficient and nearly immovable in high speed dives.

In steep dives compressibility became a concern at Mach 0.77 or around 480 mph. A sudden change of trim occurred and needed to be quickly addressed. Pilots were warned not to exceed 400 mph when dive bombing with 1,000 lb. ordinance.

The Hellcats landing gear had a very soft stroke that was developed to improve landings and avoid a tendency to bounce. This feature was most appreciated by naval carrier pilots. The landing gear could be locked down at speeds below 135 knots and were so sturdy that they could be dropped at 350 mph and used as a 'dive brake'.

Cdr. Alexander (Alex) Vraciu
VF-6 VF-16　　　19 Victories

"Throughout the war I flew the Grumman F6F Hellcat, which was designed to counter the Japanese Mitsubishi Zero, the dominant plane early in the Pacific war. The Hellcat gave us not only the speed, range and climb to compete successfully against the Zero, but it could dictate the rules of combat. It had a rugged dependability, a solid and stable gunnery platform, and distinctly was more of a pussycat than a Corsair in its carrier operations.

What better success could be attributed to the F6F than to acknowledge its kill-to-loss ratio of nineteen to one."

Lt. Franklin (Trooper) Troup
VF-29   7 Victories

"The Hellcat was the best and took a lot of punishment and still stayed in the air."

Col. Robert (Bruce) Porter
VMF-121/VMF(N)-542
5 Victories

"All I can say is my Hellcat brought me home again and again!"

Lt(jg) Benjamin (Ben) Amsden
VF-22   5 Victories

"The Hellcat was a much studier plane with superior armor plating compared to the Zero. We were considerably faster, approximately 50 mph in level flight, at all altitudes. Above 10,000 feet the F6F could match or exceed the Zero's rate of climb, and in most performance categories was superior at higher altitudes.

Because of our superior power and weight, no Zero could escape in any kind of prolonged dive. At air speeds below 230 mph, the Zero easily out maneuvered the Hellcat. At higher speeds the Hellcats could match turns with the Zeros."

Lt. Richard Bertelson
VF-29   5 Victories

"The Hellcat was a beautiful and rugged plane. It had a marvelous motor. I never had one or heard of one stopping."

Cdr. LeRoy (Robby) Robinson
VF-2   5 Victories

"The Hellcat was the nicest carrier based airplane of 1944. Its design saved many lives and allowed carrier pilots to compete with ground based aircraft. Speed and maneuverability were not sacrificed in the wing folding mechanism. Each wing held three rapid firing .50 caliber machine guns. Each gun had the capability to cut down a 12 inch diameter pine tree at 750 feet. The distance at which the six guns were bore sighted was 750 feet. Bore sighting means that each gun is aimed to hit the same target at a certain distance. Six rapid fire .50 caliber machine guns are very awesome firepower. A two second burst from six guns like those in the wings of the Hellcat, were indeed awesomely effective. The combination was devastating! I personally felt god like! Untouchable!"

Cdr. Richard H. May
VF-32   5 Victories

"I miss the Hellcat. I lived in her for nearly 500 hours of combat flying. She always brought me home to the carrier. I love her!"

Cdr. Charles Haverland Jr.
VF-20   6.5 Victories

"The F6F was by far the most advanced and capable carrier aircraft of World War 2. It was superior in performance in all respects to anything our opponents could field. The Pratt and Whitney R-2800 'round' engine was the most reliable and forgiving that was every built. Our armament, oxygen system and armor were all cutting edge at the time.

I feel I was very fortunate to be given such a fine machine to fly in combat."

Capt. Daniel Carmichael Jr.
VF-2/VBF-12   13 Victories

"The F6F was an excellent aircraft, well suited to carrier operations. It was easily adapted to all types of fighter performance, particularly air-to-air combat. It was rugged, dependable and most importantly an excellent gun platform. I flew several different fighter aircraft, and the F6F was outstanding."

Cdr. Lester Gray Jr.
VF-10   5.25 Victories

"My first Pacific tour was aboard the USS Enterprise in the Hellcat. I managed to shoot down 3.25 enemy planes. The Hellcat was an extremely dependable aircraft."

Lt. Vincent (Buck) Rieger
VF-31   5 Victories

"For carrier based operations I preferred the Hellcat as the visibility of the L.S.O. (Landing Signal Officer), was better than the Corsair for carrier landings, therefore safer for carrier based fighters."

Cdr. John M. Wesolowski
VF-5/VBF-9   7 Victories

"The Hellcat was rugged, very stable and hard to shoot down. The Hellcat had an 'escape' capability that the Zeros didn't have. We could go vertical and get away if we rotated."

Capt. Stanley (Swede) Vejtasa
VS-5/VF-10   10.25 Victories

"The F6F really served us well. That powerful engine could give us speed and climb and those six .50 caliber guns were unbeatable in their day. I guess best of all this plane was so dependable and easy to fly. It was ideal on the carriers of the day."

CHANCE VOUGHT F4U CORSAIR

12,681 Corsairs were built over ten years and were considered the best of all the piston engine fighter aircraft when finally retired in 1965.

F4Us shot down 2,140 enemy planes in World War II with only 189 lost. This remarkable kill versus loss ratio was 11.32 to 1.

The legendary Chance Vought aircraft designer Tex Beisel built the famed gull-wing design to utilize the largest engine and propeller available. The inverted gull wing configuration helped achieve necessary ground clearance and still keep the landing gear lighter and shorter than originally envisioned.

On May 29, 1940 the Corsair became the first American fighter to exceed 400 mph in level flight.

Early Corsairs were used by land based U.S.M.C. units exclusively. It was several years before the forward visibility and landing gear problems were modified and became practical for shipboard carrier use.

A massive fuselage self-sealing fuel tank was mounted in front of the pilot. This forced the cockpit to be set back 32 inches. Many photos exist of white markings on this part of the upper cowling. These white markings were actually white tape applied by ground crew to keep fumes from entering the cockpit. The elongated nose caused many taxing and landing vision problems especially when the cowl flaps were open.

The original Corsair cockpit was spacious and lent itself to tall or stocky pilots. The chief Vought Corsair designer and test pilot was 6 foot 4 inches tall. This undoubtedly had something to do with the cockpit design. However, the view from the original canopy design was very bad, and even worse when on the ground with "up" being the only safe and unrestricted viewing area.

FLIGHT AND HANDLING CHARACTERISTICS

The R-2800 Double Wasp was an easy starting, strong and reliable engine. After takeoff and once in level flight the F4U could be easily trimmed to be a "hands off" airplane.

The control harmony was judged poor with elevators being heavy and ailerons quite light even during dives. On the positive side, this allowed the Corsair to be rolled even during high speed dives. The F4U's chief opponent was the Japanese Zero and its very poor aileron control at speed gave the Americans a decisive advantage.

Stalling characteristics were very poor with little or no warning given. The Corsair also had a bad reputation of initiating a severe torque stall and at lower speeds poor aileron and elevator control.

The climb rate was nine and a half minutes to 20,000 feet.

A Corsair's ground handling was always a cause for concern. Proper braking was a necessary skill if a pilot wanted to avoid a ground-looping tendency.

Pilots enjoyed flying the F4U at its cruise settings and the low cabin noise levels often caused aviators to accidentally over-boost their engines. When flying at low speeds pilots had to stay sharp to control poor lateral control and lack of rudder feel.

Spins had to be recovered from quickly or control forces became so high that a pilot would have great difficulty in getting his plane back under control. If a pilot was still in a spin at 3,000 feet he was advised to leave the aircraft.

Along with the P-38 and P-47, the F4U ran into compressibility problems if the dive speed was allowed to get out of hand. Pilots were given strict guidelines for maximum dive speeds at various altitudes.

The Corsair had a much better rate of role than its chief rival the Grumman F6F Hellcat.

If the Corsair was properly trimmed in advance there was little tendency to swing to one side after takeoff. Once airborne, the landing gear could be quickly raised and during steep dives could be lowered without dropping the tail wheel. This acted and became a very efficient dive brake.

When sharply accelerated the Corsair would respond like a thoroughbred. Depending on altitude, it could out perform almost any opposition thrown against it.

With an expert and experienced pilot the Chance Vought Corsair was extremely deadly to its Japanese opponents. In the hands of the inexperienced it could be equally deadly to its own pilot.

Advanced models of the F4U Corsair continued to be produced and even played a modest role along side the jet fighters in Korea.

Cdr. Lester Gray Jr.
VF-10   5.25 Victories

"My second tour was aboard the USS Intrepid flying Corsairs. This aircraft was a real pleasure to fly, very light on the controls, and an excellent platform for fighting or bombing. It seemed a little more fragile than the F6F Hellcat, but was a very dependable plane."

Lt Cdr. William (Paul) Thayer
VF-26   6.5 Victories

"The Corsair is agile and rugged. The long nose was a slight problem when landing a three point on a runway-but not on a carrier landing or bore sighting the enemy.

I put on my last air show in a F4U-10 when I was 80."

Col. Dean Caswell
VMF-221   7 Victories

"The Corsair was designed and manufactured by Vought Chance Sikorski as a land and carrier based fighter-bomber. It came into limited service as an F4U-A in 1939 and became a mature design in 1942 as a F4U-1D.

I flew the Corsair in 1944 and by 1950 had accumulated over 2,000 hours of flight time in the fighter, using it in World War II and Korea. I have seen it loaded with six .50 caliber machine guns, eight five inch air-to-ground rockets and a 1,000 lb. bomb; there were many variations to loading that included additional bombs and napalm. I have registered 425 knots, straight and level, on the airspeed indicator, and backed off of compressibility in a dive. Our adversary Japanese fighters, of any type, could not match the weapons capability, the maneuverability, the speed and after dropping its loading, FIGHTING ABILITY! With additional drop tanks, 4.5 hours of flight were common-all from a carrier deck. It was probably the best in the world for its day."

CURTISS P-40 WARHAWK

The P-40 was a controversial World War II fighter. It had many critics as well as proponents throughout its operational career and was in fact the United States first modern single engine fighter to be mass produced. Though never considered a great fighter, it was at least available in large numbers early in the war when America desperately needed them.

The P-40s performance never exceeded its opponents, but thanks to its strong airframe and sturdy overall construction, its pilots at least had a plane that could absorb large amounts of battle damage and still bring them safely home.

The Curtiss fighter was never intended to be a high altitude interceptor and was intentionally built for low and medium combat heights.

Early models of the P-40 were purchased by Great Britain and designated as the Tomahawk. It was from this initial group of 1,041 planes that the 100 "shark mouthed" Flying Tigers of the American Volunteer Group (AVG), held the ground until more advanced American fighters could be developed.

When the AVG was finally disbanded and folded over into the U.S.A.A.F. they had been credited with 286 destroyed Japanese aircraft against a loss of fifteen members killed or missing in action. Claire Chennault's "Flying Tigers" produced twelve aces and had sixteen others go on to become aces with other units. Among these accomplished pilots were future Medal of Honor winners James Howard and Greg "Pappy" Boyington.

In the beginning, American pilots underestimated the quality and fighting ability of their Japanese opponents. It was soon a concrete rule that a pilot should never dogfight with their lighter and more maneuverable foes, but to instead adopt a 'slash and run' strategy that capitalized on the P-40s armor protection and superior diving ability.

In the RAF the Tomahawks were replaced with the P-40-D/E models and renamed Kittyhawk.

The largest series appeared in 1943 and was designated the P-40-N War-hawk. The basic design of the Curtiss P-40 remained unchanged throughout its production life. Most of the major improvements dealt with larger engines, changes in armament and with the radiators and oil cooler arrangement.

FLIGHT AND HANDLING CHARACTERISTICS

The P-40 excelled in making sharp turns and high speed dives. Its excellent dive qualities and sturdiness were its two most redeeming features.

Takeoffs were easy and once in flight the pilot had easy control of his plane. Ailerons were sharp and precise and the elevator light but not trouble-some. During takeoffs the pilot had to exercise caution not to raise flaps to quickly or the nose would rise and lead to a possible stall.

The longitudinal stability was considered superb and during high speed dives there were no vibrations or flutter to deal with. Even during a 400+ mph dive over 50% aileron could easily be applied. The P-40 had a low gearing between ailerons and the stick which translated into smooth and easily con-trollable turns. Elevators were also similarly balanced in control forces and were smooth and not too sensitive. P-40 pilots were very happy with the posi-tive feelings of the controls at low speeds and the lack of stiffness at high speeds.

The P-40 and the superb Spitfire were flown in mock combat on many occasions at low to medium altitudes with the Curtiss fighter often coming out on top. This was especially true while executing banked turns that the Spitfire could not match. In fact, the only area in which the Spitfire held a decisive advantage was in its ability to break off combat and escape when it was prudent. This was due to its much cleaner aerodynamic design and slightly higher top speed.

The view from the cockpit and the P-40s overall landing characteristics were considered excellent and spin recovery was very good but on many occa-sions the plane would end up in a recovery 90 degrees from where it began.

The later model P-40s had greater power and a higher altitude perfor-mance. However, this was neutralized by an increase of a half ton in gross weight. Because of this the later model P-40s had a worse takeoff and climb performance as well as being less maneuverable than its earlier siblings.

Instrumentation was adequate for combat use but the Artificial Horizon and Directional Gyro were on opposite sides of the cockpit. This was not an ideal placement for flight operations. High speed dives on later model P-40s were limited to 460 mph at 3,200 rpm. This was considered more than adequate by most pilots.

Maj. Stephen Bonner
23 FG   5 Victories

"Most of my combat missions and confirmed aerial victories were in the P-40 and I was very comfortable in flying it. One had to concentrate and be alert at all times while flying it. This was true while flying all planes, but more so in the P-40. It was not the fastest nor most maneuverable and was rather slow in climbing, but once mastered I gained confidence and became a part of the machine."

Lt Gen. George Loving Jr.
31 FG   5 Victories

"The P-40 Warhawk was the backbone of the fighter force during the early days of WW II in China, and served well in North Africa and on the continent as well. I found it lacked the agility of the Mustang, but I sensed that it was a tough airplane."

1st Lt. Paul E. Olson
359 FG   5 Victories

"We had some combat training in Waycross Georgia. This was done in both the P-39 Airacobra and the P-40 Warhawk. Both of these planes had minimal instrumentation which made it quite interesting to get our night flying time in. It sure taught us to maintain a constant altitude, how to hold a heading and time each leg of your flight pattern, as if you didn't you could end up as alligator bait in the Okefenokee Swamp."

Col. James B. Morehead
24 PG   8 Victories

"The P-40 early models were poor fighter planes, especially against the Jap Zero. The event where our two P-40s bagged three Zeros was thrilling and most memorable."

Lt Col. Donald S. Bryan
352 FG   13.33 Victories

"The P-40 was a tough aircraft. It was without a doubt the hardest aircraft ever built when it came to landings. You always had to be prepared to recover from at least two ground loops on every landing."

F/Ldr. Kenneth Jernstedt
AVG   3 Victories

"The P-40B was the best looking of the P-40s.!!

We had level speed advantage over anything the Japanese had and we had a tremendous advantage over them in a dive!! They could out turn us, but we usually had altitude on them before we started a fight. If they got on our tail all we had to do was nose over in a dive.

We had more fire-power and a lot better protection for the pilot. Our plane loss ratio was very much in our favor!"

NORTH AMERICAN P-51 MUSTANG

Many aviation experts consider the P-51 Mustang the best combat fighter produced by any nation during World War II.

The team of Raymond Rice and Edgar Schmued were primarily responsible for the ultimate design of the legendary fighter. It originally was designated the NA-73 and had every design feature that would reduce drag incorporated into the finished prototype. The original fighter prototype was completed in a record 117 days. Laminar flow wings and careful positioning of the air intake and radiator helped to create one of the cleanest and sleekest fighters ever built.

It was Major Thomas Hitchcock that firmly cemented the P-51 Mustang into the superb fighter it was to become. He reported to Washington and London that the P-51 was the best fighter airframe ever developed. It was his suggestion that the P-51's body be mated with the sensational Rolls Royce Merlin 61 engine. Eddie Rickenbacker and Air Marshall Sir Trafford Leigh-Mallory also pushed for and advanced this idea.

What resulted was the sensational P-51 that earned its mark in aerial warfare history as a plane that could and did accomplish everything that was asked of it.

The P-51 was the premier long range fighter escort of WW II. The Mustang was also produced as a superb photo-recon plane designated the F6A and also as an excellent dive bomber called the A-36A. The P-51D introduced the much appreciated 'bubble' canopy that ended pilot's poor vision complaints.

It was as a high altitude long range escort fighter that the P-51 gained its enduring fame. It was superior in maneuverability and speed over any axis fighter above 20,000 feet.

FLIGHT AND HANDLING CHARACTERISTICS

Takeoffs were quite easy with a flap setting of 15 degrees. The ailerons and rate of role was superb up to 400 mph. and controls were responsive in dives up to 500 mph.

The Mustang was very stable directionally and laterally at whatever center of gravity position was being utilized. Stalls could easily be predicted and there was little problem spinning.

G-suits were developed to keep pilots from blacking out as the Mustang could take more G-pressure that the men flying them. Pilots experienced discomfort from the early P-51 models due to the placement of the radiator and lack of an effective thermal barrier.

The Mustang was an excellent dogfighter and had great maneuverability along with superb turning and dive abilities.

Early Allison powered P-51s had trouble climbing above 25,000 feet and its rate of climb was slow. Later model Mustangs had a superb climb rate and ceiling. However, because of its increased performance during dives, compressibility became a real headache to pilots flying the 'hotter' Packard-Merlin derivatives.

Pilot's of the 1,200 horse power Allison engine "A" model were stunned by the 1,600 to 1,700 horse powered Packard-Merlin "B/C and D" Mustang. Though the Allison engine powered P-51 left a lot to be desired, especially in high altitude performance, it was at least very stable and docile to fly.

The Merlin powered Mustang could be quite vicious in the stall, and less stable directionally. Early examples also tended to overheat. All of these teething problems were soon rectified and it was hard to knock the huge jump in climbing ability. Where the Allison powered Mustang took nine minutes to reach 20,000 feet, the Packard-Merlin example took but six.

Against its adversaries the P-51 was nearly 50 mph faster and that was increased to 70 mph above 28,000 feet. The Mustang could also out dive its opponents and could turn circles and roll quicker than either the German FW-190 or the Bf.109.

Maj. Stephen Bonner
23 FG   5 Victories

"The P-51 was much easier to fly than the P-40. It was faster and had better climbing ability but didn't take the beating of a P-40.

Many of my missions in the P-51 were in support of the Chinese Army, which meant a lot of ground strafing and dive bombing. This was difficult and dangerous for both the plane and pilot. Many of our losses were from ground fire on these type missions.

Flying fighters in combat was the greatest experience of my lifetime. I feel most fortunate and honored to have been given the opportunity to serve my country in a time of need while doing the thing I loved most. This is an experience no man ever forgets, and for which he is always proud-serving his country and the people within it."

Lt Col. Donald S. Bryan
352 FG   13.33 Victories

"The P-51B was a real high performance aircraft, but I didn't like it one bit. The cockpit was very uncomfortable on long flights and EXTREMELY cold at altitude. The four .50 caliber machine guns sounded like popguns after having the eight .50s of the P-47. If you pulled any negative Gs when you fired you ended up without guns.

The P-51D was the best fighter of World War II. All of the faults I had with the Jug or the B were corrected in the D. The cockpit was really laid back, warm in winter and cool in the summer. Everything in the cockpit was JUST where it should be. I loved this aircraft and every one else that flew it did also. Not that it didn't have any weaknesses. The one big thing you wanted to do was stay out of range of ground fire if you could. One bit of lead in the cooler and you were going to have to land or jump in a very short while."

Col. David L. (TEX) HILL
AVG/23 FG   18.75 Victories

"I flew all the early fighters. My favorite aircraft was the P-51D"

1st Lt. Alden P. Rigby
352 FG   5 Victories

"I found out that as good as the Mustang was, most of the difference in combat came with the pilot. At my time after D-Day we mostly owned the skies. The Mustang was a huge factor."

Lt Gen. George Loving Jr.
31 FG   5 Victories

"It was the premier fighter airplane of World War II. More aerial victories were scored by American pilots flying Mustangs during World War II than any other fighter plane. I flew 50 missions in the Mustang during WW II escorting heavy bombers on massive air raids against targets all across Southern and Eastern Europe, and scored five victories. It was a great airplane-agile with an astonishing radius of action, an engine-air frame design that provided the speed and dive characteristics needed to defeat the enemy, and the reliability and comfort to keep the pilots happy. I loved it. I flew the Mustang for a number of years following WW II and flew some missions in the P-51 early in the Korean War. We used it as a fighter-bomber and for rocketing and strafing North Korean army forces. Although it performed well in this role, and indeed saved the day on many occasions for the embattled U.S. and South Korean troops, its liquid cooled engine made it vulnerable to ground fire. It was my favorite airplane."

Col. Clarence E. (Bud) Anderson
357 FG   16.25 Victories

"The P-51 is my favorite because it got me thru the war. It is good looking and makes a great sound. It was a great performer also."

Lt Col. Lowell Brueland
354 FG   14.5 Victories

"I was the only individual that was assigned to the 354th Fighter Group from activation to its deactivation. I was assigned with the 354th longer than any other individual.

The P-51 was as good in combat as any fighter the Germans had.

There were several times I did not think I would make it back to England or back to base.

You have to stay aggressive and show no fear in combat.

I lucked out in combat and never picked up a single bullet hole from air to air encounters with the enemy. Flying combat missions were always exciting but in 435 hours of flying over enemy territory I never found anything amusing."

BGen. Robin Olds
479 FG/8 TFC
17 Victories

"In World War II I flew the Lockheed Lightning P-38Js and North American Mustang P-51Ds. In Southeast Asia I flew the McDonnell Douglas F-4C and D models of the Phantom. Since the time lapse between the two wars was rather extensive, I have to say I had two favorite aircraft, these being the P-51 and the F-4C."

Col. James B. Tapp
15 FG   8 Victories

"On a May 29th 1945 mission I encountered a pair of Japanese 'Franks'. From the speed and maneuverability standpoint they appeared comparable to the P-51. None of the other Japanese aircraft had the same capabilities."

1st Lt. Paul E. Olson
359 FG   5 Victories

"The P-51 was the easiest of all the planes that I was assigned to fly during World War II. Others included: PT17 Stearman, BT 13 Basic Trainer, AT6 Texan, P-39 Airacobra, P-40 Warhawk, P-38 Lightning, P-47 Thunderbolt, Spitfire and B-17 bomber.

The Mustang was more maneuverable than any the enemy put in the sky. The most fun was doing aerobatics like loops, Immelmans, and slow rolls. Spins were also easy to recover from.

I flew my first operational missions on D-Day and was in the air over Europe for twelve hours.

I had to lie on my P-51Bs wing for about an hour after the mission until the circulation in my legs let me walk again. Our chutes were back packs and the seat cushion was a dingy with the inflation cylinder under the leading edge. This cut off all circulation in the legs."

Col. Arthur C. Fiedler Jr.
325 FG   8 Victories

"I had no question that the P-51 was superior to anything I would probably meet in the skies over enemy countries. The Me-262 was superior in speed but we were too gung ho to be afraid of it; just hoped we would see it before it made a pass at us. I thought the FW-190 was a fine bird. It gave me a lot more trouble than any of the 109s I encountered. I have no question that the quality and experience of a pilot was the primary factor in the success or failure of an aerial combat. A good pilot in a P-51 should probably prevail against a good pilot in a Me-109 or FW-190. A fair pilot in a P-51 against a good 109 or 190 pilot would have a chance of losing, especially at lower altitudes."

Lt Col. Charles Fischette
31 FG   5 Victories

"After the Allison inline engine was replaced with the British Rolls Royce engine, it became a top notch fighter on air to air bomber escort missions. On ground support missions it was vulnerable to ground fire because of its liquid cooled engine."

Maj. George Carpenter
4 FG   13.833 Victories

"I loved the P-51 Mustang!! It was a great fighter!"

Capt. Clayton Kelly Gross
354 FG   6 Victories

"What can I say about the P-51 Mustang that hasn't been said many times before. I was privileged to be in the first fighter group to fly the Mustang in combat and was one of the three group pilots to check out at an English base, actually flying the A-36 dive bomber version.

We transitioned to the P-51A with a three bladed prop and an Allison engine. That was a good aircraft but we then went to the P-51B with its Merlin engine and a four bladed propeller. Now we were talking GREAT fighters!

The 354th Fighter Group was the highest scoring group in the ETO in aerial victories although the 4th and 56th had a several month head start in combat. It was the Mustang that was partly responsible for that.

We did transition to the P-47s in late 1944 and flew them for two months before going back to the P-51s."

BGen. Frank Gailer Jr.
357 FG   5.5 Victories

"The torque of the P-51s engine was not much of a problem compared to that of the P-40.

The P-51 was a good airplane in its day, but, it did have some weaknesses (structurally).

I was flying with my friend on a checkout mission with Chuck Yeager. When Chuck finished wringing us out he said we were over our own field and to go on in and land. We were at around 20,000 feet or so.

I pulled over with my friend on my wing and shortly after that he called me and said his wing had folded over his canopy. He went straight in. So I loved the plane and I also hated some aspects of it!"

SUPERMARINE SPITFIRE

Even non-aviation buffs seem to know of the exploits and sleek elliptical shaped wings of the legendary British fighter.

Aircraft designer Reginald J. Mitchell developed the Spitfire fighter from the "Schneider Trophy" winning seaplane racer. When this superb aircraft had its floats removed and added the famed Rolls-Royce Merlin 12 cylinder V. liquid cooled engine, it became a truly exceptional fighter.

The Supermarine design facility produced the sleek and graceful fighter with great attention given to details. To obtain the clean aerodynamic lines of the Spitfire nothing was left to chance or overlooked. The highly waxed paint finish, curved windscreen, retractable tail wheel, ejector exhausts, special radiator design, and nearly a dozen more features gave the fighter an increase of over 40 mph in speed over its original design specifications.

Probably the best tribute given to the Spitfire came from the Germans themselves. When Herman Goering asked renowned Luftwaffe Ace Adolph Galland what he could do to help his pilots better protect their bomber formations, Galland replied, "I should like a Staffel of Spitfires for my Gruppe!"

FLIGHT AND HANDLING CHARACTERISTICS

Spitfire ailerons were light and easy to use. They were much heavier during high speed dives exceeding 400 mph though still useable and responsive. The elevator controls were equally easy for the pilot, though somewhat less so than with the ailerons.

A pronounced buffeting would occur before a stall, thus giving the pilot enough warning for a speedy response and correction.

Very few fighter aircraft handled a spin well, and the Spitfire was no exception. Very careful and planned pilot action was necessary to avoid disaster.

Cockpit canopies could not be opened above 300 mph so special break out panels were introduced on late model variants to allow a pilot to safely bail out of a stricken aircraft.

The Spitfire could out maneuver nearly any other World War II fighter except when trying to complete high speed rolls. Though the Spitfire was better in rate of role and in turns, the Mustang could achieve and still survive steeper and faster dive speeds.

The Spitfire had adequate range to protect England from German invaders but never had enough endurance to make it a decent escort fighter.

Comparisons between the Spitfire, FW-190 and Me-109 show the Supermarine fighter superior to its adversaries from 20,000 feet to maximum altitude. When attempting a zoom climb the Spitfire was clearly superior as was its sustained turning ability. The Focke Wulf 190 had a better rate of role and the Messerschmitt 109 held an advantage in sustained dives. The Spitfire was always the winner when accomplishing aerobatic turns.

Lt Gen. George Loving Jr.
31 FG   5 Victories

"The heroes of the Battle of Britain, brave young pilots of the Royal Air Force, flying Hurricanes and Spitfires, defeated the German Luftwaffe in its attempt to destroy the RAF and clear the way for a German invasion of the British Isles. Naturally, when I learned in 1943 that I was to fly the Spitfire in combat, I was intrigued and delighted. Its distinctive wing design suggested bird-like flying qualities, and that was the case.

Extremely easy to fly, light on the controls, and perhaps the most agile of the fighters in the European Theatre, it was a dream to fly.

In 1943, the Germans had nothing that could turn with it and couldn't outrun the Mark IX, but they could out-dive it.

Designed as a short-range interceptor, it excelled in that role, but lacked, as WWII progressed, the versatility to continue making notable contributions. Its short range ruled it out as an escort fighter for heavy bombers participating in the great strategic air offensive against German oil, transportation and the armament industry, and its liquid cooled engine and lack of toughness, made it unsuitable as a fighter-bomber.

But that did not alter the esteemed place it had earned in the annals of military aviation history as one of the greatest fighter airplanes ever built. I found it to be a pleasure to fly and was confident to face whatever the Luftwaffe could put against me."

MGen. Charles (Sandy) McCorkle
31 FG   11 Victories

"The Spitfire was my all-time favorite fighter. Fun to fly!"

Maj. Robert C. Curtis
52 FG   14 Victories

"I loved the Spitfire and was happy to get the chance to fly it although most of my missions were dull harbor and convoy patrols and dive bombing for which the Spit was not designed."

Col. Jerry D. Collinsworth
31 FG   6 Victories

"The Spit IX was a complete new ballgame! Although my Spitfire Mk. V could only turn inside the FW-190, I did shoot down three of them in my Mk. V. We could still out-turn the FW-190, but the Spitfire Mk. IX could also out climb and out turn him at some altitudes.

Unfortunately the Spitfire had such a short range that it wasn't able to reach into Germany far enough to get a shot at most of their fighters.

Any aircraft only performs its best when flown by a pilot who was 'serious' about learning his aircraft's capabilities versus the enemies aircraft's capabilities."

Lt Col. Charles Fischette
31 FG   5 Victories

"The Spitfire Mk V was great in air to air combat below 1,200 foot altitude, both on offense and defense. Defensively, the turn rate was better than the German Me 109 and FW 190. Consequently, the enemy fighters could not turn tight enough to lead the targeted aircraft and shoot it down. If you saw the attacking aircraft soon enough, you could turn hard into him at the right moment, frustrate his attack and add to your longevity.

High altitude was a different matter, the Spitfire Mk.V was not equipped with a supercharger and so power and speed were reduced considerably. The enemy fighter had the advantage.

The Spitfire Mk.VIII and Mk.IX were equipped with a manual and automatic control supercharger that cut in around 14,000 feet altitude. The German fighters were no match against these Spitfires."

Col. Steve Pisanos
4 FG   10 Victories

"Of all the fighters I flew during World War II, I was most impressed with the Spitfire. It was a masterpiece of harmony and power. I had flown the Hurricane, P-40 and the P-51A before I put my hands on a Spitfire when I joined the 71 Eagle Squadron at Debden Aerodrome. When I returned from my first flight with the Spit, I was so excited and most impressed about its maneuverability and turning ability in comparison to the other fighters I had flown.

When I was flying the Hurricane, my instructor, a Battle of Britain Ace, asked me: 'How do you like the Hurricane Mr. Pisanos?' *'I love it!'*, said I. 'It's the best aircraft I have ever flown!' The ace told me, 'Wait until you fly the Spitfire!'

He was right, although I did not get any kills with the Spitfire, I did ground strafing and always enjoyed hitting enemy locomotives over France with its two 20mm cannons. It was certainly a great sport.

I evaded the Germans for six months in occupied Paris just before the war was over in Europe.

Just before the war was over in Europe, I was assigned to Wright Field in Dayton Ohio as a test pilot.

After I completed the Air Force's Test Pilot school, I had the chance to fly many different types of fighters, including the Me-109, FW-190 and ME-262. I also had the opportunity to fly the Japanese Zero. Not one of these machines, including the P-80, F-102 and F-106 compare to the tremendous agility and smoothness of the Spitfire, the machine the Luftwaffe pilots feared most during the Battle of Britain and World War II."

MESSERSCHMITT Bf. 109

The most important Axis and German fighter of World War II was the Bf.109. It was produced in larger numbers than any other axis aircraft and it became adaptable for constant improvements throughout the war.

Larger engines and a variety and increases in armament were installed to keep pace with the allied fighters it operated against.

The stark, harsh lines of the Bf.109 were nearly opposite that of its chief rival, the Supermarine Spitfire. Where the Spitfire fuselage, wings and overall layout was one of eye pleasing and graceful shaping, the Messerschmitt fighter on the other hand, was designed with sharp angles that gave it a strong and ruthless appearance in flight.

Both designs obviously worked, for the Spitfire and 109 retained their basic shapes regardless of the many and constant improvements made throughout the war.

FLIGHT AND HANDLING CHARACTERISTICS

The Bf.109 had a flush riveted outer skin and was designed by Willy Messerschmitt to keep overall weight as low as possible, without sacrificing protection for the pilot as happened with the Mitsubishi Zero. One problem that was never addressed or corrected was the small and very cramped cockpit.

The Daimler-Benz engine was fuel injected and this allowed it to dogfight in the inverted position if necessary, something allied carbureted fighters could not do.

Ground characteristics of the Bf.109 were poor, having narrowly spaced landing gear and its steep, tail down position caused German pilots much anguish.

Flying controls for some reason lacked an Artificial Horizon indicator and when flying in inclement weather, darkness or clouds, pilots were susceptible to vertigo.

Upon takeoff pilots were always aware of a tendency for the left wing to dip, often times causing horrifying results if proper altitude and speed had not been attained.

Trying to land a Bf. 109 like any other contemporary fighter of its day, would again cause the left wing to drop unexpectedly. If not compensated for correctly, the result was an unavoidable crash.

Safe landings required pulling the fighter up at a steep attitude just before touch down. If this was accomplished correctly, the 109 would drop to earth in a perfect three point landing.

The poor design of the cockpit canopy that so limited the pilot's vision, was at least very tightly sealed. In very poor weather conditions such as heavy rain, the Messerschmitt pilot would still have some forward visibility. In similar bad weather British pilots were forced to severely reduce speed and open the canopy or be totally blinded.

Lateral oscillations could be severe at low speeds and there was no warning before entering a stall.

Aileron control was excellent at normal flight speeds and was quick and responsive.

However, at speeds approaching 400 mph they became nearly impossible to operate.

Fighter comparisons between the Bf.109 and the British Spitfire were thoroughly tested and explored. In dogfighting scenarios the Spitfire could easily perform a half-roll followed by diving. Elevators on the allied plane would allow an easy completion to the maneuver. The German pilot was totally out of his element when attempting a similar move.

Bf.109s had problems performing loops and upward rolls. The climb rate at all altitudes was inferior to the Spitfire. As mentioned earlier, the cockpit of the 109 fighter was very cramped and also provided its pilots with very poor visibility. With the addition of multiple fuselage bulges containing various scoops and breech covers for its nose mounted machine guns, forward and downward viewing was very difficult and I'm sure exasperating for the German pilots.

Allied test pilots who flew the Messerschmitt felt that if handled properly, the 109 was a match for the legendary Spitfire, and indeed in some combat modes even superior. The Bf.109s direct injection engine was superior in gaining quick bursts of speed and dog fighting scenarios were more often decided on the quality of pilots, not airplanes.

1ˢᵗ Lt. Alden P. Rigby
352 FG   5 Victories

"As good as the Mustang was, most of the difference in combat came with the pilot. The Bf. 109 was a very worthy aircraft, and the experienced pilots used this to some limited advantage."

FOCKE WULF FW-190

The second most important German fighter of World War II was the FW-190. Though it came later than its stable mate the Bf.109, it was in many ways the premier axis fighter of the war.

Designed by the brilliant and renowned Kurt Tank the Technical Director of Focke Wulf, the handsome fighter proved to be a new and painful thorn to the allies when it was first encountered in 1941.

The FW-190 was powered by the powerful B.M.W. air-cooled 801 radial engine and was very aerodynamic, fast and strong.

The Focke Wulf fighters were excellent in any role they undertook. The FW-190 A-S/U3 was a fighter bomber and the V-13 was developed as a high altitude interceptor with cabin pressurization. The long nose D "Dora" model was extremely fast and had an upgraded 30mm nose cannon.

The final derivative of the FW-190 was also designed by Kurt Tank and was designated the Ta-152. Though it was manufactured in relatively small quantities, it out performed every other piston engine fighter in the world. The newly developed engine had added nitrous oxide boosting and could obtain 472 mph at over 40,000 feet. Ceiling was near 50,000 feet and maneuverability was up to the same high standard and was more than a match for any allied fighter it met.

FLIGHT AND HANDLING CHARACTERISTICS

The cockpit was comfortable and the nearly transparent canopy gave excellent visibility. Not only was the fighter pleasing to the eye and very maneuverable and hard hitting, but was also well built and relatively easy to maintain.

The B.M.W. engine was however, prone to overheat and pilots often complained of temperatures of 130 degrees in the cockpit. Many felt as if they had 'their feet in a fireplace' while flying the FW-190. The cabin also leaked vast amounts of exhaust fumes while waiting to get airborne. Pilots also had real and imagined fears of hitting the tail plane if forced to bail out.

Even with a wider landing gear than the Me-109, the Focke Wulf fighter had poor ground handling and 15 degrees of flap was essential to keep a take-off swing from causing a disaster.

In flight, the FW-190 was superior to the British Spitfire in most areas and was a pilots dream to fly. Controls were very responsive and the stalling speed was quite high. High speed maneuvers were easy and crisp and re-trimming the airplane was hardly ever necessary.

The powerful BMW 801 engine often ran rough and pilots had little faith in its reliability. This was especially alarming when flying long missions and on flights over the English Channel.

Night flying was never smart or pleasant in a FW-190. The engine exhaust was very bright and easily seen by an enemy. The cockpit also lacked proper instrumentation.

The Spitfire, Mustang and FW-190 were tested together and it was found that the German fighter was noticeably faster at all altitudes and had a clear climb, dive and recovery advantage as well. It also had the best aileron controls of all three planes. The Focke Wulf could change speeds and directions with great ease and from other aircraft it looked like a *flick roll* was being completed.

The German fighter was superb in aerobatics in all areas tested except in performing loops.

Col. Jerry D. Collinsworth
31 FG   6 Victories

"The FW-190 was a great aircraft!

The famous FW-190 Ace Kurt Buhligen (112 victories), shot down Merlin Mitchell my Flight Leader on March 8th 1943, Southeast of the Kasserine Pass.

He was over here at the Champlin Fighter Museum a few years ago, but I only learned of it the day after he left!"

Capt. William Y. Anderson
354 FG   7 Victories

"The FW-190 was a toughie! Especially the D model."

MITSUBISHI ZERO A6M

The Zero was the first carrier based fighter that had higher performance than its land based rivals.

The Zero was the symbol of Japan's new emergence as a world class power. It carried a profound significance as a symbol Japan could rally behind just as the Spitfire had accomplished for Great Britain.

Unlike the legendary British Spitfire, the Zero fighter symbolized the offensive war Japan had unleashed against her enemies. As great as the Supermarine Spitfire was, it would always be remembered as a short-ranged defensive weapon that saved England during the Battle of Britain. The A6M Zero's extremely long range allowed the Japanese Navy to operate hundreds of miles beyond the reach of her aircraft carriers. The Zero often flew long missions of nearly 1,500 miles or over twice that of their allied opponents.

Saburi Sakai the famed Japanese fighter Ace and survivor of World War II, set a record low fuel consumption rate of less than 17 gallons per hour. The Zeros normal fuel capacity was 182 gallons. In comparison, the massive American built Thunderbolt drank nearly 85 gallons an hour at normal cruise settings. Sakai was a master at long distance flying at low speeds. He would drop the propeller revolutions to 1,700 and hang on the brink of losing engine power and stalling for flights of up to eleven hours!

The Zero-Sen was the much heralded replacement for the Type 96 (A5M) fighter, the first Japanese naval monoplane. The power plant for the new fighter was the Mitsubishi MK2 Zuisei 13 (Auspicious Star).

Much design time went into developing and utilizing Extra-Super Duralumin (E.S.D.), which became the chief alloy used in the light weight wings and fuselage assemblies. The wing system of the A6M2 was modified in 1940 with the tips allowed to 'fold up'. In early 1941 the Model 21 was given new aileron balancing tabs which reduced the stick forces needed in high speed maneuvers. This was the type of fighter that was prominently used in the attack of Pearl Harbor on December 7, 1941.

Also flown in 1941 was the modified A6M3 with the folding wing tips removed and the Model 32 became the so-called 'clipped-wing' fighter. When first encountered in action near New Guinea in the fall of 1942, the Allies thought this to be a completely new type of Japanese fighter. It was therefore given the code name 'Hap'. This was later changed to 'Hamp', so as to not embarrass General 'Hap' Arnold. When it was finally realized that the so-called 'new' fighter was just another modified Zero, the Allied Code name was again changed. It would now be known as the infamous 'Zeke 32' or 'Zeke'.

In 1943 with the war turning against Japan a new fighter development was urgently needed. Instead of a new and advanced fighter design, the navy received a face-lifted Zero designated the A6M5 (Model 52). Only minor wing refinements and thrust augmented exhaust stacks emerged. This was helpful, but not nearly good enough to match the powerful Hellcats and Corsairs of the United States.

It was in early 1944 that Japan felt the need to finally take measures to protect pilot and aircraft with bullet proof glass and a fire extinguishing system. The fighter that emerged was the A6M5 (Model 52 B&C). The down side was that what they gained in protection it lost in maneuverability, speed and range.

This was followed in late 1944 with the A6M6 with the new Sakae 31 engine and this plane was largely built by Nakajima. The A6M6 was truly a disappointment to the military as the additional engine power did not materialize and its fuel injection system gave maintenance personal much trouble and difficulty.

Late in the war, with time running out for Japan, it was decided to replace the Zero's long range belly tanks with 500 lb. bombs and turn the once lethal fighter into the (Devine Wind) Kamikaze aircraft. Air Group 201 was formed in the Philippines for just this purpose.

In May of 1945 a further development of the Zero-Sen became the Model 63 A6M7. This plane had reinforced and near fool proof bomb dropping mechanisms and a new and stronger tail unit. This plane was used exclusively as dive bombers or in 'suicide missions'.

The Type O, Model 64, A6M8 was the final swan song for the legendary fighter series. Many improvements were made including additional wing armament and engine changes. This led to a higher top speed, decent pilot and plane armor and improved climb ability. This aircraft was given such high priority that eight major factories were ear-marked to produce them.

Unfortunately, time ran out for Japan and the once touted Mitsubishi Zero.

FLIGHT AND HANDLING CHARACTERISTICS

First viewed with disbelief by the American military, the A6Ms' legendary deeds were nearly 'myth-like' and allowed the Zero to hold complete dominance in the Pacific air war until the Battle Of Midway in 1942. Actually the

Zeros reputation far surpassed what it had in fact, actually accomplished or was capable of achieving.

Almost as important as breaking Japan's top secret military code, was the discovery of an accessible Zero fighter that had crashed in 1942 during an emergency landing on the small island of Aktan. American intelligence personal were able to dissect the nearly intact Zero and learn first-hand of its true capabilities and equally important, its many faults and shortcomings.

The Zeros strengths were many but it also had many glaring weaknesses. The A6M was very light structurally, and had no armor protection for its pilot or fuel. Even a few well placed .50 caliber machine gun hits would often cause a total structural failure or a dramatic and fiery explosion.

Having a high degree of low level maneuverability built in meant a trade off of poor high altitude performance and the inability to out roll or out dive its American opponents. For these reasons American fighter pilots were told never to dogfight with the Zero at low altitudes. Not heeding this warning often led to a pilot's demise.

One of the Mitsubishi fighter's most glaring faults was the way in which the wing, wing spar and fuselage was constructed. It took many hours to produce a Zero and the intricate building techniques made mass production impossible and field repairs difficult at best.

Another major under-estimated weakness was the lack of trained and experienced fighter pilots. By June, 1942 and the Battle Of Midway, many of Japan's best and most capable combat pilots had been shot down or lost in carrier sinking. When flown by poorly trained or inexperienced pilots the once fabled Zero was now little more than a death trap.

More Zero fighters were produced than any other aircraft type. Mitsubishi built 3,879 planes, Nakajima produced 6,215 and Sasebo, Hitachi and Nakajima combined to make 844 trainers and float plane variants.

ZERO FIGHTER INDIVIDUAL MODELS AND CHARACTERISTICS

A6M1	First seen in 1939.
A6M2 (Model 21)	Folding wingtips for carrier use.
A6M2 (Model 11)	First actual production model.A6M2-N

A6M3 (Model 32)	Wing tips clipped and squared.
A6M3 (Model 22)	Full wing tips, including folding mechanisms.
A6M2-K	Two seat trainer version.
A6M5 (Model 52)	Clipped but rounded wingtips and individual exhaust stubs.
A6M5 (Model 52 A)	Heavier wing sturdiness and diving speed.
A6M5 (Model 52 B)	Larger caliber cowl machine guns.
A6M5 (Model 52 C)	Increased fuel. Armor and protected fuel tanks. Lower top speed.
A6M6 (Model 53 C)	Water-methane fuel injection led to unreliable engine. Few made
A6M7 (Model 63)	Designed solely as a fighter-bomber.
A6M8 (Model 64)	Final production version. Had much greater climb rate.

With the vast number of model variations it is easy to see why American pilots and intelligence officers were often unsure in identification.

NORTH AMERICAN F-86 SABRE VERSUS THE MIKOYAN-GUREVICH MiG 15

The F-86 Sabre was one of the most successful combat aircraft of all time. The North American fighter had superb performance qualities and was very easy to fly and dog fight with.

The MiG-15 had a better rate of climb and power thrust-to-weight ratio, but lacked the Sabre's maneuverability and range. A strange problem surfaced in late 1952 that was never fully explained. 54 MiGs went into uncontrollable lethal spins without being engaged in actual combat. As time went on either the planes or pilots became better as the un-explained deadly spins seemed to stop. Eventually all the more serious problems with the MiG-15 were ironed out and what emerged was a very capable fighter-interceptor. The first radar equipped MiG-15 was the SP-1 with a less reliable but adequate radar scanning system than the F-86 Sabre.

The F-86A used the German swept wing technology and was originally designed as a day fighter. It used the General Electric J47-6E-1 4,850 lb. thrust turbojet engine. As originally tested, the first Sabre XP-86 could exceed 700 mph at sea level. In fact, it is possible that this F-86 may have unofficially broken the sound barrier prior to Chuck Yeager's October 14, 1947 historic flight in the Bell XS-1.

The MiG-15 was the primary fighter opposition of the F-86 Sabre in Korea and was the first fighter to take advantage of German research in swept-back wing design. The Soviet built Mig had a swept wing of 35 degrees and was first flown on December 30, 1947.It was powerfully armed with three cannon and a higher altitude ceiling than the American F-86 Sabre.

The MiG-15 lacked the ability to fly as a fighter-bomber and was lighter and less sophisticated than the United States Air Force F-86 jet fighter.

As originally designed, the MiG-15 had many inherit deficiencies. The servo aileron controls needed to be strengthened as well as the elevator balancing, wing box structure, air brakes, leading wing edge and the tall vertical tail unit.

The early F-86 A was not without its own problems. Pilots were frustrated with faulty gun chargers and never were able to gain altitude advantage on their MiG opponents. Though highly trained F-86 pilots developed tactics to effectively counter MiG-15s in most combat scenarios, the MiG fighter always controlled the ability to pick when and if to engage in combat.

The F-86 and MiG-15 were approximately equal in flight speed and with the Sabre's better aerodynamics it enjoyed a marked advantage in dive speeds and had a better dive recovery rate.

The second main Sabre model was the F-86 E and was first flown in September of 1950 with the addition of the 'all flying tail' assembly.

F-86 F Sabres followed in 1952 and had a modified wing assembly and engines with a higher power output.

In April of 1953 the slightly larger and better armed F-86 H variant appeared in the Korean skies.

There was somewhat of a controversy as to whether the MiG or the Sabre had the better armament package. The Sabre pilot had a better gun-sight, a more stable firing platform and could put a lot of bullets on target in a short span of time.

The MiG pilot's cannon armament, though slower firing, only needed a few hits to down their F-86 foe.

The much revered Soviet Ace Yevgeni Pepelyaev claimed the MiG could absorb a larger number of .50 caliber hits and still continue fighting.

Both the F-86 Sabre and the MiG-15 were very well protected. Both planes had effective self-sealing fuel tanks and superb windscreen and cockpit armor protection.

There has always been debate on the actual number of MiG versus Sabre kills. Both the United States and North Korea originally claimed widely exaggerated victory totals.

The final U.S.A.F. revised totals indicate 379 MiGs downed and 103 F-86s lost in combat or a kill ratio of Sabre over MiG-15 approximately 3.5 to 1.

F-86 SABRE		MiG-15
677 MPH	**SPEED**	667 MPH
48,300 ft.	**CEILING**	51,000 ft.
(6) .50 cal.	**ARMAMENT**	(1) 37 mm cannon
		(2) 23 mm cannon

BGen. Robinson Risner
4 FIW   8 Victories

"Since the F-86 was my favorite plane during my 33 years of flying in the Air Force, I'll be happy to briefly make some comments about those days.

Although the Sabre Jet was a bit heavier than the Russian made MiG-15, it could pull more G's, out dive the MiG and was more maneuverable. Even though I was able to shoot down eight enemy MiG-15s the thing that gave me the most satisfaction was being able to push my wingman back to safety after he flamed out deep in enemy territory.

To me, the F-86 Sabre Jet was the greatest fighter of it's time."

Col. Cecil G. Foster
51 FIW   9 Victories

"I considered the F-86E the finest fighter aircraft that I ever flew, primarily because of its versatility and simplicity. The response of this aircraft to the slightest control input was positive and precise. Its fuel consumption was frugal and the redundancy that the engineers built in was a great safety factor and provided great confidence to the pilot.

The AICM gun-sight was radar computing and provided (when used by pilots who understood radar), kill capacity at extreme ranges. In fact, I scored my last three MiG-15 victories at ranges which exceeded 4,000 feet. My conversations with other F-86 pilots who had WW II experience, convinced me that they did not understand or trust the gun sight.

I felt that the MiG-15 was a very good fighter aircraft and could be used very effectively against the USAF when using its built in advantages-i.e.; higher service ceiling and better climb capability. However, it could not withstand battle damage as well as the F-86.

The F-86 was such a great experience and a joy to fly. I still consider it the most enjoyable aircraft that I have ever flown."

Maj. Richard (Dick) Becker
4 FIW   5 Victories

"In my opinion the F-86 Sabre was by far the best fighter I ever flew. The advantages versus the MiG-15 are:

1.   Better gun platform and gun sight.

2.   Better pilot comfort.

3.   It could out dive the MiG-15.

4.   Best of all was better trained pilots in the cockpit.

During my tour our pilots had flown together for over one and a half years prior to going to Korea, (February 1949 thru December 1950).

The MiG-15 could out climb and out turn the Sabre as well as fly at a higher altitude. It also had 23 mm as well as a 37mm cannon, which if it hit you, could destroy a Sabre with a very few rounds, compared to the Sabres six

.50 caliber machine guns which required more rounds into the MiG before it went down."

CAMOUFLAGE ON WORLD WAR II AIRCRAFT

The art of trying to hide or blend in an aircraft to its environment started and flourished during World War I, especially with the early British warplanes.

After the end of hostilities many nations became literal 'bill boards' for paint manufacturing companies.

Gaudy yellow wings, red noses and green tails graced many fighting aircraft during the 1920's and 30s.

However, with war on the horizon, countries once again began to try to make combat aircraft indistinguishable from their element, whether that was in flight or sitting on the ground.

GREAT BRITAIN

Official mandates regulated and standardized camouflage patterns and colors. Aircraft colors, usually two-toned and aptly chosen to represent the area in which they operated were either: TEMPERATE = dark green and brown. SEA DUTY TEMPERATE CLIMATE AREA = dark grey and green. MIDDLE EAST COLOR SCHEME = dark brown and medium to light tan.

Later in the war the temperate climate color combinations were changed to dark grey and green.

Early in the war lower portions of British aircraft were painted half black and half white, and then later changed to a pale, duck egg blue color. During the final months of World War II, it was further modified to a very pale sky (type S).

GERMANY

For a country beset with strict rules and regulations, the German combat aircraft camouflage colorations were very often original, seldom regulated and were many times left to the discretion of individual units to decide what patterns and colors should be adopted.

Normally planes were painted in geometric patterns in shades of green or grey. In desert climates shades of brown and tan were used. The undersides of German combat aircraft were usually painted a pale or light blue.

Night fighters were covered in dark grey or black, with even the national insignia often over coated in a subdued grey or left off entirely.

Winter saw an adoption of white splotches or hand applied white washed finishes. The blotchy finishes were very effective in the harsh forward areas from Finland to Russia.

While national insignia were finished in black or grey, the individual unit insignia could and were often times brightly colored and personalized. Often cartoon characters or mascots graced the sides or nose of fighters, while victory or *kill* markings were normally applied to the sides of the horizontal stabilizer.

FRANCE

French combat aircraft were usually painted in the 1939 adopted pattern of dark brown and green with a grey coloring added in a random application. The lower surfaces of wings and fuselage were normally painted in light grey or blue shades.

ITALY

Italian aircraft had probably the most simplistic form of camouflage. Two basic color combinations covered everything.

In the desert regions planes were painted in a tan color with irregular splotches of medium to dark green. This pattern was commonly referred to as '*sand and spinach*'. Shades of dark green or grey were used in all other areas.

When fighters were sent from the Italian countryside to the desert or mountain regions, ochre or tan was over painted in a series of random spots. This motif covered the entire upper surface and sides of the aircraft.

The undersides of Italian combat planes were painted a light sea green, grey, or an ivory-cream color.

SOVIET UNION

Russian aircraft had a very strict guideline concerning the colors to be employed for camouflage purposes.

During winter conditions either an overall solid color of very dark green or white was incorporated. Along with the solid green a two toned wavy pattern of green and dark brown was used. Light gray was the color of choice for the lower portions of the wing, tail and fuselage.

The Russian national red star insignia was at times out-lined in yellow. Unlike other countries, the Soviet Union usually left the upper wings free of national markings.

Brightly colored nationalistic slogans were often seen along the sides of the fuselage. These were normally painted in red, yellow or white colors.

JAPAN

Though strict guidelines were laid out for the colorization of Japanese aircraft, the further away from the home islands a squadron was based, the easier and more common it was to vary from the strict rules governing camouflage.

Often the poor quality of paint left aircraft multi-colored even when it wasn't the intention to do so. Grey or dark green were common upper surface colors and were sometimes mixed in a mottling affect.

Larger aircraft were often painted in a wavy olive green and brown pattern.

The lower surfaces of Japanese warplanes were usually painted a light shade of grey or very pale blue. A yellow band was incorporated on the wings leading edge to help with identification in combat.

Late in the war many combat planes had a white, yellow, red or blue stripe painted around the aft fuselage for the same purpose.

The cowling of radial engine fighters were usually painted in a blue-black color. Propellers were normally left in natural metal finish or painted in a brownish or red primer color.

Ace pilots or squadron leaders were allowed to have bright colors painted along the fuselage with unique and striking stylized symbols and shapes adorning the vertical tail surfaces of their aircraft. Lightning bolts in various configurations were a favorite design choice of many high scoring pilots.

UNITED STATES

After Pearl Harbor America's combat aircraft quickly converted to very drab colors. Gone were the bright and gaudy colors that once graced the aircraft of the 1920s and 30s. In their place the Army Air Corps adopted shades of olive green or drab, greenish-brown colors.

Considerations were made for desert combat areas where tan and even pinkish shades were incorporated. This was especially true for larger aircraft like the B-25 Mitchell and B-24 Liberator bombers.

However, in general, the rule was the more drab the better, and along with normal weathering from combat duty, aircraft definitely did not draw attention to themselves.

The lower portions of Army Air Corps planes were usually painted in an intermediate, dull gray color.

Rapid identification to determine if an aircraft was friend or foe, was a problem every combatant nation faced during World War II.

Many times similar looking aircraft or national insignias led to a 'shoot and then think' attitude among other pilots and ground based anti-aircraft batteries.

In spring of 1942 the red center circle was painted out on American aircraft to avoid any quick confusion with the Japanese red circle 'meatball' national insignia.

Also in the early months of 1942, field maintenance personal began receiving permission to delete the large black 'U.S. Army' identification letters from the lower wing surfaces of combat aircraft. The bold lettering had drained many man hours of labor and gallons of paint to accomplish and actually defeated the main intention to produce an 'invisible' or neutral and non-identifiable aircraft.

Naval aircraft were originally painted an overall gull gray, with off white or light gray undersurfaces.

In 1943 a new paint scheme was adopted that included upper surfaces painted a dark, opaque blue that blended into a blue-grey and then dull white on the lower surfaces of the wings and fuselage.

Once air superiority was attained, the Army allowed great latitude in the color schemes used by both fighters and bombers.

Gone were the drab colors of the early war years and in their place fighter groups and squadrons painted bright colors on spinners, cowlings, and tails. The leaders of individual fighter groups were aware of the personal pride and competitiveness of their pilots and allowed colors to be used for both recognition and identification purposes.

Late in the war many fighter and bomber units reverted back to their aircraft's original natural metal finish. These were often highly waxed and in the bright sunlight could be seen many miles away. A slight increase in overall speed could be obtained by doing this and with air superiority achieved, the need for hiding, blending in or concealment of aircraft seemed redundant and unnecessary.

American Army Air Corps fighter and bomber pilots were allowed great latitude in developing individual nose art and colorful and original names for their aircraft. Many cartoon characters or sultry and risqué '*Max Vargas*' type female forms and nudes adorned individual fighters and bombers.

The U.S. Navy and Marine Corps kept a stricter control of markings and colors throughout the war years.

Few Navy or Marine pilots were allowed to individualize their planes with personal markings. **Captain Joe McGraw's** F4F '*Mah Baby*', **Captain David McCampbell's** F6F '*Monsoon Maiden*' and later '*Minsi*', **Captain Hugh Winters, Jr.** '*Hanger Lily*' and **Colonel R. Bruce Porter's** F6F '*Black Death*' are a few notable exceptions.

A pilot was usually given a specific aircraft to fly, as well as a loyal and well trained ground crew to maintain it. However, some units including the famed '*BLACK SHEEP*' of VMF-214, handed out whichever aircraft was serviceable and in flying condition. At the VMF-214 reunion held at Eden Prairie, Minnesota in 2005, **BGen. Bruce Matheson** explained that planes were handed out in random order on the flight line. A F4U Corsair was either in flight condition or it wasn't. "Our planes all flew the same. After all they were built on assembly lines just like Fords and Chevys!"

FIGHTER AIRCRAFT ARMAMENT OF WORLD WAR II AND KOREA

Many a fighter ace has confided to me that their aircraft were no more than a *'gun platform'*. Each combatant country developed their own weapon systems for their pilots. As was discussed in earlier pages of this book, every aircraft had different flying characteristics. Some fighting aircraft had good qualities, some great, some poor, but to be a great fighting aircraft, everything had to come together in *harmony*. Reliability, maneuverability, speed, climb and dive characteristics, range and ceiling were *ALL* very important, but if a pilot's aircraft was not a stable gun platform, its use for its intended purpose, ie; to *'shoot down enemy aircraft'*, is questionable.

GREAT BRITAIN

Great Britain endorsed and used .303 caliber ammunition as their primary source of armament in nearly every fighter it fielded in World War II.

Biplanes usually carried two in World War I, where the legendary Spitfires and Hurricanes of World War II could carry between eight and twelve.

The development of the so called *'universal wing'* allowed British fighters to carry combinations of machine guns and 20 mm cannon armament.

Tank busting duties went to the powerful 40mm cannon armed fighters of the RAF. The superb and deadly Typhoons and Tempests were most adept at these low level assaults on enemy ground targets.

ITALY

Italy developed fighter aircraft that were highly maneuverable but were lightly armed. Italian fighter aircraft were usually armed with just two or three rifle caliber machine guns and had a difficult time downing the well built and armored Allied aircraft they faced in combat.

Later aircraft carried heavy armament to try to compete with their allied counterparts. The Fiat G.55 and Regianne Re.2005 were typical, each carrying wing and nose mounted German designed 20mm cannon and twin cowl mounted machine guns.

GERMANY

At the beginning of the war German aircraft used the MG-15 machine gun in the standard 7.92 mm, or the MG-81 machine gun manufactured by Mauser.

Later the 13 mm Rheinmetall machine gun was adopted to try and equal the heavier fire power of the Americans .50 caliber guns.

Probably Germany's best aircraft weapon was its version of the Swiss Oerlikon 15mm cannon. This superb functioning cannon was later upgraded to 20 mm. and produced by Mauser, was arguably the finest cannon produced during World War II. The Mauser cannon was very reliable, had a high rate of fire and a very respectable muzzle velocity.

The other prominent weapon used with great success in German fighters was the Mk 108, 30mm cannon. Many of Germany's most advanced fighters including the Me-262 'Swallow', and the Me-163 rocket fighter used these to great effect, especially against large four engine bomber formations.

JAPAN

Japan's early aircraft were notoriously under armed. As with pilot armor and protection for fuel tanks, heavy armament was considered unnecessary for the light and maneuverable fighters and in fact was often purposely ignored.

The A6M-2 Reisen modified this thinking and adopted the type 99, 20mm wing mounted cannon to supplement its cowl mounted 7.7 mm machine guns.

Normally only twin engine bomber interceptors or night fighters carried heavier armament.

Japan held to the belief that aircraft of minimum weight and high maneuverability were a fighter's most important attributes.

Near the end of the war the Kawasaki Ki-102 was designed to carry a 37mm and twin 20 mm cannon. Though only built in small numbers, this Japanese bomber interceptor was quite effective when finally used as intended.

UNITED STATES

America relied almost entirely on the .50 caliber Browning machine gun to arm their fighter aircraft.

Some early fighters such as the Curtiss P-40 Tomahawk and the Bell P-39 Airacobra mixed .30 and .50 caliber weapons. The P-39 Airacobra was an interesting hi-bred that combined .30 caliber and .50 caliber machine guns along with a heavy 37mm cannon that fired through the propeller hub. The only other widely used U.S. fighter to utilize a cannon with great effectiveness was the superb P-38. The Lightning combined four .50 caliber machine guns and a 20mm cannon in the nose of its revolutionary twin engine fighter. This nose mounted armament allowed the pilot a much easier task of hitting his adversary.

USMC F4U Corsairs, USAAF P-51 Mustangs and Navy Hellcats and Wildcats usually operated with six .50 caliber mountings. Only the huge, P-47 Thunderbolt carried eight of these reliable and hard-hitting weapons.

During the Korean War in the 1950s, The United States still relied on the tried but true .50 caliber guns to arm its F-86 Sabre. The six Browning guns grouped in the Sabre's nose gave a very effective rate of fire against its MiG-15 adversaries.

NORTH KOREA

North Korea using Russian built MiG-15 fighter jets adopted two 23mm and one 37mm cannon as its primary weapons.

It would seem a toss up as to whether the United States or North Korea had a better weapon system. The six nose mounted Browning machine guns of the F-86 could pour out a tremendous rate of fire in a few seconds, but it only took a few rounds to make contact from the MiGs cannons to cripple or shot down its American counterpart.

FIGHTER AIRCRAFT GUN SIGHTS

The most widely used gun sights in use during World War II were the standard *'optical reflector'* type. A ring of light with a center bead would be projected on a transparent mirror at the bottom of the windscreen. The pilot would then have to line his target up with the ring of light before firing. These early gun sights required that the aircraft, guns and sight all be aligned before accurate firing could be accomplished.

Having ones weapons directly in front of the pilot as with the P-38 Lightning was the easiest and simplest way to achieve results in combat. If an aircraft's armament was wing mounted, guns had to be *'harmonized'* to converge on a particular point at a pre-determined distance. The pilots only other choice was to give a *'spray pattern'* of bullets over the entire range of his machine guns.

The hardest targets to hit were those flying across ones field of vision. As in hunting with a shotgun, a person must *'lead'* the target, or shoot to where you believe the target will be when your bullets finally reach it.

In late 1944 the K-14 gyro computing gun sight was introduced. This was an early form of computer and made it much easier to hit an enemy target. Fighter pilot victories tripled after the new invention was introduced and adopted on allied fighters.

The K-14 optical gun sight was such a revelation that it was still in wide use with jet fighters in the 1950s.

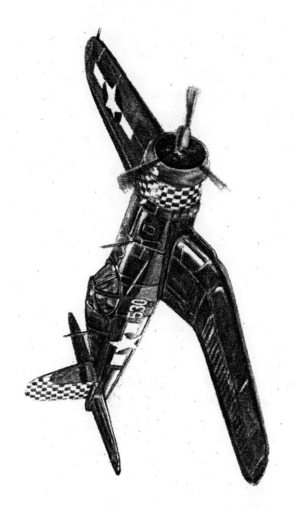

Chance Vought F4U Corsair Illustration by Scott Oleson

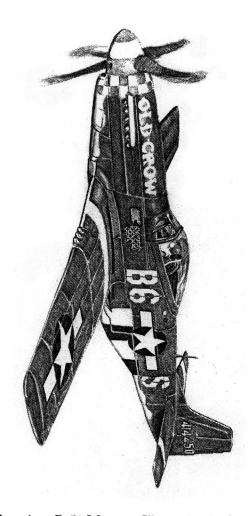

North American P-51 Mustang Illustration by Scott Oleson

Grumman F6F Hellcat Illustrated by Scott Oleson

Curtiss P-40 Warhawk Illustrated by Patrick Oleson

North American F-86 Sabre Illustrated by Scott Oleson

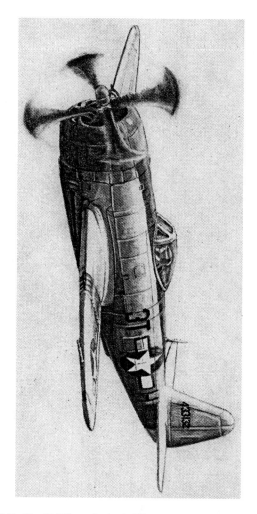

Republic P-47 Thunderbolt Illustrated by Scott Oleson

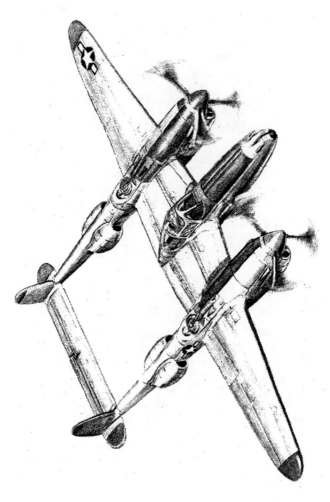

Lockheed P-38 Lightning Illustrated by Scott Oleson

Part III

INTRODUCTION

If there is one thing that I hope the reader will take to heart, ponder and remember, it is just how dangerous it is to fly combat aircraft.

As anyone who has ever piloted an aircraft knows, flying can be a true joy. Flying makes one feel exhilarated, free, and can leave you marveling at the sheer accomplishment of being able to shake one's earthly bonds.

Flying can also be dangerous, deadly and at times a terrifying experience, especially in combat or when testing a new aircraft type.

Not everyone who wanted to fly a fighter aircraft had the opportunity or the necessary skills to do so.

America has always had more than their share of eager, young pilot candidates for its military training program. A great share of these novice and youthful pilots were *washed out* or had dangerous or deadly accidents while in flight school trying to master their aircraft. Even the most docile of military training aircraft could be considered *hot* when compared with their civilian counterparts.

The American Fighter Aces are an elite group of aviators. They are the 'crème de la crème', the best trained, had the best aircraft and ground maintenance available, and still many died due to combat battle damage, aircraft failure, navigation error, poor weather conditions or just plain bad luck.

Imagine flying a fighter aircraft that was often unforgiving, into bad weather, in close formation with other aircraft, and then into combat against a determined and skilled enemy, and you have some idea of what America's fighter aces endured on a daily basis. Imagine surviving your ordeal and then facing the possibility of trying to fly a crippled aircraft, alone and separated

189

from your fellow pilots, low on fuel and with many long, agonizing miles left to travel. After all that you still have to face the dangers of landing when extremely tired or wounded, often in the twilight or even darkness.

Be prepared to experience this again tomorrow, and every other day of your combat tour, and you have some idea of what it was like to be an ace fighter pilot! Reality was far different then the glamorous and envied life usually portrayed in Hollywood movies.

The American fighter aces from all conflicts numbered 1,473. Nearly 50% of all air combat victories were scored by just 5% of our fighter pilots. These illustrious combat veterans shot down 10,527.25 enemy planes for an average of 7.15 *kills* each. 160 of our aces were killed in World War II and Korea, and a further 124 died in non-combat related flying accidents. In World War I there were 117 American Aces that flew for the United States, France and Great Britain. 17 of these pilots died in combat, while another 13 died in non-combat flying accidents.

These figures are indeed sobering. Nearly 20% of all World War II American Aces died while flying and a staggering 30% died in World War I. These high fatality numbers included many of our *best* and most successful fighter pilots. Countless additional brave aviators were killed *before* they could reach the lofty plateau of *"ACE"* status.

To sum up I wish to discuss the illustrious career of test pilot Scott Crossfield.

Scott Crossfield's flight accomplishments are unparalleled in aviation history. He became the first pilot to break MACH 2, (twice the speed of sound), on November 20, 1953 in the Skyrocket D-558-II. Crossfield logged more than 100 rocket flights during the 1950s to make him the worlds foremost rocket test pilot. He was enshrined in both the *National Aviation Hall of Fame* and the *International Space Hall of Fame.*

Late in 2005 I received the following personal letter from the legendary test pilot and aeronautical engineer:

"All of my experiences have been documented many times. I have **never** been injured by an airplane. I have **never** bailed out of an airplane. I have enjoyed flying and living with every plane I ever flew.

In my day the sky was the laboratory and the aircraft the experiment. Today the airplane is the laboratory and the payload is the experiment. Times have changed which is progress."

I am very proud and honored that Scott Crossfield was my friend, and deeply saddened to hear of his tragic and unnecessary death on April 19, 2006 at age 84.

After speaking to a group of Air Force Officers at Maxwell Air Force Base in Alabama, he was piloting his single engine Cessna 210A back to Virginia and crashed during a severe thunderstorm into a mountainous region of Georgia.

As great a pilot as he was, Scott Crossfield put himself at risk doing what he loved the most, and paid the ultimate price for doing so.

Make no mistake, flying is a very serious business. Even the most accomplished and experienced pilot can lose their life in a flying mishap.

Appendix A

AMERICAN FIGHTER ACES THAT WERE KIA OR MIA

NAME	PLANE FLOWN	DATE	AGE
Capt. Fletcher Adams	P-51 Mustang	May 30, 1944	22
1st Lt. Robert Adams	P-38 Lightning	September 2, 1943	23
Capt. Charles F. Anderson Jr.	P-51 Mustang	April 19, 1944	-
!st Lt. William Aron	P-51 Mustang	April 22, 1945	-
Lt(jg) Douglas Baker	F6F Hellcat	December 14, 1944	23
Ens. Edgar Bassett	F4F Wildcat	June 4, 1942	28
Lt.Col. Harold Bauer	F4F Wildcat	November 14, 1942	33
Capt. Edward Beavers	P-51 Mustang	November 27, 1944	24
Maj. Donald Beerbower	P-51 Mustang	August 9, 1944	22
Ens. Jack Berkheimer	F6F Hellcat	December 16, 1944	20
1st Lt. Hipolitus Biel	P-51 Mustang	April 24, 1944	-
Lt. Walter Bishop	F6F Hellcat	December 14, 1944	24

AMERICAN FIGHTER ACES THAT WERE KIA OR MIA (Continued)

NAME	PLANE FLOWN	DATE	AGE
Cdr. Charles Brewer	F6F Hellcat	June 19, 1944	33
Lt. Mark Bright	F6F Hellcat	June 17, 1944	25
Maj. Meade Brown	P-51 Mustang	August 24, 1950	34
Capt. William Brown Jr.	F4U Corsair	February 24, 1952	28
Capt. James Browning	P-51 Mustang	February 9, 1945	27
Lt. William Burkhalter	F6F Hellcat	June 11, 1944	22
Lt(jg) Howard Burriss	F4U Corsair	January 31, 1944	22
Maj. Philip Chapman	P-51 Mustang	March 28, 1945	25
Lt.Cdr. Leonard Check	F6F Hellcat	January 4, 1945	33
Maj. Henry Condon II	P-38 Lightning	January 2, 1945	-
Maj. Edward Cragg	P-38 Lightning	December 26, 1943	25
Capt. Arthur Cundy	P-51 Mustang	March 11, 1945	21
Capt. Frank Cutler	P-51 Mustang	May 13, 1944	23
Lt.Col. George Davis Jr.	F-86 Sabre	February 10, 1952	32
Capt. Frederick Doersch	P-51 Mustang	October 29, 1944	24
2nd Lt. Cecil Doyle	F4F Wildcat	November 7, 1942	22
Capt. Walter Duke	P-38 Lightning	June 6, 1944	22
1st Lt. Hoyt Eason	P-38 Lightning	March 3, 1943	28
Capt. Joseph Egan Jr.	P-47 Thunderbolt	July 19, 1944	27

AMERICAN FIGHTER ACES THAT WERE KIA OR MIA (Continued)

NAME	PLANE FLOWN	DATE	AGE
Capt. Lee Everhart	P-38 Lightning	October 12, 1944	26
Maj. Selvan Feld	P-47 Thunderbolt	August 13, 1944	-
Capt. Ernest Fiebelkorn	F-82 Twin Mustang	July 6, 1950	27
Maj. Virgil Fields	Spitfire IX	February 6, 1944	22
Lt. George Formaneck Jr.	F6F Hellcat	April 23, 1944	24
Lt. Doris Freeman	Kamikaze (Bunker Hill)	May 11, 1945	25
Capt. Earl Fryer	P-51 Mustang	November 8, 1944	27
Capt. Robert Gibb	F-84 Thunderjet	December 16, 1951	29
Lt. John Gilder	Kamikaze (Bunker Hill)	May 11, 1945	24
Capt. Lindol Graham	P-38 Lightning	March 18, 1944	-
1st Lt. Robert Griffith	P-38 Lightning	July 26, 1944	-
Col. William Halton	P-51 Mustang	May 21, 1952	24
Mar.Gun. Henry Hamilton	F4F Wildcat	October 21, 1942	34
Capt. John Hampshire Jr.	P-40 Warhawk	May 2, 1943	-
Lt. Christopher Hanseman	P-51 Mustang	July 29, 1944	19
1st Lt. Robert Hanson	F4U Corsair	February 3, 1944	23
Lt. William Harris Jr.	FG-1D	August 9, 1945	26
Lt. Frank Hayde	F6F Hellcat	July 15, 1944	23

AMERICAN FIGHTER ACES THAT WERE KIA OR MIA (Continued)

NAME	PLANE FLOWN	DATE	AGE
Capt. Cotesworth Head	P-38 Lightning	January 18, 1944	27
Lt. Paul Henderson Jr.	F6F Hellcat	June 15, 1944	27
Maj. Edwin Hernan Jr.	F4U Corsair	July 19, 1951	30
Maj. Edwin Hiro	P-51 Mustang	September 19, 1944	28
1st Lt. Ralph Hofer	P-51 Mustang	July 2, 1944	23
1st Lt. James Hoffman Jr.	P-51 Mustang	August 22, 1944	21
1st Lt. James Holloway	P-38 Lightning	June 18, 1945	26
Lt(jg) Robert Humphrey	-	June 13, 1952	28
1st Lt. Edward Hunt	P-51 Mustang	November 8, 1944	25
2nd Lt. Joe W. Icard	P-47 Thunderbolt	March 8, 1944	-
Capt. Clarence Johnson	P-51 Mustang	September 23, 1944	24
Flt.Lt. Paul G. Johnson	Spitfire IX	July 18, 1944	24
1st Lt. Cyril Jones Jr.	P-51 Mustang	September 12, 1944	23
Capt. Frank Jones Jr.	P-51 Mustang	August 8, 1944	24
Flt.Lt. Ripley Jones	Spitfire V	October 17, 1942	27
Col. Neel Kearby	P-47 Thunderbolt	March 5, 1944	33
2ndLt. Charles Kendrick	F4F Wildcat	October 2, 1942	28
Lt. Lenton Kirkland Jr.	P-38 Lightning	December 24, 1944	24

AMERICAN FIGHTER ACES THAT WERE KIA OR MIA (Continued)

NAME	PLANE FLOWN	DATE	AGE
Lt. William Knight	F6F Hellcat	November 5, 1944	25
1st Lt. Ward Kuentzel	P-38 Lightning	June 19, 1944	22
Capt. Kenneth Ladd	P-38 Lightning	October 14, 1944	24
Capt. Joseph Lang	P-51 Mustang	October 14, 1944	22
Maj. Donald Larson	P-51 Mustang	August 4, 1944	29
Lt.(jg) John Leppla	F4F Wildcat	October 26, 1942	26
Flt.Ldr. Robert Little	P-40E (AVG)	May 22, 1942	25
Capt. Paul Lucas	P-38 Lightning	January 15, 1945	25
1st Lt. Lowell Lutton	P-38 Lightning	November 2, 1943	25
Lt.Col. Thomas Lynch	P-38 Lightning	March 8, 1944	27
Lt.Col. Grant Mahoney	P-38 Lightning	January 3, 1945	26
Lt. William Marontate	F4F Wildcat	June 15, 1943	23
1st Lt. Donald McDowell	P-51 Mustang	May 28, 1944	27
Capt. Bernard McGratten	P-51 Mustang	June 6, 1944	-
Maj. Thomas McGuire Jr.	P-38 Lightning	January 7, 1945	24
Lt.Col. George McMillan	P-38 Lightning	June 24, 1944	27
Maj. Michael McPharlin	P-51 Mustang	June 6, 1944	20
Maj. George Merritt Jr.	P-51 Mustang	June 7, 1944	28

AMERICAN FIGHTER ACES THAT WERE KIA OR MIA (Continued)

NAME	PLANE FLOWN	DATE	AGE
1st Lt. Donald Meuten	P-40 Warhawk	May 7, 1944	-
Capt. Henry Miklajcyk	P-51 Mustang	November 2, 1944	23
Lt. Henry Mitchell Jr.	F6F Hellcat	April 3, 1945	23
Ens. Arthyr Mollenhauer	F6F Hellcat	October 29, 1944	20
Maj. John T. Moore	P-47 Thunderbolt	October 8, 1944	27
Capt. John Morgan Jr.	F4U Corsair	March 28, 1945	23
Lt. Stanley Morrill	B-24 (Bomb explosion)	March 29, 1945	26
Lt. William Moseley	F6F Hellcat	July 4, 1944	27
Capt. Alva Murphy	P-51 Mustang	March 2, 1945	26
1st Lt. Jennings Myers	P-38 Lightning	December 22, 1943	26
Lt. Joseph Narr	F4F Wildcat	November 11, 1942	26
Ens. Robert K. Nelson	F6F Hellcat	November 19, 1944	21
Sqn.Ldr. John Newkirk	P-40 (AVG)	March 24, 1942	28
Lt.Cdr. Edward O'Hare	F6F Hellcat	November 26, 1943	29
Capt. Norman E. Olson	P-51 Mustang	April 8, 1944	29
Cdr. Charles Ostrom	Liscombe Bay sinking	November 24, 1943	35
Flt.Ldr. John Petach	P-40 (AVG)	July 10, 1942	27
Maj. Hyde Phillips	AU-1	August 14, 1952	27

AMERICAN FIGHTER ACES THAT WERE KIA OR MIA (Continued)

NAME	PLANE FLOWN	DATE	AGE
1st Lt. Joseph Pierce	P-51 Mustang	May 21, 1944	22
Ens. Claude Plant Jr.	F6F Hellcat	September 12, 1944	24
Lt. Zenneth Pond	F4F Wildcat	September 10, 1942	22
Capt. Ernest Powell	F4U Corsair	July 18, 1943	24
Capt. Joseph Powers Jr.	F-51 Mustang	June 8, 1951	30
Maj. George Preddy Jr.	P-51 Mustang	December 25, 1944	25
Lt. William Reese	P-51 Mustang	May 21, 1944	23
Lt.Col. Elwin Righetti	P-51 Mustang	April 17, 1945 (Birthday)	30
Lt. Thomas Roach	F4F Wildcat	July 25, 1943	24
Capt. Daniel Roberts Jr.	P-38 Lightning	November 9, 1943	25
1st Lt. LeRoy Ruder	P-51 Mustang	June 6, 1944	22
Capt. William Rynne	P-47 Thunderbolt	March 28, 1944	-
1st Lt. Philip Sangermann	P-51 Mustang	December 9, 1944	20
Lt. John Sargent Jr.	Kamikaze (Bunker Hill)	May 11, 1945	26
Cdr. Gordon Schecter	F6F Hellcat	March 18, 1945	32
Maj. Glen Schiltz Jr.	F-51 Mustang	October 6, 1950	32
Capt. Al Schlegal	P-51 Mustang	August 28, 1944	25
Lt. Frank Schneider	F6F Hellcat	January 9, 1944	23

AMERICAN FIGHTER ACES THAT WERE KIA OR MIA (Continued)

NAME	PLANE FLOWN	DATE	AGE
Maj. Leroy Schreiber	P-47 Thunderbolt	April 15, 1944	26
1st Lt. Robert Seidman	P-38 Lightning	May 14, 1944	-
1st Lt. William Simmons	P-51 Mustang	April 25, 1944	-
Lt. Frank Sistrunk	-	September 3, 1951	29
2nd Lt. John C. Smith	P-38 Lightning	September 9, 1943	23
Col. Meryl Smith	P-38 Lightning	December 7, 1944	26
Maj. Robert E. Smith	P-38 Lightning	June 22, 1944	27
1st Lt. Virgil Smith	P-38 Lightning	December 30, 1942	23
Maj. Robert Stout	FG-1A	March 4, 1945	26
P/O James Thorne	Mustang III	September 10, 1944	23
Lt.Cdr. Ross Torkelson	F4F Wildcat	July 22, 1943	29
2nd Lt. Grant Turley	P-47 Thunderbolt	March 6, 1944	23
Capt. Arnold Vinson	Spitfire VB	April 3, 1943	-
Lt.Col. Sidney Weatherford	F-84 Thunderjet	August 11, 1952	31
P/O Claude Weaver III	Spitfire IX	January 28, 1944	20
Lt.Col. Robert Westbrook Jr.	P-38 Lightning	November 22, 1944	27
1st Lt. John Wolford	P-38 Lightning	May 19, 1943	-
Maj. Sun-Shui Wong	Polikarpov I-15	March 16, 1941	27

AMERICAN FIGHTER ACES THAT WERE KIA OR MIA (Continued)

NAME	PLANE FLOWN	DATE	AGE
Ens. Walter Wood Jr.	F6F Hellcat	October 18, 1944	23

APPENDIX B

NON-COMBAT FLYING ACCIDENTS OF AMERICAN FIGHTER ACES (KIFA)

NAME	DEATH	LOCATION OF CRASH	PLANE FLOWN
Ens. Fred Ackerman	34	Doerun, Georgia (Storm)	-
Maj. Donald Adams	32	Detroit, Michigan	F-89
Lt.Col. Frank Adkins	31	Freepont, Texas	P-38
Capt. Donald Aldrich	29	Chicago, Illinois	F4U
Lt. Robert Anderson	27	Stockton, Maryland	F6F
Maj. Jack Bade	42	New York	F-105
Lt. James Barnes	31	-	F6F
Capt. Hampton Boggs	31	Madison, Wisconsin (Weather)	F-86
Maj. Dick Bong	34	Burbank, California	F-80
Lt.Cdr. William Bonneau	28	Philadelphia, Pennsylvania	F8F
Lt. Gerald Boyle	27	Ocean crash	F6F
Maj. Michael Brezas	30	Korea	F-84

NON-COMBAT FLYING ACCIDENTS OF AMERICAN FIGHTER ACES (KIFA) (Continued)

NAME	DEATH	LOCATION OF CRASH	PLANE FLOWN
Lt.Cdr. Sam Brocato	39	Pacific Ocean	F6F
Lt(jg) James Bryce	33	Banning, California	F6F
Capt. John Carder	41	New Orleans, Louisiana	Civil A/C
1st Lt. Walt Carroll	28	Cajon Pass, California	P-38
Lt.Col. William Crowe	42	Rufugio, Texas	AD-6
Maj. William Daley	24	Coulommiers (Take-off collision)	P-47
Capt. Fernley Damstrong	21	Luzon	P-38
1st Lt. Richard Deakins	24	(Flew into mountain)	P-47
Lt. Robert Dibb	23	Inyokern, California	F6F
Capt. Eugene Dillow	25	Atlantic, North Carolina	F4U
1st Lt. John Samuel Dunaway	22	Kaohe Bay	P-38
Lt.Col. John England	31	Toul, France	F-86
Lt.Col. Marion Felts	39	Avon Park, Florida	F-105
Maj. Manuel (Pete) Fernandez	55	Grand Bahama Island	-
1st Lt. William Fiedler	-	Guadalcanal (struck by P-38 during takeoff)	P-39
Capt. Ed Fisher	29	Norristown, Pennsylvania	AT-6F
Col. Patrick Fleming	38	Tracy, California	B-52
Lt. George Formanek Jr.	23	Hollandia (Crashed into tree)	F6F
Lt.Col. Robert Foy	34	Phoenix, Arizona (Explosion)	B-25

NON-COMBAT FLYING ACCIDENTS OF AMERICAN FIGHTER ACES (KIFA) (Continued)

NAME	DEATH	LOCATION OF CRASH	PLANE FLOWN
Capt. Magnus Francis	30	Muric Air Force Base, California	C-47
Maj. Robert Fraser	30	Santa Barbara, California	F6F
Lt.Col. Ken Frazier	39	Sourland Mountain, New Jersey	FJ-3
Capt. Al Froning	53	Clinton, Iowa	Civil plane
Maj. Fred Glover	28	Hazelhurst, Georgia	-
Maj. Mathew Gordon	23	Kalaikunda, India	P-51
Lt.Cdr. John Gray	29	San Clemente, California	FR-1
Maj. Rockford Gray	30	NW of Borokoe Air Drome	P-47
Capt. Billy Gresham	21	Biak (Bad Parachute)	P-38
1st Lt. Charley Gumm Jr.	23	East Angela, England	P-51
Col. William Halton	34	Korea	P-51
Maj. Ernest Harris	32	Augsburg, Germany	F-80
Capt. Fred Harris	22	Buna Bay	P-38
Capt. Cameron Hart	27	Craig Field, Alabama	P-47
Ens. Horace Heath	23	Hawaii	F4U
Lt. Lloyd Heinzen	27	Beacon, New York (Bad weather)	JRB-4
Capt. William Hennon	23	Long Island, New York	BT-14
Lt.Col. John Hebst	36	San Diego, California	P-80
Maj. Edwin Hiro	28	Vreden, Ahaus	P-51
1st Lt. James Hoffman Jr.	21	Czechoslovakia (Collision)	P-51

NON-COMBAT FLYING ACCIDENTS OF AMERICAN FIGHTER ACES (KIFA) (Continued)

NAME	DEATH	LOCATION OF CRASH	PLANE FLOWN
1st Lt. James Holloway	25	Moulmein (Weather)	P-38
1st Lt. William Hood	22	Indiania/Michigan	F4U
Cdr. Robert Jennings	34	Memphis, Tennessee	F2H-4
Capt. Alvin Jensen	28	Patuxent River	F2H-4
Col. Gerald R. Johnson	25	Ie Shima, Tokyo, Japan (Bad weather)	B-25
Capt. William Kane	45	Augusta, Georgia	TV-2
Capt. Ivan Kincheloe	30	Edwards Air Force Base, California	F-104
1st Lt. Wayne Laird	23	New Herbides	F4U
Capt. Robert Latshaw Jr.	30	Boca del Rio, Venzuela	T-33
1st Lt. Larry Liebers	26	Victorville, California	AT-7C
Capt. Ray Littge	25	Maupin, Oregon	F-84
Capt. Gregory Loesch	24	Santa Barbara, California	F4U
Maj. John Lombard	24	Tungting Lake	P-40
Capt. Virgil Lusk	26	NAS, San Diego, California	P-38
Lt Col. John Lynch	35	Okinawa	F-84
Capt. William Maguire	34	Great Dunmow (Bad weather)	P-51
Capt. T.H. McArthur	23	Between Bone and Berteaux	P-38
Maj. William McDonough	24	Port Moresby (Parachute failed to open)	P-47
Maj. Pierce McKennon	27	San Antonio, Texas	AT-6D
Lt.Col. Leland Molland	32	Taegu (Bad weather)	T-33

NON-COMBAT FLYING ACCIDENTS OF AMERICAN FIGHTER ACES (KIFA) (Continued)

NAME	DEATH	LOCATION OF CRASH	PLANE FLOWN
Maj. Lonnie Moore	35	Elgin Air Force Base, Florida	F-101
Capt. Paul Mullen	26	Kikuma, Japan (Collision)	FG-1D
Lt.Cdr. Cleveland Null	31	Portugal	F3D-2
Capt. Donald Owen	28	South Pacific (Carrier Take-off crash)	F4U
Col. Carl Payne	35	Torbay Airport, St. John's Newfoundland	T-33
Capt. James Peck	23	Christchurch, England	P-38
Lt(jg) Eugene Redman	30	(Take-off accident)	F4U
Lt.Col. William Reed	27	(Killed Bailing out)	P-40
Lt.(jg) Francis Register	25	Holtz Bay, Attu Island	F4F
Col. Ben Rimerman	32	Great Dunmin (Bad weather)	P-51
Lt(jg) Ross Robinson	24	NAS, Jacksonville, Florida	F8F
Sqn.Ldr. Robert Sandell	26	Rangoon, Burma	P-40
Maj. Frank Schiel	25	Stuming, China	F-4
Capt. Alex Sears	29	San Angelo, Texas	T-6
Cdr. Kenneth D. Smith	38	Maryland	YF3
Maj. Kenneth G. Smith	33	Searsport, Maine	P-47
Lt(jg) Irl Sonner Jr.	25	(Landing accident)	F6F
Cdr. James Southerland 2nd	37	Jacksonville, Florida (Take-off accident)	F4U
Capt. Kenneth Sparks	24	Muroc, California	P-38
Capt. Harold Spears	24	El Toro, California	SBD

NON-COMBAT FLYING ACCIDENTS OF AMERICAN FIGHTER ACES (KIFA) (Continued)

NAME	DEATH	LOCATION OF CRASH	PLANE FLOWN
Col. Gordon Stanley	34	Lakke Michigan (Near Fort Sheridan, Ill.	F9F
1st Lt. Francis Terrill	25	Shreveport, Louisiana (Ground collision)	F4U
Capt. Wilbur Thomas	26	Old Saddleback Mtn, Calif. (Bad weather)	F7F
Lt(jg) Ed Toaspern	26	Barryville, New York	-
Lt(jg) Eugene Townsend	33	Ontario, California	-
Lt. Donald Umphfres	25	NAS, Patuxent River, Maryland	P-80
Capt. James Varnell Jr.	33	Florida	P-40
Wing Cdr. Lance Wade	29	Foggia, Italy	-
Lt.Col. Boyd Wagner	36	Elgin Field, Florida	P-40
Capt. John Wainwright	31	Germany	P-47
Capt. George Welch	36	Edwards Air Force Base, California	F-100
Maj. Robert Welch	27	Luke Air Force Base, Arizona	F-84
Capt. Art Wenige	65	Ashville, North Carolina	Civil plane
Maj. Raymond Wetmore	27	Otis Air Force Base, Massachusetts	F-86
Maj. John White	29	Amarillo, Texas	C-45
Maj. Felix Williamson	35	March Field, California	FP-80
Capt. William Wilson	30	Havava, Arkansas	B-25
Lt. John Wirth	27	Alpine, California	-

<u>NON-COMBAT FLYING ACCIDENTS OF AMERICAN FIGHTER ACES (KIFA)</u> (Continued)

NAME	DEATH	LOCATION OF CRASH	PLANE FLOWN
Maj. Judge Wolf	32	Williams Air Force Base, Arizona	F-80
Ens. Harold Yeremian	29	Santee, California	-

APPENDIX C

AMERICAN FIGHTER ACE POWs

NAME	PLANE FLOWN	DATE	FATE
Capt. Richard Alexander	P-51 Mustang	May 30, 1944	POW
1st Lt. Dudley Amoss	P-51 Mustang	March 21, 1945	POW
Lt.Col. Stephen Andrew	P-51 Mustang	July 2, 1944	POW
Capt. David Archibald	P-51 Mustang	December 18, 1944	POW
Maj. Robert Aschenbrener	P-38 Lightning	December 25, 1944	EVADED and RETURNED (January 17, 1945)
Lt.Col. Rudy Augarten	P-47 Thunderbolt	June 10, 1944	EVADED and RETURNED (August 14, 1944)
Maj. Raymond Bank	P-51 Mustang	March 2, 1945	POW
Col. Rex Barber	P-38 Lightning	April 29, 1944	EVADED
1st Lt. Aaron Beardon	P-38 Lightning	September 3, 1944	POW
Col. Walter Beckham	P-47 Thunderbolt	February 22, 1944	POW

AMERICAN FIGHTER ACE POWs (Continued)

NAME	PLANE FLOWN	DATE	FATE
Lt.Col. Duane Beeson	P-51 Mustang	April 5, 1944	POW
Lt.Col. Louis Benne	P-38 Lightning	June 14, 1944	POW
Capt. Joseph Bennett	P-51 Mustang	May 25, 1944	POW
Col. Steve Bettinger	F-86 Sabre	July 20, 1953	POW
Capt. Robert Booth	P-51 Mustang	June 8, 1944	POW
Col. Gregory Boyington	F4U Corsair	January 3, 1944	POW
Maj. Michael Brezas	P-38 Lightning	April 2, 1945	POW
Lt.Col. John Bright	P-38 Lightning	August 30, 1943	POW and ESCAPED (September 1943)
Col. Gerald Brown	P-51 Mustang	September 5, 1944	EVADED and RETURNED (September 6, 1944)
Col. Gerald Brown	-	November 30, 1950	POW KOREA (3 YEARS)
Col. Henry Brown	P-51 Mustang	October 3, 1944	POW
Maj. Quince Brown	P-47 Thunderbolt	September 6, 1944	MURDERED by GERMAN SS (September 6, 1944)
Col. Richard Candelaria	P-51 Mustang	April 13, 1945	POW
Capt. John Carder	P-51 Mustang	May 12, 1944	POW

AMERICAN FIGHTER ACE POWs (Continued)

NAME	PLANE FLOWN	DATE	FATE
Col. Raymond Care	P-51 Mustang	April 15, 1944	POW
Lt.Col. Ken Carlson	P-51 Mustang	February 25, 1945	POW
Maj. George Carpenter	P-51 Mustang	April 18, 1944	POW
Col. Oscar Coen	Spitfire VB	October 20, 1941	EVADED and RETURNED (December 1941)
Col. Robert Coffey Jr.	P-47 Thunderbolt	July 11, 1944	EVADED and RETURNED (August 6, 1944)
Lt.Col. Charles Cole Jr.	P-51 Mustang	February 25, 1945	POW
BGen. Frank Collins Jr.	P-47 Thunderbolt	July 10, 1945	POW
Capt. William Cullerton	P-51 Mustang	April 8, 1945	POW
Lt.Col. Louis Curdes	P-38 Lightning	August 27, 1943	POW
Sqn.Ldr. John Curry	Spitfire Vb	March 2, 1944	EVADED and RETURNED (May 1944)
Lt. Edward Czarnecki	P-38 Lightning	October 23, 1943	EVADED and RETURNED (February 1944)
Col. Perry Dahl	P-38 Lightning	November 10, 1944	EVADED and RETURNED (December 10, 1944)
Capt. Kenneth Dahlberg	P-51 Mustang	August 16, 1944	EVADED and RETURNED (August 16, 1944)

AMERICAN FIGHTER ACE POWs (Continued)

NAME	PLANE FLOWN	DATE	FATE
Capt. Kenneth Dahlberg	P-51 Mustang	December 14, 1945	POW
Lt.Col. Clayton Davis	P-51 Mustang	August 17, 1944	EVADED and RETURNED (September 6, 1944)
Col. Glendon V. Davis	P-51 Mustang	April 28, 1944	EVADED and RETURNED (November 1944)
Maj. Cecil Dean	P-51 Mustang	July 2, 1944	POW
Capt. Elliott Dent Jr.	P-38 Lightning	November 1, 1944	EVADED and RETURNED (November 15, 1944)
Col. Glenn Duncan	P-47 Thunderbolt	July 7, 1944	EVADED until LIBERATED (April 4, 1945)
Col. Billy Edens	P-47 Thunderbolt	September 10, 1944	POW
Lt.Col. Sheldon Edner	P-51 Mustang	March 8, 1944	POW
Lt.Col. Sheldon Edner	(light plane)	January 21, 1949	MURDERED in GREECE by COMMUNISTS SAME DAY
Capt. Wallace Emmer	P-51 Mustang	August 9, 1944	POW
Col. Benjamin Emmert Jr.	P-51 Mustang	September 1, 1944	POW
MGen. Andrew Evans Jr.	F-86 Sabre	March 27, 1953	POW in KOREA (RELEASED September 1953)
Lt.Col. Roy Evans	P-51 Mustang	February 14, 1945	POW

AMERICAN FIGHTER ACE POWs (Continued)

NAME	PLANE FLOWN	DATE	FATE
Sqn.Ldr. David Fairbanks	Tempest V	February 28, 1945	POW
Maj. Selvan Feld	P-47 Thunderbolt	August 13, 1944	POW
Lt.Col. Marion Felts	P-38 Lightning	November 2, 1944	EVADED and RETURNED (December 12, 1944)
Col. Harold Fischer	F-86 Sabre	April 7, 1953	POW
Col. Harry Fisk	P-47 Thunderbolt	January 13, 1945	POW
Maj. Nelson Flack Jr.	P-40 Warhawk	February 14, 1944	EVADED and RETURNED (March 12, 1944)
Ens. Kenneth Flynn	F6F Hellcat	October 13, 1944	POW (DIED JAPANESE PRISON July 24, 1945)
Col. Francis Gabreski	P-47 Thunderbolt	July 20, 1944	POW
Brig.Gen. Frank Gailer Jr.	P-51 Mustang	November 27, 1944	POW
Col. Vermont Garrison	P-51 Mustang	March 3, 1944	POW
Capt. Edward Gimbel	Spitfire IX	April 4, 1943	EVADED and RETURNED (late 1943)
Capt. Edward Gimbel	P-51 Mustang	April 16, 1945	POW
Maj. William Giroux	P-47 Thunderbolt	September 1, 1943	EVADED and RETURNED
Maj. Fred Glover	P-51 Mustang	April 30, 1944	EVADED and RETURNED (May 28, 1944)

AMERICAN FIGHTER ACE POWs (Continued)

NAME	PLANE FLOWN	DATE	FATE
Maj. John Godfrey	P-51 Mustang	August 24, 1944	POW
Lt. Burdett Goodrich	P-38 Lightning	June 6, 1944	POW (DIED IN PRISON CAMP January 1, 1945)
Maj. James Goodson	P-51 Mustang	June 20, 1944	POW
Capt. Lee Gregg	P-38 Lightning	May 6, 1944	EVADED
Lt. Thomas L. Harris	P-51 Mustang	May 27, 1944	POW
Lt.Col. Edward Heller	F-86 Sabre	January 23, 1953	POW
Col. Donald Hillman	P-47 Thunderbolt	October 7, 1944	POW
Cdr. Hollis Hills	F6F Hellcat	September 22, 1944	SHOT DOWN and RESCUED SAME DAY
Maj. John Hockery	P-47 Thunderbolt	November 26, 1944	POW
Capt. William Hodges	P-51 Mustang	May 11, 1944	EVADED and RETURNED (September 1944)
Lt. Bernard Howes	P-51 Mustang	March 3, 1945	POW
Col. Mark Hubbard	P-38 Lightning	March 18, 1944	POW
Capt. Jack Ilfrey	P-38 Lightning	June 13, 1944	EVADED
Lt.Gen. Gerald W. Johnson	P-47 Thunderbolt	March 27, 1944	POW
Capt. Alwin Juchheim Jr.	P-47 Thunderbolt	May 28, 1944	POW

AMERICAN FIGHTER ACE POWs (Continued)

NAME	PLANE FLOWN	DATE	FATE
Col. James Kasler	F-105 Thunderchief	August 8, 1966	POW NORTH VIETNAM (RELEASED March 4, 1973)!
BGen. Benjamin King	P-38 Lightning	July 17, 1943	EVADED and RETURNED (September 17, 1943)
Lt.Col. Claude Kinsey Jr.	P-38 Lightning	April 5, 1943	POW until (October 29, 1943)
Lt.Col. Walter Koraleski	P-51 Mustang	April 15, 1944	POW
Col. John Landers	P-40 Warhawk	December 26, 1942	EVADED and RETURNED (January 2, 1943)
2ndLt. Franklin Lathrope	P-38 Lightning	May 10, 1944	EVADED and RETURNED (May 31, 1944)
Capt. Charles Lenfest	P-51 Mustang	October 3, 1944	POW
Lt.Col. Brooks Liles	P-51 Mustang	March 3, 1945	POW
Maj. James Low	F4D Phantom	December 16, 1967	POW (RELEASED August 1968)
Capt. Wayne Lowry	P-51 Mustang	October 7, 1944	POW
Lt.Col. Carl Luksic	P-51 Mustang	May 24, 1944	POW
Col. Mort Magoffin	P-47 Thunderbolt	August 10, 1944	POW
Flt.Ldr. Jackson Mahon	Spitfire Vb	August 19, 1942	POW

AMERICAN FIGHTER ACE POWs (Continued)

NAME	PLANE FLOWN	DATE	FATE
Col. Walker Mahurin	P-47 Thunderbolt	March 27, 1944	EVADED and RETURNED (May 7, 1944)
Col. Walker Mahurin	F-86 Sabre	May 13, 1952	POW (RELEASED September 1953)
Capt. Thomas Maloney	P-38 Lightning	August 19, 1944	EVADED and RETURNED late August 1944
Col. Bert Marshall	P-51 Mustang	August 18, 1944	SHOT DOWN and RESCUED SAME DAY
Col. Kenneth Martin	P-51 Mustang	February 11, 1944	POW
Lt.Col. Paul McArthur	P-40 Warhawk	June 10, 1943	SHOT DOWN and RESCUED SAME DAY
W/Man. William McGarry	P-40 (AVG)	April 24, 1942	POW and REPATRIATED in (May 1945)
Maj. Pierce McKennon	P-51 Mustang	April 28, 1944	EVADED and RETURNED (September 22, 1944)
Maj. Pierce McKennon	P-51 Mustang	March 18, 1945	SHOT DOWN and RESCUED SAME DAY
Lt.Col. Joseph McKeon	P-51 Mustang	October 7, 1944	POW
Lt.Col. Nicholas Megura	P-51 Mustang	May 22, 1944	INTERNED IN SWEDEN until (June 28, 1944)
Col. Virgil Meroney	P-51 Mustang	April 8, 1944	POW

AMERICAN FIGHTER ACE POWs (Continued)

NAME	PLANE FLOWN	DATE	FATE
2ndLt. Thomas Miller	P-51 Mustang	August 7, 1944	POW
Maj.Gen. Willard Millikan	P-51 Mustang	May 30, 1944	POW
Maj. Henry Mills	P-51 Mustang	March 6, 1944	POW
Lt.Col. James Morris	P-38 Lightning	July 7, 1944	POW
Col. Frank O'Connor	P-51 Mustang	November 5, 1944	POW
1st Lt. Paul Olson	P-51 Mustang	December 18, 1944	POW
1st Lt. PLoyd Overfield	P-51 Mustang	August 7, 1944	EVADED and RETURNED (August 12, 1944)
Col. Forrest Parham	P-51 Mustang	April 2, 1945	EVADED and RETURNED (April 25, 1945)
Col. Heywood Paxton Jr.	P-51 Mustang	January 14, 1945	EVADED and RETURNED (January 27, 1945)
MGen. Chelsey Peterson	P-47 Thunderbolt	April 15, 1943	BAILED OUT and RESCUED SAME DAY
Lt.Col. Sammy Pierce	P-40 Warhawk	October 13, 1943	EVADED and RETURNED (October 21, 1943)
Flt.Ldr. Donald Pieri	Spitfire IX	May 3, 1945	POW
Col. Steve Pisanos	P-51 Mustang	March 5, 1944	EVADED and RETURNED (September 9, 1944)

AMERICAN FIGHTER ACE POWs (Continued)

NAME	PLANE FLOWN	DATE	FATE
Lt.Col. Lawrence Powell	P-51 Mustang	January 14, 1945	SHOT DOWN and became POW (January 16, 1945)
Col. Roger Pryor	F-6D Mustang	March 26, 1945	POW until LIBERATED (May 1, 1945)
Capt. John Purdy	P-38 Lightning	December 11, 1944	EVADED and RETURNED SAME DAY
Capt. John Purdy	P-38 Lightning	January 9, 1945	EVADED and RETURNED (January 24, 1945)
Maj. Donald Quigley	P-40 Warhawk	August 10, 1944	POW
Col. Michael Quirk	P-47 Thunderbolt	September 10, 1944	POW
Capt. Robert Reynolds	P-51 Mustang	September 12, 1944	POW
Capt. Paul Riley	P-51 Mustang	April 24, 1944	POW
BGen. Robinson Risner	F-105 Thunderchief	March 22, 1965	RESCUED SAME DAY
BGen. Robinson Risner	F-105 Thunderchief	September 16, 1965	POW until RELEASED (December 12, 1973)!
BGen. Wiltz Segura	P-40 Warhawk	August 7, 1944	EVADED and RETURNED SAME DAY
Maj. Ernest Shipman	P-51 Mustang	February 3, 1944	SHOT DOWN by P-38 and became POW
Lt. Robert Shoup	P-51 Mustang	May 12, 1944	POW

AMERICAN FIGHTER ACE POWs (Continued)

NAME	PLANE FLOWN	DATE	FATE
Col. Clyde Slocumb Jr.	P-51 Mustang	April 2, 1945	EVADED and RETURNED (April, 25, 1945)
2ndLt. John C. Smith	P-38 Lightning	September 2, 1943	EVADED and RETURNED (September 21, 1943)
Maj. Kenneth G, Smith	P-51 Mustang	March 21, 1944	POW
Col. Walter Starck	P-51 Mustang	November 27, 1944	POW
Lt.Col. Richard Suehr	P-38 Lightning	January 1, 1945	EVADED and RETURNED (February 4, 1945)
Col. Charles Sullivan (O'Sullivan)	P-38 Lightning	September 18, 1943	EVADED and RETURNED (October 11, 1943)
Capt. William Sykes	P-51 Mustang	December 24, 1944	POW
Capt. Kun Tan	P-40 Warhawk	May 16, 1944	EVADED and RETURNED LATER
Maj. Fred Trafton	P-51 Mustang	April 23, 1944	POW and ESCAPED (July 28, 1944)
Capt. Richard West	P-38 Lightning	November 1, 1944	EVADED and RETURNED LATE 1944
Lt.Col. James Williams	P-40 Warhawk	September 10, 1943	EVADED and RETURNED LATER
Lt.Col. James Williams	P-51 Mustang	December 1, 1943	EVADED and RETURNED (December 17, 1943)

AMERICAN FIGHTER ACE POWs (Continued)

NAME	PLANE FLOWN	DATE	FATE
Col. Sidney Woods	P-51 Mustang	April 16, 1945	POW
BGen. Charles Yeager	P-51 Mustang	March 5, 1944	EVADED and RETURNED (May 27, 1944)
Col. Hubert Zemke	P-47 Thunderbolt	October 30, 1944	POW
Lt.Col. Charles Zubarik	P-38 Lightning	May 24, 1943	POW

APPENDIX D

TOP SCORING AMERICAN FIGHTER ACES OF WORLD WAR II AND KOREA

(230 AMERICAN FIGHTER ACES WITH TEN OR MORE VICTORIES)

VICTORIES	PILOT	COMBAT UNITS	FIGHTER TYPES
40	Maj. Richard Bong	49th FG	P-38 Lightning
38	Maj. Thomas McGuire	475th FG	P-38 Lightning
34.5	Col. Francis Gabreski	56th FG/4th & 51st FIW	P-47/F-86
34	Capt. David McCampbell	VF-15	F6F Hellcat
27	Lt.Col. Robert S. Johnson	56th FG	P-47 Thunderbolt
27	Col. Charles MacDonald	475th FG	P-38 Lightning
26.833	Maj. George Preddy Jr.	352nd FG	P-47/P-51
26	BGen. Joseph Foss	VMF-121	F4F Wildcat

TOP SCORING AMERICAN FIGHTER ACES OF WORLD WAR II AND KOREA (230 AMERICAN FIGHTER ACES WITH TEN OR MORE VICTORIES) (Continued)

VICTORIES	PILOT	COMBAT UNITS	FIGHTER TYPES
26	Gen. John C. Meyer	352nd FG/4th FIW	P-47/P-51/F-86
25	Lt. Robert Hanson	VMF-214 & 215	F4U Corsair
24.25	Col. Walker "Bud" Mahurin	56th FG/3rd (Cdo)/51st FIW	P-47/P-51/F-86
24	Col. Gregory "Pappy" Boyington	AVG/VMF-214	P-40/F4U
24	Capt. Cecil Harris	VF-27 & 18	F4F/F6F
23	Cdr. Eugene Valencia	VF-9	F6F Hellcat
23	Wing Cdr. L.C. "Lance" Wade	33 Sqn/145 Sqn.	Hurricane/Spitfire
22.5	Col. David Schilling	56th FG	P-47 Thunderbolt
22	Col. Gerald R. Johnson	49th FG	P-38 Lightning
22	Col. Neel Kearby	348th FG	P-47 Thunderbolt
22	Lt.Gen. Jay Robbins	8th FG	P-400/P-38
21.833	Maj. Don Gentile	133rd Sqn/4th FG	Spitfire/P-47/P-51
21.5	Col. Fred Christensen Jr.	56th FG	P-47 Thunderbolt
21.25	Maj. Ray Wetmore	359th FG	P-47/P-51
21	Lt.Col. George Davis Jr.	348th FG/4th FIW	P-47/F-86
21	Col. John Voll	31st FG	P-51 Mustang
21	Lt.Col. Kenneth Walsh	VMF-124 & 222	F4U Corsair
21	Col. William Whisner	352nd FG/4th & 51st FIW	P-47/P-51/F-86

TOP SCORING AMERICAN FIGHTER ACES OF WORLD WAR II AND KOREA (230 AMERICAN FIGHTER ACES WITH TEN OR MORE VICTORIES) (Continued)

VICTORIES	PILOT	COMBAT UNITS	FIGHTER TYPES
20.5	Col. Glenn Eagleston	354th FG/4th FIW	P-51/F-86
20	Capt. Thomas Aldrich	VMF-215	F4U Corsair
20	Lt.Col. Thomas Lynch	35th FG	P-400/P-38
20	Lt.Col. Robert Westbrook Jr.	18th & 347th FG	P-40/P-38
19.5	Col. Glenn Duncan	353rd FG	P-47 Thunderbolt
19	Col. Patrick Fleming	VF-80	F6F Hellcat
19	Lt.Cdr. Cornelius Nooy	VF-31	F6F Hellcat
19	Col. John Smith	VMF-223	F4F Wildcat
19	Cdr. Alex Vraciu	VF-6 & 16	F6F Hellcat
18.75	Col. David "Tex" Hill	AVG & 23rd FG	P-40/P-51
18.5	M.Gen. Marion Carl	VMF-221 & 223	F4F/F4U
18.5	Col. Leonard "Kit" Carson	357th FG	P-51 Mustang
18.5	Capt. Wilbur Thomas	VMF-213	F4U Corsair
18	Col. Walter Beckham	353rd FG	P-47 Thunderbolt
18	Maj. Michael Gladych	303rd & 302nd Sqn/56th FG	Spitfire/P-47
18	Col. Herschel Green	325th FG	P-40/P-47/P-51
18	Lt.Col. John Herbst	23rd FG	P-51/P-40
18	Lt.Col. Charles Older	AVG/23rd FG	P-40/P-51
18	Col. Wiltold Urbanowicz	145th & 303rd Sqn/23rd FG	PZL P.XIc/ Hurricane/P-40
17.75	Col. Hubert Zemke	56th & 479th FG	P-47/P-51

TOP SCORING AMERICAN FIGHTER ACES OF WORLD WAR II AND KOREA (230 AMERICAN FIGHTER ACES WITH TEN OR MORE VICTORIES) (Continued)

VICTORIES	PILOT	COMBAT UNITS	FIGHTER TYPES
17.5	Lt.Col. John England	357th FG/4th FIW	P-51/F-86
17.33	Lt.Col. Duane Beeson	4th FG	P-47/P-51
17.33	Col. Vermont Garrison	4th FG/4th FIW	P-47/F-86
17.25	Lt.Col. John Thornell Jr.	352nd FG	P-47/P-51
17	BGen. Robin Olds	479th FG/8th TFW	P-38/P-51/F4C
17	Capt. James Varnell Jr.	52nd FG	P-51 Mustang
16.5	Lt.Gen. Royal Baker	31st/48th/348th FG & 4th FIW	Spitfire/P-47/F-86
16.5	Col. James Jabara	363rd FG & 4th FIW	P-51/F-86
16.5	Lt.Gen. Gerald W. Johnson	56th/356th FG	P-47 Thunderbolt
16.33	Lt.(j.g.) Douglas Baker	VF-20	F6F Hellcat
16.33	Maj. John Godfrey	4th FG	P-47/P-51
16.25	Col. Clarence E. "Bud" Anderson	357th FG	P-51 Mustang
16	BGen. William Dunham	348th FG	P-47/P-51
16	Lt.Col. William "Bill" Harris	347th & 18th FG	P-38 Lightning
16	Lt.Cdr. Ira Kepford	VF-17	F4U Corsair
16	Capt. Joseph McConnell Jr.	51st FIW	F-86 Sabre
16	Cdr. Charles Stimpson	VF-11	F4F/F6F
16	Capt. George Welch	15th PG & 8th FG	P-40/P-39/P-38

**TOP SCORING AMERICAN FIGHTER ACES OF WORLD WAR II AND KOREA
(230 AMERICAN FIGHTER ACES WITH TEN OR MORE
VICTORIES) (Continued)**

VICTORIES	PILOT	COMBAT UNITS	FIGHTER TYPES
15.5	Maj. Don Beerbower	354th FG	P-51 Mustang
15.5	Maj. Samuel Brown	31st FG	P-51 Mustang
15.5	Maj. Richard Peterson	357th FG	P-51 Mustang
15.5	Col. James Swett	VMF-221	F4F/F4U
15	Col. Jack T. Bradley	354th FG	P-51 Mustang
15	Maj. Edward Cragg	8th FG	P-38 Lightning
15	Lt.Col. Robert Foy	357th FG	P-51 Mustang
15	Lt. Ralph Hofer	4th FG	P-47/P-51
15	Maj. Cyril Homer	8th FG	P-38 Lightning
15	Col. John Mitchell	347th/15th/21st FG & 51st FIW	P-39/P-38/P-51/ F-86
15	Capt. Harold Spears	VMF-215	F4U Corsair
14.5	Col. Donald Blakeslee	401/133rd FS & 4th FG	Spitfire/P-51
14.5	Lt.Col. Lowell Brueland	354th FG & 51st FIW	P-51/F-86
14.5	Maj. Manuel "Manny" Fernandez	4th FIW	F-86 Sabre
14.5	Col. James Hagerstrom	49th FG & 4th FIW	P-40/F-86
14.5	Col. John Landers	49th/55th/357th/ 78th FG	P-40/P-51
14.5	Capt. Joseph Powers Jr.	56th FG	P-47 Thunderbolt
14.5	Capt. Edward Shaw	VMF-213	F4U Corsair
14.2	Col. Henry Brown	355th FG	P-51 Mustang

**TOP SCORING AMERICAN FIGHTER ACES OF WORLD WAR II AND KOREA
(230 AMERICAN FIGHTER ACES WITH TEN OR MORE
VICTORIES) (Continued)**

VICTORIES	PILOT	COMBAT UNITS	FIGHTER TYPES
14	Maj. Robert C. Curtis	52nd FG	Spitfire/P-51
14	Capt. Kenneth Dahlberg	354th FG	P-51/P-47
14	Col. Robert DeHaven	49th FG	P-38 Lightning
14	Col. Archie Donahue	VMF-112/451	F4U Corsair
14	Capt. Wallace Emmer	354th FG	P-51 Mustang
14	Maj. James Goodson	4th/31st FG	P-47/P-51
14	Capt. Arthur Hawkins	VF-31	F6F Hellcat
14	Capt. Cotesworth Head Jr.	18th FG	P-40/P-38
14	Col. Arthur Jeffrey	479th FG	P-38/P-51
14	Col. Edward McComas	23rd FG	P-51 Mustang
14	Capt. Daniel Roberts Jr.	8th/475th FG	P-400/P-38
14	Capt. Richard West	8th FG	P-40/P-38
14	Lt. John Wirth	VF-31	F6F Hellcat
13.83	Lt.Col. Donald Bockay	357th FG	P-51 Mustang
13.83	Maj. George Carpenter	4th FG	P-47/P-51
13.5	Capt. George Duncan	VF-15	F6F Hellcat
13.5	Capt. E. Scott McCuskey	VF-42/VF-3/VF-8	F4F/F6F
13.5	MGen.Donald Strait	356th FG	P-47/P-51
13.33	Lt.Col. Donald Bryan	352nd FG	P-47/P-51
13.166	Col. Phillip DeLong	VMF-212/312	F4U Corsair
13	Capt. James Brooks	31st FG	P-51 Mustang

TOP SCORING AMERICAN FIGHTER ACES OF WORLD WAR II AND KOREA (230 AMERICAN FIGHTER ACES WITH TEN OR MORE VICTORIES) (Continued)

VICTORIES	PILOT	COMBAT UNITS	FIGHTER TYPES
13	Capt. Daniel Carmichael	VF-21	F6F Hellcat
13	Lt.Col. Clyde East	10th PRG	F6C/D Mustang
13	BGen. Robert Galer	VMF-224	F4F Wildcat
13	Capt. John Hampshire Jr.	23rd FG	P-40 Warhawk
13	Gen. Bruce Holloway	23rd FG	P-40 Warhawk
13	Lt.Col. John Lynch	71st/249th Sqn.	Supermarine Spitfire
13	Lt. William Marontate	VMF-121	F4F Wildcat
13	MGen. William Millikan	4th FG	P-47/P-51
13	BGen. Glennon Moran	352nd FG	P-47/P-51
13	Sqn.Ldr. Robert Neale	AVG	P-40 Tomahawk
13	Capt. Harry Parker	325th FG	P-51 Mustang
13	Lt. Roy Rushing	VF-15	F6F Hellcat
13	Col. Robert Stephens	354th FG	P-51 Mustang
13	Lt. Wendell Van Twelves	VF-15	F6F Hellcat
13	Maj. Felix Williamson	56th FG	P-47 Thunderbolt
12.5	Sqn.Ldr. David Fairbanks	501st/274th/3rd Sqn.	Spitfire/Tempest
12.5	Lt.Col. Kenneth Frazier	VMF-223	F4F/F4U
12.5	Capt. James Shirley	VF-27	F6F Hellcat
12.5	P/O Claude Weaver III	185th/403rd Sqn.	Supermarine Spitfire
12.33	Maj. Quince Brown	78th FG	P-47 Thunderbolt

**TOP SCORING AMERICAN FIGHTER ACES OF WORLD WAR II AND KOREA
(230 AMERICAN FIGHTER ACES WITH TEN OR MORE
VICTORIES) (Continued)**

VICTORIES	PILOT	COMBAT UNITS	FIGHTER TYPES
12	Lt.Col. John Bolt Jr.	VMF-214 & 51st FIW	F4U/F-86
12	Maj. Michael Brezas	14 FG	P-38 Lightning
12	MGen. Levi Chase Jr.	33rd/1 (Prov) FG	P-40/P-51
12	MGen. George Gleason	479th FG	P-38/P-51
12	R.Adm. Roger Hedrick	VF-17/84	F4U Corsair
12	Maj. Deacon Hively	4th FG	P-47/P-51
12	Capt. Kenneth Ladd	8th FG	P-38 Lightning
12	Lt.Cdr. William Masoner Jr.	VF-11/19	F4F/F6F
12	Cdr. Hamilton McWhorter III	VF-9/12	F6F Hellcat
12	Maj. Robert W. Moore	15th FG	P-40/P-51
12	Maj. Leroy Scheiber	56th FG	P-47 Thunderbolt
12	Maj. Harold Segal	VMF-221/211	F4U Corsair
12	Capt. Norman Skogstad	31st FG	P-51 Mustang
12	Lt.Col. William Sloan	82nd FG	P-38 Lightning
12	Col. James Watkins	49th FG	P-40/P-38
11.83	Lt.Col. Nicholas Megura	4th FG	P-51 Mustang
11.75	Cdr. Clement Craig	VF-22	F6F Hellcat
11.5	Lt. George Carl	VF-15	F6F Hellcat
11.5	Lt.Col. Paul Conger	56th FG	P-47 Thunderbolt

**TOP SCORING AMERICAN FIGHTER ACES OF WORLD WAR II AND KOREA
(230 AMERICAN FIGHTER ACES WITH TEN OR MORE
VICTORIES) (Continued)**

VICTORIES	PILOT	COMBAT UNITS	FIGHTER TYPES
11.5	Col. William Hovde	355th FG & 4th FIW	P-47/P-51/F-86
11.5	Maj. John Kirla	357th FG	P-51 Mustang
11.5	Lt.Col. Norm McDonald	52nd/325th FG	Spitfire/P-51
11.5	Capt. William Snider	VMF-221	F4U Corsair
11.5	Lt.Col. James C. Stewart	56th FG	P-47 Thunderbolt
11.5	R.Adm. Albert Vorse Jr.	VF-3/2/6/80	F4F/F6F
11.5	BGen. Charles Yeager	357th FG	P-51 Mustang
11	Lt.Col. Harold Bauer	VMF-212	F4F Wildcat
11	Capt. John "Tom" Blackburn	VF-17	F4U Corsair
11	Capt. William Dean Jr.	VF-2	F6F Hellcat
11	Capt. Carl Frantz Jr.	354th FG	P-51 Mustang
11	Lt. James French	VF-9	F6F Hellcat
11	Lt.Col. Robert Goebel	31st FG	P-51 Mustang
11	Col. James K. Johnson	404th FG & 4th FIW	P-47/F-86
11	Capt. John "Barry" Lawler	52nd FG	P-51 Mustang
11	Capt. Francis Lent	475th FG	P-38 Lightning
11	Col. William Leverette	14th FG	P-38 Lightning
11	Col. John Loisel	475th FG	P-38 Lightning
11	Capt. Wayne Lowry	325th FG	P-47/P-51
11	MGen. Charles "Sandy" McCorkle	31st FG	Spitfire/P-51

**TOP SCORING AMERICAN FIGHTER ACES OF WORLD WAR II AND KOREA
(230 AMERICAN FIGHTER ACES WITH TEN OR MORE
VICTORIES) (Continued)**

VICTORIES	PILOT	COMBAT UNITS	FIGHTER TYPES
11	Maj. Pierce McKennon	4th FG	P-47/P-51
11	Lt. Loyd Overfield	354th FG	P-51 Mustang
11	Lt.Cdr. Harvey Picken	VF-18	F6F Hellcat
11	Col. Michael Quirk	56th FG	P-47 Thunderbolt
11	Ens. James Reber Jr.	VF-30	F6F Hellcat
11	Capt. Robert Riddle	31st FG	P-51 Mustang
11	Capt. James Rigg	VF-15	F6F Hellcat
11	Cdr. Donald Runyon	VF-6/18	F6F Hellcat
11	Lt.Col. Murray Shubin	347th FG	P-38 Lightning
11	Col. Cornelius "Corky" Smith	8th FG	P-38 Lightning
11	Capt. Kenneth Sparks	35th FG	P-38 Lightning
11	Lt.(j.g.) John Symmes	VF-21/15	F4F/F6F
11	Lt.Col. Richard Turner	354th FG	P-51 Mustang
10.75	Col. Frank O'Connor	354th FG	P-51 Mustang
10.5	Capt. Marshall Beebe	VF-17	F6F Hellcat
10.5	Col. George Ceullers	364th FG	P-38/P-51
10.5	Lt.Col. James Clark Jr.	4th FG	Spitfire/P-47/P-51
10.5	Col. George Doersch	359th FG	P-47/P-51
10.5	Col. William Halton	352nd FG	P-47/P-51
10.5	Capt. Raymond Littge	352nd FG	P-51 Mustang
10.5	Lt.Col. Leland "Tommy" Mollard	31st FG	Spitfire/P-51
10.5	Col. George Ruddell	406th FG & 51st FIW	P-47/F-86

**TOP SCORING AMERICAN FIGHTER ACES OF WORLD WAR II AND KOREA
(230 AMERICAN FIGHTER ACES WITH TEN OR MORE
VICTORIES) (Continued)**

VICTORIES	PILOT	COMBAT UNITS	FIGHTER TYPES
10.5	Lt.Col. John Storch	357th FG	P-51 Mustang
10.33	Maj. Fred Glover	4th FG	P-51 Mustang
10.33	Lt.Cdr. Robert Murray	VF-29	F6F Hellcat
10.33	Lt.Col. Louis Norley	4th FG	P-47/P-51
10.25	Capt. Stanley "Swede" Vejtasa	VS-5 & VF-10	SBD-3/F4F
10	Capt. Charles Anderson Jr.	4th FG	P-47/P-51
10	Maj. Robert Aschenbrener	49th FG	P-40/P-38
10	Maj.Gen. Frederick Blesse	4th FIW	F-86 Sabre
10	Cdr. Carl Brown Jr.	VF-27	F6F Hellcat
10	F/Ldr. George Burgard	AVG	P-40 Tomahawk
10	Lt.Cdr. Leonard Check	VF-7	F6F Hellcat
10	Capt. Thaddeus Coleman Jr.	VF-6/83	F6F Hellcat
10	Maj. Philip Colman	5 (Prov) FG & 4th FIW	P-40/F-86
10	Col. Jack Conger	VMF-223/212	F4F Wildcat
10	Capt. Walter Duke	459th FG	P-38 Lightning
10	Col. James England	311th FG	P-51 Mustang
10	Col. Loren Everton	VMF-212/113	F4F/F4U
10	Col. Harold Fischer	51st FIW	F-86 Sabre
10	Capt. Walter Goehausen	31st FG	P-51 Mustang

**TOP SCORING AMERICAN FIGHTER ACES OF WORLD WAR II AND KOREA
(230 AMERICAN FIGHTER ACES WITH TEN OR MORE
VICTORIES) (Continued)**

VICTORIES	PILOT	COMBAT UNITS	FIGHTER TYPES
10	Maj. Ernest Harris	49th FG	P-40 Warhawk
10	Capt. Ted Lines	4th FG	P-51 Mustang
10	Flt.Ldr. Robert Little	AVG	P-40 Tomahawk
10	Col. Herbert Long	VMF-121/122/451	F4F/F4U
10	Lt.Cdr. Charles Mallory	VF-18	F6F Hellcat
10	Cdr. Harris Mitchell	VF-9	F6F Hellcat
10	Maj. Lonnie Moore	4th FIW	F-86 Sabre
10	Col. Ralph Parr	4th FIW	F-86 Sabre
10	Col. Robert Rankin	56th FG	P-47 Thunderbolt
10	Lt. Thomas Reidy	VBF-83	F4U Corsair
10	Col. Donald Sapp	VMF-222	F4U Corsair
10	BGen. Robert S. Scott Jr.	23rd FG	P-40
10	Lt. Arthur Singer	VF-15	F6F Hellcat
10	Capt. Armistead "Chick" Smith	VF-9	F6F Hellcat
10	Capt. John M. Smith	VF-17/84	F4U Corsair
10	Lt.Cdr. Richard Stambook	VF-27	F6F Hellcat
10	Col. Paul Stanch	35th FG	P-38 Lightning
10	Lt. James S. Stewart	VF-31	F6F Hellcat
10	Maj. Elliott Summer	475th FG	P-38 Lightning
10	BGen. Harrison Thyng	31st/413th FG & 4th FIW	Spitfire/P-47/F-86

TOP SCORING AMERICAN FIGHTER ACES OF WORLD WAR I

VICTORIES	PILOT	COMBAT UNITS	FIGHTER TYPES
26	Capt. Edward Rickenbacker	94th Aero Squad.	Nieuport 28/Spad XIII
20	Capt. Frederick W. Gillet	RAF NO. 79 Squad.	Sopwith Dolphin
19	Capt. Wilford Beaver	RFC/RAF NO. 20 Squad.	Bristol F2B Brisfit
19	Capt. Harold A. Kullberg	RAF NO. 1 Squad.	SE-5A
18	Capt. William C. Lambert	RAF NO. 24 Squad.	SE-5A
18	2nd Lt. Frank Luke Jr.	USAS 27th Aero Squad.	Spad XIII
17	Capt. August T. Iaccaci	RAF NO. 20 Squad.	F2B Brisfit
17	Lt. Paul T. Iaccaci	RAF NO. 20 Squad.	F2B Brisfit
16	Lt. Eugene S. Coler	RAF NO. 11 Squad.	F2B Brisfit
16	SOUS-Lt. Gervais Raoul Lufbery	Escadrille Americaine NO. 124	Nieuport 11
16	Capt. Oren J. Rose	RAF NO. 92 Squad.	SE-5A
16	Capt. Elliott W. Springs	USAS NO. 85 Squad.	Sopwith Camel
14	Lt. Kenneth R. Unger	NO. 210 Squad.	Sopwith Camel
13	Sergeant Lt. David E. Putnam	MS. 156	Spad XIII
13	Capt. George A. Vaughn	USAS NO. 84 Squad.	SE-5A/Sopwith Camel

TOP SCORING AMERICAN FIGHTER ACES OF WORLD WAR I

VICTORIES	PILOT	COMBAT UNITS	FIGHTER TYPES
12	Sergeant Frank L. Baylies	Escadrille SPA. 3	Spad XIII
12	Lt. Louis Bennett Jr.	RAF NO. 40 Squad.	SE-5A
12	!st Lt. Field E. Kindley	USAS NO. 65 Squad.	Sopwith Camel
12	Maj. Reed G. Landis	USAS NO. 40 Squad.	SE-5A
12	Capt. Frederick I. Lord	RAF NO. 79 Squad.	Sopwith Dolphin
12	Capt. James W. Pearson	RAF NO. 23 Squad.	Sopwith Dolphin
12	Capt. Clive W. Warman	RFC NO. 23 Squad.	Spad VII
10	1st Lt. Lloyd A. Hamilton	USAS NO. 3 Squad.	Sopwith Camel
10	1st Lt. Duerson Knight	USAS NO. 1 Squad.	SE-5A
10	Capt. Oliver C. Leboutillier	RAF NO. 9 Squad.	Sopwith Triplane
10	1st Lt. Jacques M. Swaab	USAS 22nd Aero Squad.	Spad XIII

APPENDIX E

AMERICAN FIGHTER ACES WITH THE MOST VICTORIES

AIRCRAFT	10 OR MORE	AIRCRAFT	10 OR MORE
	VICTORIES		VICTORIES
P47 THUNDERBOLT		P47 THUNDERBOLT	
Lt.Col. Francis "Gabby" Gabreski	28	Capt. Joseph Powers	14.5
Lt.Col. Robert S. Johnson	27	Maj. Felix Williamson	13
Col. David Schilling	22.5	Maj. Quince Brown	12.3
Col. Neel Kearby	22	Maj. Leroy Schreiber	12
Col. Fred Christensen	21.5	Lt.Col. Paul Conger	11.5
Col. Walker "Bud" Mahurin	19.75	Lt.Col. James C. Stewart	11.5
Col. Glenn Duncan	19.5	Lt.Col. Duane Beeson	11
Col. Walter Beckham	18	Col. Michael Quirk	11
Lt.Gen. Gerald W. Johnson	16.5	Col. Vermont Garrison	10
Col. Hub Zemke	15.25	Maj. Michael Gladych	10
BGen. William Dunham	15	Col. Robert Rankin	10

AMERICAN FIGHTER ACES WITH THE
MOST VICTORIES (Continued)

AIRCRAFT	10 OR MORE VICTORIES	AIRCRAFT	10 OR MORE VICTORIES
P-51 MUSTANG		**P-51 MUSTANG**	
Maj. George Preddy	23.83	Col. William Whisner	14.5
Gen. John Meyer	21	Col. Henry Brown	14.2
Col. John Voll	21	Capt. Wallace Emmer	14
Lt.Col. John Herbst	19	Lt.Col. Donald Bochkay	13.83
Col. Leonard Carlson	18.5	Maj. John Godfrey	13.83
Col. Glenn Eagleston	18.5	Capt. James Brooks	13
Lt.Col. John England	17.5	Maj. Robert C. Curtis	13
Maj. Raymond Wetmore	17	Lt.Col. Clyde East	13
Col. C.E. "Bud" Anderson	16.25	Lt. Ralph Hofer	13
Maj. Samuel Brown	15.5	Capt. Harry Parker	13
Maj. Donald Beerbower	15.5	Col. Robert Stephens	13
Maj. Samuel Brown	15.5	Maj. George Carpenter	12.83
Maj. Donald Gentile	15.5	Lt. Col. Lowell Brueland	12.5
Maj. Richard Peterson	15.5	Lt. Col. John Thornell, Jr.	12.5
Col. Jack T. Bradley	15	BGen. Glen Moran	12
Lt.Col. Robert Foy	15	Lt. Col. Nicholas Megura	11.83
Capt. James Varnell	15	Maj. John Kirla	11.5

AMERICAN FIGHTER ACES WITH THE
MOST VICTORIES (Continued)

AIRCRAFT	10 OR MORE VICTORIES	AIRCRAFT	10 OR MORE VICTORIES
P-51 MUSTANG		**P-51 MUSTANG**	
Col. Edward McComas	14	BGen. Charles "Chuck" Yeager	11.5
Capt. Carl Frantz	11	Capt. Ray Littge	10.5
Lt.Col. Robert Goebel	11	Lt.Col. John Storch	10.5
Capt. John "Barry" Lawler	11	Maj.Gen. Donald Strait	10.5
Capt. Wayne Lowrey	11	Maj. Fred Glover	10.33
Maj. Robert W. Moore	11	Col. James England	10
Lt. Loyd Overfield	11	Capt. Walter Goehausen Jr.	10
Capt. Robert Riddle	11	Capt. Ted Lines	10
Col. Richard Turner	11	Maj.Gen. Willard Millikan	10
Lt. Frank O'Connor	10.75	Lt.Col. Louis Norley	10
P-38 LIGHTNING		**P-38 LIGHTNING**	
Maj. Richard Bong	40	Capt. Daniel Roberts Jr.	12
Maj. Thomas McGuire Jr.	38	Lt.Col. William Sloan	12
Col. Charles MacDonald	27	Capt. Francis Lent	11
Col. Gerald R. Johnson	22	Col. William Leverette	11
Lt.Gen. Jay Robbins	22	Col. John Loisel	11
Lt.Col. Thomas Lynch	17	Lt.Col. Murray Shubin	11

AMERICAN FIGHTER ACES WITH THE
MOST VICTORIES (Continued)

AIRCRAFT	10 OR MORE VICTORIES	AIRCRAFT	10 OR MORE VICTORIES
P-38 LIGHTNING		**P-38 LIGHTNING**	
Lt.Col. William "Bill" Harris	16	Col. Cornelius "Corky" Smith	11
Maj. Edward Cragg	15	Col. James Watkins	11
Maj. Cyril Homer	15	Capt. Walter Duke	10
Lt.Col. Robert Westbrook	13	Maj. Ken Giroux	10
Maj. Michael Brezas	12	Col. Paul Stanch	10
Capt. Kenneth Ladd	12		
F6F HELLCAT		**F6F HELLCAT**	
Capt. David McCampbell	34	Cdr. Alex Vraciu	19
Capt. Cecil Harris	23	Lt.(jg) Douglas Baker	16.33
Col. Patrick Fleming	19.5	Capt. Art Hawkins	14
Lt.Cdr. Cornelius Nooy	19	Lt. John Wirth	14
Cdr. Eugene Valencia	19	Capt. George Duncan	13.5
Lt. Roy Rushing	13	Cdr. Carl Brown Jr.	10.5
Capt. John Strane	13	Lt.Cdr. Robert E. Murray	10.3
Lt. Wendell Van Twelves	13	Lt.Cdr. Leonard Check	10
Capt. James Shirley	12.5	Capt Thad Coleman	10
Cdr. Hamilton McWhorter	12	Lt.Cdr. Charles Mallory	10

AMERICAN FIGHTER ACES WITH THE
MOST VICTORIES (Continued)

AIRCRAFT	10 OR MORE VICTORIES	AIRCRAFT	10 OR MORE VICTORIES
F6F HELLCAT		**F6F HELLCAT**	
Cdr. Clement Craig	11.75	Lt.Cdr. William Masoner Jr.	10
Lt.(jg) George Carr	11.5	Cdr. Harris Mitchell	10
Capt. William Dean	11	Lt. Arthur Singer	10
Lt. James French	11	Capt. Armistead "Chick" Smith Jr.	10
Lt.Cdr. Harvey Picken	11	Lt.Cdr. Richard Stambook	10
Ens. James Reber	11	Lt. James S. Stewart	10
Capt. James Rigg	11	Cdr. Charles Stimpson	10
Capt. Marshall Beebe	10.5		
F4U CORSAIR		**F4U CORSAIR**	
Lt. Robert Hanson	25	Col. Phillip DeLong	13.166
Col. Gregory "Pappy" Boyington	22	Col. James Cupp	12
Lt.Col. Kenneth Walsh	21	R.Adm. Roger Hedrick	12
Capt. Donald Aldrich	20	Capt. John "Tom" Blackburn	11
Capt. Wilbur Thomas	18.5	Col. Herbert Long	10
Lt.Cdr. Ira Kepford	16	Lt. Thomas Reidy	10
Capt. Harold Spears	15	Col. Donald Sapp	10
Capt. Edward Shaw	14.5	Capt. John M. Smith	10
Col. Archie Donahue	14		

AMERICAN FIGHTER ACES WITH THE
MOST VICTORIES (Continued)

AIRCRAFT	10 OR MORE VICTORIES	AIRCRAFT	10 OR MORE VICTORIES
F4F WILDCAT		**F4F WILDCAT**	
BGen. Joseph Foss	26	Lt. William Marontate	13
Col. John L. Smith	19	Lt.Col. Kenneth Frazier	11.5
MGen. Marion Carl	16.5	Lt.Col. Harold Bauer	11
BGen. Robert Galer	13	Col. Jack Conger	10
F-86 SABRE JET		**F-86 SABRE JET**	
Capt. Joseph McConnell	16	Col. Harold Fischer	10
Col. James Jabara	15	Col. James K. Johnson	10
Maj. Manuel "Manny" Fernandez	14.5	MGen. Frederick "Boots" Blesse	10
Lt.Col. George Davis	14	Maj. Lonnie Moore	10
Lt.Gen. Royal Baker	13	Col. Ralph Parr	10
P-40 WARHAWK		**SUPERMARINE SPITFIRE**	
Col. David L. "Tex" Hill	13.25	Lt.Col. John J. Lynch	13
Capt. John Hampshire	13	P/O Claude Weaver	12.5
Gen. Bruce Holloway	13		
Sqn.Ldr. Robert Neale	13	Wing Cdr. L.C. "Lance" Wade	10

AMERICAN FIGHTER ACES WITH THE
MOST VICTORIES (Continued)

AIRCRAFT	10 OR MORE VICTORIES	AIRCRAFT	10 OR MORE VICTORIES
P-40 WARHAWK			
Flt.Ldr. George Burgard	10		
MGen. Levi Chase	10	**HAWKER HURRICANE**	
Col. Robert DeHaven	10		
Maj. Ernest Harris	10	Col. Wiltold Urbanowicz	15
Flt/Ldr. Robert Little	10	Wing Cdr. L.C. "Lance" Wade	13
Lt.Col. Charles Older	10	P/O Claude Weaver	12.5
BGen. Robert S. Scott Jr.	10		
HAWKER TEMPEST			
Sqn.Ldr. David Fairbanks	11.5		

APPENDIX F

PILOTS THAT BECAME ACES IN MORE THAN ONE AIRCRAFT TYPE

NAME	PLANE FLOWN AND VICTORIES	TOTAL
	FOR EACH TYPE	VICTORIES
Lt.Col. Duane Beeson	P-47 Thunderbolt (12)/P-51 Mustang (5.3)	17.33
Lt.Col. John Bolt	F4U Corsair (6)/F-86 Sabre (6)	12
Lt.Col. George Davis	P-47 Thunderbolt (7)/F-86 Sabre (14)	21
Col. Francis Gabreski	P-47 Thunderbolt (28)/F-86 Sabre (6.5)	34.5
Col. Vermont Garrison	P-47 Thunderbolt (10)/F-86 Sabre (6.33)/P-51 Mustang (1)	17.33
Maj. Michael Gladych	P-47 Thunderbolt (10)/Spitfire (8)	18
Maj. James Goodson	P-51 Mustang (9)/P-47 Thunderbolt (5)	14
Col. James Hagerstrom	F-86 Sabre (8.5)/P-40 Warhawk (6)	14.5
Capt. Cotesworth Head	P-40 Warhawk (8)/P-38 Lightning (6)	14

PILOTS THAT BECAME ACES IN MORE THAN
ONE AIRCRAFT TYPE (Continued)

NAME	PLANE FLOWN AND VICTORIES	TOTAL
	FOR EACH TYPE	VICTORIES
MGen. Charles McCorkle	P-51 Mustang (6)/Spitfire (5)	11
Capt. Elbert Scott McCuskey	F6F Hellcat (7)/F4F Wildcat (6.5)	13.5
R Adm. Roger Mehle	F6F Hellcat (8)/F4F Wildcat (5.33)	13.33
Lt.Col. Charles Older	P-40 Warhawk (10)/P-51 Mustang (8)	18
BGen. Robin Olds	P-51 Mustang (8)/P-38 Lightning (5)/ F4 Phantom (4)	17
Cdr. Charles Stimpson	F6F Hellcat (10)/F4F Wildcat (6)	16
Col. James Swett	F4U Corsair (8.5)/F4F Wildcat (7)	15.5
Lt.(jg) John Symmes	F4f Wildcat (5.5)/F6F Hellcat (5.5)	11
BGen. Harrison Thyng	Spitfire (5)/F-86 Sabre (5)	10
R Adm. Albert Vorse Jr.	F6F Hellcat (6)/F4F Wildcat (5.5)	11.5
Wing Cdr. Lance Wade	Hurricane (13)/Spitfire (10)	23
Capt. Richard West	P-38 Lightning (8)/P-40 Warhawk (6)	14
Lt.Col. Robert Westbrook Jr.	P-38 Lightning (13)/P-40 Warhawk (7)	20
Col. William Whisner	P-51 Mustang (14.5)/F-86 Sabre (5.5)/ P-47 Thunderbolt (1)	21

APPENDIX G

AMERICAN FIGHTER PILOTS THAT BECAME "ACE IN A DAY"

ACE	UNIT	PLANE TYPE	DATE	VICTORIES
Maj. William Allen	55th FG	P-51 Mustang	September 5, 1944	(5 German Training Aircraft)
Lt. Alexander Anderson	VF-80	F6F Hellcat	February 16, 1945	(Zeke/2 Oscars/ Tony/Tojo)
1st Lt. Richard H. Anderson	318th FG	P-47 Thunderbolt	May 25, 1945	(5 Zekes)
Lt. Robert Anderson	VF-80	F6F Hellcat	December 14, 1944	(5 Zekes)
Capt. David Archibald	359th FG	P-51 Mustang	December 18, 1944	(5 FW-190s)
Lt. Gen. George Axtell	VMF-323	F4U Corsair	April 22, 1945	(5 Vals)
Col. Ernest Bankey	364th FG	P-51 Mustang	December 27, 1944	(4 FW-190s/1.5 Bf-109s)
Capt. Lloyd Barnard	VF-2	F6F Hellcat	June 15, 1944	(5 Zeros)

AMERICAN FIGHTER PILOTS THAT BECAME
"ACE IN A DAY" (Continued)

ACE	UNIT	PLANE TYPE	DATE	VICTORIES
Capt. Marshall Beebe	VF-17	F6F Hellcat	March 18, 1945	(2 Zekes/3 Franks)
Capt. William Beyer	361st FG	P-51 Mustang	September 27, 1944	(5 FW-190s)
Lt. Col. Wayne Blickenstaff	353rd FG	P-51 Mustang	March 24, 1945	(3 FW-190s/2 Bf.109s)
Maj. Lawrence Blumer	367th FG	P-38 Lightning	August 25, 1944	(5 FW-190s)
Col. Gregory Boyington	VMF-214	F4U Corsair	September 16, 1943	(4 Haps/Zeke)
Cdr. Charles Brewer	VF-15	F6F Hellcat	June 19, 1944	(3 Zekes/2 Judys)
Cdr. Carl A. Brown	VF-27	F6F Hellcat	October 24, 1944	(5 Zekes)
Lt Col. Donald S. Bryan	352nd FG	P-51 Mustang	November 2, 1944	(5-Bf.109s)
Lt. Cdr. Robert Buchanan	VF-29	F6F Hellcat	October 16, 1944	(2 Franks/2 Jills/ Zeke)
Col. Bruce Carr	354th FG	P-51 Mustang	April 2, 1945	(3 FW-190s/2 Bf-109s)
Lt. George Carr	VF-15	F6F Hellcat	June 19, 1944	(5 Judys)
Col. Leonard "Kit" Carson	357th FG	P-51 Mustang	November 27, 1944	(5 FW-190s)
Col. Fred Christensen Jr.	56th FG	P-47 Thunderbolt	July 7, 1944	(6 JU-52s)
Capt. Arthur Cleaveland	57th FG	P-40 Warhawk	April 18, 1943	(5 JU-52s)
Capt. Robert Coats	VF-17	F6F Hellcat	March 18, 1945	(5 Zekes)

AMERICAN FIGHTER PILOTS THAT BECAME
"ACE IN A DAY" (Continued)

ACE	UNIT	PLANE TYPE	DATE	VICTORIES
Capt. William Collins Jr.	VF-8	F6F Hellcat	October 12, 1944	(2 Zekes/2 Oscars/Betty)
Lt. Cdr. Thomas Conroy	VF-27	F6F Hellcat	October 24, 1944	(3 Zekes/3 Tojos)
Cdr. Clement Craig	VF-22	F6F Hellcat	January 21, 1945	(5 Tojos)
Cdr. John "Ted" Crosby	VF-17	F6F Hellcat	April 16, 1945	(3 Jacks/Zeke/ Val)
Cdr. Kenneth Dahms	VF-30	F6F Hellcat	April 6, 1945	(2 Zekes/3 Vals)
Maj. J.S. "Jim" Daniel	339th FG	P-51 Mustang	November 26, 1944	(5 FW-190s)
Col. Jefferson DeBlanc	VMF-112	F4F Wildcat	January 31, 1943	(2 Float Biplanes/ 3 Zeros)
Col. Archie Donahue	VMF-451	F4U Corsair	April 12, 1945	(3 Vals/2 Zeros)
Maj. Jefferson Dorroh	VMF-323	F4U Corsair	April 22, 1945	(6 Vals)
2nd Lt. Richard E. Duffy	324th FG	P-40 Warhawk	April 18, 1943	(5 JU-52s)
Lt. Bert Eckard	VF-9	F6F Hellcat	May 11, 1945	(5 Zekes)
Lt. Cdr. William Edwards Jr.	VF-80	F6F Hellcat	February 16, 1945	(2 Nates/2 Zekes/ Oscar)
Col. Robert Elder	353rd FG	P-51 Mustang	March 24, 1945	(4 FW-190s/1 Bf-109)
Capt. Alfred Fecke	VF-29	F6F Hellcat	October 16, 1944	(Frances/4 Jills)
Col. Patrick Fleming	VF-80	F6F Hellcat	February 16, 1945	(5 Zekes)

AMERICAN FIGHTER PILOTS THAT BECAME
"ACE IN A DAY" (Continued)

ACE	UNIT	PLANE TYPE	DATE	VICTORIES
BGen. Joseph Foss	VMF-121	F4F Wildcat	October 25, 1942	(5 Zeros)
Ens. Carl Foster	VF-30	F6F Hellcat	April 6, 1945	(2 Tojos/Zeke/3 Vals)
Capt. Harold Funk	VF-26	FM-2 Wildcat	October 24, 1944	(3 Sallys/Zeke/ Betty/Irving)
Lt. Vernon Graham	VF-11	F4F Wildcat	June 12, 1943	(5 Zekes)
Col. Herschel Green	325th FG	P-47 Thunderbolt	January 30, 1944	(4 JU-52s/MC 202/Do-217)
Capt. Eugene "Ralph" Hanks	VF-16	F6F Hellcat	November 23, 1944	(3 Haps/2 Zekes)
Maj. Harry Hanna	14th FG	P-38 Lightning	October 9, 1943	(5 JU-87s)
Lt. Robert Hanson	VMF-215	F4U Corsair	January 14, 1944	(5 Zeros)
Cdr. Willis "Bill" Hardy	VF-17	F6F Hellcat	April 6, 1945	(2 Vals/2 Judys/ Zeke)
Lt. Everett Hargreaves	VF-2	F6F Hellcat	June 24, 1944	(5 Zekes)
1st Lt. Herbert Hatch	1st FG	P-38 Lightning	June 10, 1944	(5 FW-190s)
Capt. Arthur Hawkins	VF-31	F6F Hellcat	September 13, 1944	(5 Oscars)
Flt. Ldr. Robert Hedman	AVG	P-40 Warhawk	December 25, 1941	(4 Type 97 Bombers/Zero)
Capt. Ken Hippe	VC-3	FM-2 Wildcat	October 24, 1944	(5 Lilys)
Col. William Hovde	355th FG	P-51 Mustang	December 5, 1945	(4.5 FW-190s/1 Bf-109)

AMERICAN FIGHTER PILOTS THAT BECAME
"ACE IN A DAY" (Continued)

ACE	UNIT	PLANE TYPE	DATE	VICTORIES
Lt. Robert Hurst	VF-18	F6F Hellcat	October 29, 1944	(4 Zekes/Tojo)
Col. Neel Kearby	348th FG	P-47 Thunderbolt	October 11, 1944	(2 Zekes/2 Haps/ 2 Tonys)
Capt. Leroy Keith	VF-80	F6F Hellcat	February 16, 1945	(2 Oscars/Val/ Nate/Zeke)
Lt.(jg) Robert Kidwell Jr.	VF-45	F6F Hellcat	February 16, 1945	(Claude/3 Tonys/ Zeke)
Cdr. Philip Kirkwood	VF-10	F6F Hellcat	April 16, 1945	(4 Nates/2 Vals)
Lt(jg) Alfred Lerch	VF-10	F4U Corsair	April 16, 1945	(6 Nates/Val)
Capt. Joseph Lesicka	18th FG	P-40 Warhawk	July 15, 1943	(3 Zeros/Kate/ Betty)
Col. William Leverette	14th FG	P-38 Lightning	October 9, 1943	(7 JU-87s)
Col. William H. Lewis	55th FG	P-51 Mustang	September 5, 1944	(5 German Training Aircraft)
Lt.Col. Carl Lucksic	352nd FG	P-51 Mustang	May 8, 1944	(3 FW-190s/2 Bf-109s)
Capt. Virgil Lusk	14th FG	P-38 Lightning	November 24, 1942	(5 SM-Transports)
Lt.Cdr. Charles Mallory	VF-18	F6F Hellcat	September 21, 1944	(Betty/4 Tonys)
Lt.Cdr. William Masoner Jr.	VF-19	F6F Hellcat	October 24, 1944	(Betty/Dinah/4 Nells)
Capt. David McCampbell	VF-15	F6F Hellcat	June 19, 1944	(5 Judys/2 Zekes)
Capt. David McCampbell	VF-15	F6F Hellcat	October 24, 1944	(5 Zekes/2 Oscars/2 Hamp

AMERICAN FIGHTER PILOTS THAT BECAME
"ACE IN A DAY" (Continued)

ACE	UNIT	PLANE TYPE	DATE	VICTORIES
Col. Edward McComas	23rd FG	P-51 Mustang	December 23, 1944	(5 Oscars)
Capt. E. Scott McCuskey	VF-3	F4F Wildcat	June 4, 1943	(3 D.B./2 Zeros)
1st Lt. Gordon McDaniel	325th FG	P-51 Mustang	March 14, 1945	(5 FW-190s)
Cdr. Johnnie Miller	VF-30	F6F Hellcat	April 6, 1945	(Tojo/Zeke/3 Vals)
1st Lt. Robert Milliken	474th FG	P-38 Lightning	September 12, 1944	(5 FW-190s)
Lt.(jg) Henry Mitchell Jr.	VF-17	F6F Hellcat	September 21, 1945	(5 Bettys)
Ens. Arthur Mollenhauer	VF-18	F6F Hellcat	October 12, 1944	(Sally/4 Oscars)
Lt.Cdr. Cornelius Nooy	VF-31	F6F Hellcat	September 21, 1944	(2 Zekes/Tony/2 Tojos)
Lt.Cdr. Edward "Butch" O'Hare	VF-3	F4F Wildcat	February 20, 1942	(5 TE-VBs)
1st Lt. Jerry O'Keefe	VMF-323	F4U Corsair	April 22, 1945	(5 Vals)
1st Lt. Paul Olson	359th FG	P-51 Mustang	December 18, 1944	(5 FW-190s)
R.Adm. Edward Outlaw	VF-32	F6F Hellcat	April 29, 1944	(5 Zekes)
1st Lt. Oscar Perdomo	507th FG	P-47 Thunderbolt	August 13, 1945	(4 Oscars/Willow)
Lt.Cdr. Harvey Picken	VF-18	F6F Hellcat	September 21, 1944	(2 Bettys/2 Tonys/ Helen)
Lt.Col. MacArthur Powers	324th FG	P-40 Kittyhawk	April 8, 1943	(4 JU-52s/Bf-109)

AMERICAN FIGHTER PILOTS THAT BECAME
"ACE IN A DAY" (Continued)

ACE	UNIT	PLANE TYPE	DATE	VICTORIES
Maj. George Preddy Jr.	352nd FG	P-51 Mustang	August 6, 1944	(6 Bf-109s)
Col. Robert Rankin	56th FG	P-47 Thunderbolt	March 12, 1944	(5 Bf-109s)
Capt. Russell Reiserer	VF-10	F6F Hellcat	June 19, 1944	(5 Vals)
Capt. James Rigg	VF-15	F6F Hellcat	September 12, 1944	(Tojo/4 Zekes)
Lt. Roy Rushing	VF-15	F6F Hellcat	October 24, 1944	(4 Zekes/Oscar/ Hamp)
Cdr. Gordon Schector	VF-45	F6F Hellcat	February 16, 1945	(3 Zekes/Oscar/.5 Dinah/.5 Claude)
Col. David Schilling	56th FG	P-47 Thunderbolt	December 23, 1944	(3 Bf-109s/2 FW-190s)
Capt. James Shirley	VF-27	F6F Hellcat	October 24, 1944	(Zeke/Nick/3 Tojo)
Lt.Col. William Shomo	71 TRG	F6-D Mustang	January 6, 1945	(6 Tonys/Betty)
Lt.Col. Murray Shubin	347th FG	P-38 Lightning	June 16, 1943	(5 Zekes)
Cdr. Charles Stimpson	VF-11	F6F Hellcat	October 14, 1944	(3 Hamps/2 Zekes)
1st Lt. Robert Stone	318th FG	P-47 Thunderbolt	June 10, 1945	(4 Zekes/Betty)
Col. James Swett	VMF-221	F4F Wildcat	April 7, 1943	(7 Aichi 99s)
Lt. Eugene Townsend	VF-27	F6F Hellcat	October 24, 1944	(5 Tojos)
Ens. Myron Truax	VF-83	F6F Hellcat	May 4, 1945	(4 Type 93s/Val/ Oscar)

AMERICAN FIGHTER PILOTS THAT BECAME
"ACE IN A DAY" (Continued)

ACE	UNIT	PLANE TYPE	DATE	VICTORIES
Lt.Cdr. Edward Turner	VF-14	F6F Hellcat	October 18, 1944	(4 Zekes/Oscar)
Cdr. Eugene Valencia	VF-9	F6F Hellcat	April 17, 1945	(6 Franks)
Maj. Herbert Valentine	VMF-312	F4U Corsair	May 25, 1945	(2 Tojos/2 Zekes/ 1.5 Val
Capt. Stanley "Swede" Vejtasa	VF10	F4F Wildcat	October 26, 1942	(5 Mitsubishi 97 VT/2 Aichi 99 DB)
Lt.Col. John E. Vogt	318th FG	P-47 Thunderbolt	May 28, 1945	(5 Zekes)
Cdr. Alex Vraciu	VF-16	F6F Hellcat	June 19, 1944	(6 Judys)
Capt. John Wainwright	404th FG	P-47 Thunderbolt	September 24, 1944	(6 Bf-109s)
Lt. Wilbur Webb	VF-2	F6F Hellcat	June 19, 1944	(6 Vals)
Maj. Elmer Wheadon	18th FG	P-40 Warhawk	July 1, 1943	(4 Vals/Zeke)
Col. William Whisner	352nd FG	P-51 Mustang	November 21, 1944	(5 FW-190s)
Maj. Felix Williamson	56th FG	P-47 Thunderbolt	January 14, 1945	(4 Bf-109s/ FW-190)
Col. Sidney Woods	49th FG	P-51 Mustang	March 22, 1945	(5 FW-190s)
Cdr. George Wren	VF-72	F4F Wildcat	October 26, 1942	(4 VTs/DB)
BGen. Charles "Chuck" Yeager	357th FG	P-51 Mustang	October 12, 1944	(5 Bf-109s)

APPENDIX H

NICKNAMES OF AMERICAN FIGHTER ACES

RANK, NAME, NICKNAME	FIGHTER TYPE	FIGHTER GROUP OR UNIT	TOTAL VICTORIES
Maj. Donald "Bunny" Adams	F-86 Sabre	51st FIW	6.5
Capt. Richard "Dixie" Alexander	Spitfire/P-51B Mustang	52nd FG	5
Lt.Col. Wyman "Porky" Anderson	P-40 Warhawk	79th FG	6
Capt. Bruce "Booty" Barackman	F6F-3 Hellcat	VF-50	5
Lt.Col. Harold "Coach" Bauer	F4F-4 Wildcat	VMF-212	11
Lt.Cdr. Redman "Beattle" Beatley	F6F-5 Hellcat	VF-18	6
Maj. Don "Buzz" Beerbower	P-51B Mustang	354th FG	15.5
Lt.COL. Duane "Bee" Beeson	P-47/P-51	4th FG	17.333
Ens. Jack "Berky" Berkheimer	F6F-5 Hellcat	VF(N)-41	7.5
Cdr. Foster "Crud" Blair	F4F-4/F6F-3	VF-5/VF-6	5

NICKNAMES OF AMERICAN FIGHTER ACES (Continued)

RANK, NAME, NICKNAME	FIGHTER TYPE	FIGHTER GROUP OR UNIT	TOTAL VICTORIES
Lt(jg) Richard "Razor" Blaydes	F6F-3/5 Hellcat	VF-2	5
MGen. Frederick "Boots" Blesse	F-86E Sabre	4th FIW	10
Maj. Laurence "Scrappy" Blumer	P-38J Lightning	367th FG	6
Maj. Richard "Bing" Bong	P-38F/G Lightning	49th FG	40
Capt. Robert "Posty" Booth	P-47D/P-51B	359th FG	8
Cdr. Clarence "Spike" Borley	F6F-3/5 Hellcat	VF-15	5
Col. Gregory "Pappy" Boyington	P-40C/F4U-1	AVG/ VMF-214	24
Lt. Mark "High Pockets" Bright	F4F-4/F6F-3	VF-5/VF-16	9
Col. Henry "Baby" Brown	P-51B/D Mustang	355th FG	14.2
Lt. Franklin "Chink" Burley	F6F-5 Hellcat	VF-18	7
Lt(jg) Howard "Teeth" Burriss	F4U-1 Corsair	VF-17	7.5
Lt.Col. Raymond "Cab" Callaway	P-40N Warhawk	3rd (Prov) FG	6
Capt. John "The Blade" Carder	P-51B Mustang	357th FG	7
Col. Leonard "Kit" Carson	P-51B/D Mustang	357th FG	18.5
Lt. Creighton "Shrimp"/ "Spud" Chandler	F4U-1 Corsair	VMF-215	6

NICKNAMES OF AMERICAN FIGHTER ACES (Continued)

RANK, NAME, NICKNAME	FIGHTER TYPE	FIGHTER GROUP OR UNIT	TOTAL VICTORIES
Capt. Robert "Dynamo" Coats	F6F-5 Hellcat	VF-18/VF-17	9.333
Lt.Col. Charles "Tink" Cole Jr.	P-51D Mustang	20th FG	5
BGen. Frank "Spot" Collins	P-40F/P-47D	325th FG	9
Col. Harold "Bunny" Comstock	P-47C/D Thunderbolt	56th FG	5
Maj. Ralph "Slick" Cox	P-51D Mustang	359th FG	5
BGen. Arthur "Growing Boy" Cruikshank Jr.	P-40K/N Warhawk	23rd FG	8
Sqn.Ldr. John "Crash" Curry	Spitfire Vc	601 Sqn	7.333
Col. Perry "Pee Wee"/ "Lucky" Dahl	P-38 Lightning	475th FG	9
Lt.Col. George "Curley" Davis Jr.	P-47D/F-86E	348th FG/4th FIW	21
1st.Lt. Edwin "Indian Joe" DeGraffenreid	P-38 Lightning	8th FG	6
Lt. Robert "Ram" Dibb	F4F-4/F6F-3	VF-18	7
Col. George "Pop" Doersch	P-47D/P-51	359th FG	10.5
Capt. Landis "Blood" Doner	F6F-3 Hellcat	VF-2	8
Capt. Charles "Duck" Drake	F4U-1D Corsair	VMF-323	5
BGen. William "Dinghy" Dunham	P-47D/P-51K	348th FG	16
Lt.Cdr. William "Bulldog" Edwards Jr.	F6F-5 Hellcat	VF-80	7.5
Lt.Col. John "Moon" Elder Jr.	P-47D/P-51	355th FG	8

NICKNAMES OF AMERICAN FIGHTER ACES (Continued)

RANK, NAME, NICKNAME	FIGHTER TYPE	FIGHTER GROUP OR UNIT	TOTAL VICTORIES
Capt. Lee "Scaly" Everhart	P-40N/P-38J	8th FG	6
Sqn.Ldr. David "Foob" Fairbanks	Spitfire/Tempest	501st/274th/ 3rd Sqn	12.5
Lt.Col. Robert "Father" Foy	P-51B/D Mustang	357th FG	15
Lt. John "Tubby" Franks	F6F-3/5 Hellcat	VF-9/VF-12	7
Maj. Robert "Fearless" Fraser	F4F-4/F4U-1	VMF-112	6
Col. Francis "Gabby" Gabreski	P-47D/F-86	56th FG/4th/ 51st FIW	34.5
Cdr. Dwight "Salty" Galt Jr.	F6F-3/5 Hellcat	VF-31	5
Maj. Frank "Wildman" Gaunt	P-40/P-38	18th FG	8
Capt. Grover "Goon" Gholson Jr.	P-39F/P-38H	8th/475th FG	5
Col. Ralph "Hoot" Gibson	F-86A Sabre	4th FIW	5
Capt. Donald "Flash" Gordon	F4F-4/F6F-3	VF-10	5
Col. Herschel "Herky"/ "Kentucky" Green	P-40/P-47/P-51	325th FG	18
Lt.Col. William "Beel" Grosvenor Jr.	P-40 Warhawk	23rd FG	5
Col. William "Wild Bill" Halton	P-47D/P-51D	352nd FG	10.5
Capt. Frederick "Squareloop" Harris	P-38H Lightning	475th FG	8
!st Lt. Herbert "Stub" Hatch	P-38 Lightning	1st FG	5
Col. David "Tex" Hill	P-40/P-51	AVG/23rd FG	18.75

NICKNAMES OF AMERICAN FIGHTER ACES (Continued)

RANK, NAME, NICKNAME	FIGHTER TYPE	FIGHTER GROUP OR UNIT	TOTAL VICTORIES
Maj. Howard "Deacon" Hively	P-47/P-51	4th FG	12
1st.Lt. Ralph "Kid" Hofer	P-47/P-51	4th FG	15
Capt. Jack "Happy Jack" Ilfrey	P-38F Lightning	1st FG/20th FG	7.5
Lt.Col. James "Impossible" Ince	P-38 Lightning	8th FG/475th FG	6
1st.Lt. Otto "Dittie" Jenkins	P-51 Mustang	357th FG	8.5
Capt. Clarence "Tuffy" Johnson	P-38/P-51	82nd/479th/ 352nd FG	7
Maj. John "Super Mouse" Johnston	F6F-5 Hellcat	VBF-17	8
Capt. William "Killer" Kane	F6F-3 Hellcat	VF-10	6
Capt. Charles "Little Horse" Koenig	P-51B/D Mustang	354th FG	6.5
Cdr. Dean "Diz" Laird	F4F-4/F6F-5	VF-4	5.75
Lt.Col. George "Lambie Pie" Lamb	P-51B/D Mustang	354th FG	7.5
Col. John "Firewall"/"Big Ass" Landers	P-40E/P-38J/ P-51D	49th/55th/ 357th/78th FG	14.5
Capt. John "Shady" Lane	P-38F Lightning	35th FG	6
Lt. Ned "Grandma" Langdon	F6F Hellcat	VF-18/VF-17	5
Lt.Col. Charles "Cousin" Lasko	P-51B Mustang	354th FG	7.5
Capt. Joseph "Jumpin' Joe" Lesicka	P-40/P-38	18th FG	9

NICKNAMES OF AMERICAN FIGHTER ACES (Continued)

RANK, NAME, NICKNAME	FIGHTER TYPE	FIGHTER GROUP OR UNIT	TOTAL VICTORIES
Col. Herbert "Trigger" Long	F4F/F4U	VMF-121/ 122/451	10
Maj. Yim-Qun "Long Legged" Louie	Gladiator	5th Grp Chinese	5
Maj. James "Dad" Low	F-86 Sabre	4th FIW	9
Lt.Cdr. Charles "Punchy" Mallory	F6F-5 Hellcat	VF-18	10
1st.Lt. William "Guts" Marontate	F4F-4 Wildcat	VMF-121	13
Lt.Gen. Winton "Bones" Marshall	F-86 Sabre	4th FIW	6.5
Col. Joe "Red Dog" Mason	P-47/P-51	352nd FG	5
Lt.Col. Donald "Fibber" McGee	P-39/P-38/P-51	8th FG/357th FG	6
Lt.Col. John "Earthquake" McGinn	P-38/P-51	347th FG/ 55th FG	5
Capt. Selva "Ace" McGinty	F4U-1 Corsair	VMF-441	5
Cdr. Hamilton "One Slug" McWhorter III	F6F Hellcat	VF-9/VF-12	12
Lt.Col. Nicholas "Cowboy" Megura	P-51 Mustang	4th FG	11.833
Gen. John "Whips" Meyer	P-47/P-51/F-86	352nd FG/ 4th FIW	26
2nd.Lt. Thomas "Gnomee" Miller	P-51B Mustang	354th FG	5.25
Col. Leslie "Loogoo" Minchew	P-51 Mustang	355th FG	5.5

NICKNAMES OF AMERICAN FIGHTER ACES (Continued)

RANK, NAME, NICKNAME	FIGHTER TYPE	FIGHTER GROUP OR UNIT	TOTAL VICTORIES
BGen. Glennon "Bubbles" Moran	P-47/P-51	352nd FG	13
Col. James "Madman" Morehead	P-40/P-38	24th PG & 49th/1st FG	8
1st.Lt. Stanley "Fats" Morrill	P-47 Thunderbolt	56th FG	9
Lt.Col. James "Slick" Morris	P-38J Lightning	20th FG	7.333
Capt. Paul "Blue Eyes" Murphy Jr.	P-38 Lightning	8th FG	6
Lt.Cdr. Robert "Bird" Murray	F6F-5 Hellcat	VF-29	10.333
Lt.Cdr. Cleveland "One Fault" Null	F6F Hellcat	VF-16	7
Col. Frank "Pinky" O'Connor	P-51B Mustang	354th FG	10.75
Lt. John "Jump" O'Neill	P-38 Lightning	49th FG	8
Col. Ernest "Hawk" Osher	P-38 Lightning	82nd FG	5
Col. John "Rabbit" Pietz Jr.	P-38 Lightning	475th FG	5
Cdr. Albert "Always Jolly" Pope	F6F-5 Hellcat	VF-13	7.25
Maj. George "Ratsy" Preddy Jr.	P-47/P-51	352nd FG	26.833
Col. Robert "Shorty" Rankin	P-47D Thunderbolt	56th FG	10
Lt(jg) Francis "Cash" Register	F4F-4 Wildcat	VF-6/VF-5	7
Cdr. Daniel "Fat Man" Rehm Jr.	F6F-3/5 Hellcat	VF-50/VF-8	9
Lt. Thomas "Squawky" Rennemo	F6F-5 Hellcat	VF-18	6

NICKNAMES OF AMERICAN FIGHTER ACES (Continued)

RANK, NAME, NICKNAME	FIGHTER TYPE	FIGHTER GROUP OR UNIT	TOTAL VICTORIES
Lt.Col. Elwyn "Eager El" Righetti	P-51D Mustang	55th FG	7.5
Capt. Paul "Rip" Riley	P-47/P-51	4th FG	6.5
Lt.Gen. Jay "Cock" Robbins	P-400/P-38	8th FG	22
Col. Herbert "Herbie The Boat Sinker" Ross	P-38 Lightning	14th FG	7
Capt. Jimmie "Doc" Savage	F6F Hellcat	VF-11	7
Capt. Albert "Smiley" Schlegel	P-47/P-51	4th FG	8.5
Capt. Louis "Screwy Louie" Schriber Jr.	P-38 Lightning	8th FG	5
Maj. Harold "Murderous Manny" Segal	F4U-1 Corsair	VMF-221/ VMF-211	12
Capt. Armistead "Chick" Smith Jr.	F6F Hellcat	VF-9/VBF-12	10
Cdr. James "Pug" Southerland 2nd	F4F/F6F	VF-5/VF-83/ VF-23	5
Col. Walter "Blouse" Starck	P-47/P-51	352nd FG	7
Cdr. Charles "Skull" Stimpson	F4F/F6F	VF-11	16
Lt(jg) John "Super" Symmes	F4F-4/F6F-3	VF-21/VF-15	11
Cdr. Ray "Smokey" Taylor Jr.	F6F-3 Hellcat	VF-14	6.5
Lt(jg) Franklin "Trooper" Troup	F6F-5 Hellcat	VF-29	7
Capt. John "Lucky" Truluck Jr.	P-47 Thunderbolt	56th FG	7

NICKNAMES OF AMERICAN FIGHTER ACES (Continued)

RANK, NAME, NICKNAME	FIGHTER TYPE	FIGHTER GROUP OR UNIT	TOTAL VICTORIES
Capt. Stanley "Swede" Vejtasa	SBD-3/F4F-4	VS-5/VF-10	10.25
Capt. Harold "Honest Hal" Vita	F4F-4/F6F-5	VF-9/VF-12	6
R.Adm. Albert "Scoop" Vorse Jr.	F4F/F6F	VF-3/VF-2/ VF-6/VF-80	11.5
Lt.Col. Boyd "Buzz" Wagner	P-40E/P-39D	24th PG	8
Capt. Thomas "Bloody" Walker	P-38 Lightning	347th FG	6
Capt. Jack "Cut Bank Kid" Warner	P-51D Mustang	354th FG	5
Capt. Jack "Walrus Jack" Warren	P-51B Mustang	357th FG	5
Capt. Edward "Pee Wee" Waters	P-38G Lightning	82nd FG	7
Col. James "Duckbutt" Watkins	P-40/P-38	49th FG	12
Capt. Oran "Pretty Boy" Watts	P-51 Mustang	23rd FG	5
Lt. Wilbur "Spider" Webb	F6F Hellcat	VF-2	7
Capt. George "Wheaties" Welch	P-40/P-38	15th PG/8th FG	16
Lt.Col. William "Westcoast" Wescott	F-86E Sabre	51st FIW	5
Cdr. John "Weasel" Wesolowski	F4F-4/F6F-5	VF-5/VBF-9	7
Maj. Raymond "Bright Eyes" Wetmore	P-47/P-51	359th FG	21.25

NICKNAMES OF AMERICAN FIGHTER ACES (Continued)

RANK, NAME, NICKNAME	FIGHTER TYPE	FIGHTER GROUP OR UNIT	TOTAL VICTORIES
1st.Lt. William "Gooney Bird" Whalen	P-51 Mustang	4th Fg/2nd SF	6
Lt. Bruce "Mohawk" Williams	F6F Hellcat	VF-19	7
Lt. John "Boom Boom" Wirth	F6F Hellcat	VF-31	14
Maj. Sun-Shui "Buffalo" Wong	Boeing 248/ Gladiator	5th Group Chinese	8.5

APPENDIX I

NICKNAMES OF AMERICAN ACES' FIGHTER PLANES

ACE	PLANE	NICKNAME
Capt. Fletcher Adams	P-51 Mustang	"Southern Belle"
Col. C.E. "Bud" Anderson	P-51 Mustang	"Old Crow"
Capt. Willie Y. Anderson	P-51 Mustang	"Swede's Steed"
Lt. Col. Wyman Anderson	P-40 Warhawk	"Hokus-Pokus"
Lt. Col. Stanley Andrews	P-38 Lightning	"Lil Woman 2nd"
Lt. Col. Richard Asbury	P-47 Thunderbolt	"Queenie"
Col. Donald Baccus	P-47 Thunderbolt	"The Bloody Shaft"
Lt.Gen. Royal Baker	F-86 Sabre	"Angel Face"
Maj. Raymond Bank	P-51 Mustang	"Fire Ball"
Col. Ernest Bankey	P-51 Mustang	"Lucky Lady"
Col. William Banks	P-47 Thunderbolt	"Sunshine"
Col. Rex Barber	P-38 Lightning	"Diablo"
Col. Robert Baseler	P-47 Thunderbolt	"Big Stud"
Col. Walter Beckham	P-47 Thunderbolt	"Little Demon"
Col. Walter (Jim) Benz	P-47 Thunderbolt	"Dirty Old Man"
Maj. Henry Bille	P-51 Mustang	"Prune Face"

NICKNAMES OF AMERICAN ACES' FIGHTER PLANES (Continued)

ACE	PLANE	NICKNAME
Maj. Larry Blumer	P-38 Lightning	"Scrapiron IV"
Lt. Col. Donald Bochkay	P-51 Mustang	"Winged Ace Of Clubs"
Col. Victor Bocquin	P-51 Mustang	"Devil May Care"
Capt. Robert Booth	P-47 Thunderbolt	"Oiley Bird"
Col. George Bostwick	P-47 Thunderbolt	"Ugly Duckling"
Lt. Col. Harley Brown	P-51 Mustang	"Brownies Ballroom"
Col. Henry Brown	P-51 Mustang	"Hun Hunter"
Capt. James Browning	P-51 Mustang	"Gentleman Jim"
Lt.Col. Lowell Brueland	P-51 Mustang	"Grim Reaper/Wee Speck"
Lt Col. Donald Bryan	P-51 Mustang	"Little One"
MGen. William Bryan	P-51 Mustang	"Big Noise"
Capt. Clinton Burdick	P-51 Mustang	"Do-Do"
Col. Richard Candelaria	P-51 Mustang	"My Pride And Joy"
Capt. John Carder	P-51 Mustang	"Taxpayer's Delight"
Col. Raymond Care	Supermarine Spitfire	"Calamity Jane"
Col. Bruce Carr	P-51 Mustang	"Angel's Playmate"
Col. Leonard "Kit" Carson	P-51 Mustang	"Nooky Booky"
Lt.Col. Frederick Champlin	P-38 Lightning	"Buffalo Blitz/We Dood It"
Col. Van Chandler	P-51 Mustang	"Wheezy"
Col. Fred Christensen Jr.	P-47 Thunderbolt	"Miss Fire"
Maj. Dallas Clinger	P-40 Warhawk	"Hold'n My Own"
Col. Robert Coffey	P-47 Thunderbolt	"Coffey's Pot"
Col. Jerry Collinsworth	Supermarine Spitfire	"Dimples II"

NICKNAMES OF AMERICAN ACES' FIGHTER PLANES (Continued)

ACE	PLANE	NICKNAME
Col. Gordon Compton	P-51 Mustang	"Little Bouncer"
Lt.Col. Paul Conger	P-47 Thunderbolt	"Hollywood High Hatter"
Capt. Warren Cooley	P-51 Mustang	"Lonesome Pole-Cat"
Col. Merle Coons	P-51 Mustang	"The Worry Bird"
Maj. Edward Cragg	P-38 Lightning	"Porky II"
Col. Niven Cranfill	P-51 Mustang	"Deviless"
Lt.Col. Claude Crenshaw	P-51 Mustang	"Heat Wave"
Capt. Art Cundy	P-51 Mustang	"Alabama Rammer Jammer"
Lt.Col. Louis Curdes	P-51 Mustang	"Bad Angel"
Capt. Frank Cutler	P-51 Mustang	"Soldier's Vote"
Col. Perry Dahl	P-38 Lightning	"Skidoo"
Capt. Kenneth Dahlberg	P-51 Mustang	"Dahlberg's Dilemma"
Col. William Daniel	P-51 Mustang	"Tempus Fugit"
Col. Barrie Davis	P-51 Mustang	"Honey Bee"
Col. Glendon V. Davis	P-51 Mustang	"Pregnant Polecat"
Maj. Cecil Dean	P-51 Mustang	"Sawtooth Apache"
Col. Robert DeHaven	P-38 Lightning	"Shooting Orchid"
Capt. Elliott Dent Jr.	P-40 Warhawk	"Grade A"
Capt. Michael Dikovitsky	P-47 Thunderbolt	"Cleveland Cleaver"
Col. George Doersch	P-51 Mustang	"Ole' Goat"
Col. Irwin Dregne	P-51 Mustang	"Ah Fung Goo"
Maj. Urban Drew	P-51 Mustang	"Detroit Miss"
Lt(jg) Paul Drury	F6F Hellcat	"Paoli Local"
Maj. James Duffy Jr.	P-51 Mustang	"Dragon Wagon"

NICKNAMES OF AMERICAN ACES' FIGHTER PLANES (Continued)

ACE	PLANE	NICKNAME
Col. Glenn Duncan	P-47 Thunderbolt	"Dove Of Peace"
Capt. Richard Dunkin	P-51 Mustang	"Thisizit"
Lt.Col. William Dunn	P-47 Thunderbolt	"Posterius Ferrous"
Lt.Col. John Elder	P-51 Mustang	"Moon"
Capt. Wallace Emmer	P-51 Mustang	"Arson's Reward"
Lt. Col. James Empey	P-51 Mustang	"Little Ambassador"
Lt. Col. John England	P-51 Mustang	"U've Had It"
Col. Herman Ernst	P-61 Black Widow	"Borrowed Time"
MGen. Andrew Evans	P-51 Mustang	"Little Sweetie"
Capt. Ernest Fiebelkorn	P-51 Mustang	"June Night"
Col. Harold Fischer	F-80/F-86	"Kismet/Heavens Above"
Col. Harry Fisk	P-51 Mustang	"Duration Plus"
Lt.Col. Joesph Forster	P-38 Lightning	"Florida Cracker"
Col. Cecil Foster	F-86 Sabre	"Four Kings And A Queen"
Lt.Col. Robert Foy	P-51 Mustang	"Reluctant Rebel/Little Shrimp"
Capt. Earl Fryer	P-51 Mustang	"Spunk Town"
Col. Kenneth Gallup	P-47 Thunderbolt	"Rat A Dat"
Capt. William Garry	P-47 Thunderbolt	"Rough & Ready"
Maj. Frank Gaunt	P-40 Warhawk	"The Twerp"
Capt. Steven Gerick	P-47 Thunderbolt	"Tally Ho Chaps"
Capt. Edward Gimbel	P-51 Mustang	"Hard Luck!"
Maj. Kenneth Giroux	P-38 Lightning	"Dead Eye Daisey"
Maj. George Gleason	P-51 Mustang	"Hot Toddy"
Maj. Maxwell Glenn	P-38 Lightning	"Sluggo-V"

NICKNAMES OF AMERICAN ACES' FIGHTER PLANES (Continued)

ACE	PLANE	NICKNAME
Maj. Fred Glover	P-51 Mustang	"Rebel Queen"
Maj. John Godfrey	P-47/P-51	"Reggie's Reply"
Lt.Col. George Goebel	P-51 Mustang	"Flying Dutchman"
Lt.Gen. Gordon Graham	P-51 Mustang	"Down For Double"
Lt. Col. Marvin Grant	P-47 Thunderbolt	"Racine Belle"
Capt. Billy Gresham	P-38 Lightning	"Black Market Babe"
Col. Joseph Griffin	P-40/P-38	"Hellzapoppin"
Capt. Clayton Gross	P-47/P-51	"Live Bait"
Col. William Halton	P-51 Mustang	"Slender, Tender & Tall"
1st Lt. Thomas Harris	P-51 Mustang	"Lil' Red's Rocket"
Capt. Kenneth Hart	P-38 Lightning	"Pee Wee V"
Capt. Russell Hayworth	P-51 Mustang	"Krazy Kid"
Lt.Col. Edwin Heller	P-51 Mustang	"Hell-er Bust"
Maj. Allen Hill	P-38 Lightning	"Hill's Angels"
Col. David "Tex" Hill	P-51 Mustang	"Bull Frog"
Maj. Edward Hiro	P-51 Mustang	"Horses Itch"
Maj. Howard Hively	P-47/P-51	"The Deacon"
Capt. William Hodges	P-47 Thunderbolt	"Channel Chariot"
1st Lt. Ralph Hofer	P-47 Thunderbolt	"The Missouri Kid/Sho-Me"
Lt.Col. Roy Hogg	P-47 Thunderbolt	"Thunderbolt Lad"
Lt.Col. Besby Holmes	P-38 Lightning	"Ole 100"
Col. Wallace Hopkins	P-51 Mustang	"Ferocious Frankie"
Lt.Col. A.T. House Jr.	P-40 Warhawk	"Poopy"
BGen. James Howard	P-51 Mustang	"Ding Hao!"
1st Lt. Bernard Howes	P-51 Mustang	"My Little Honey"

NICKNAMES OF AMERICAN ACES' FIGHTER PLANES (Continued)

ACE	PLANE	NICKNAME
Capt. Edward Hoyt	P-47 Thunderbolt	"Hoyt's Hoss"
1st Lt. Edward Hunt	P-51 Mustang	"Ready Eddy"
Capt. Jack Ilfrey	P-51 Mustang	"Happy Jack's Go Buggy"
Lt.Col. James Ince	P-38 Lightning	"Impossible Ince"
BGen. Clayton Isaacson	P-38 Lightning	"Almost A Draggin II"
Col. Willie Jackson	P-51 Mustang	"Hotstuff"
Col. Arthur Jeffrey	P-51 Mustang	"Boomerang Jr."
1st Lt. Otto Jenkins	P-51 Mustang	"Toolin' Fool's Revenge"
Maj. Evan Johnson	P-51 Mustang	"The Comet"
Lt. Col. Gerald W. Johnson	P-47 Thunderbolt	"The Mood"
Lt.Col. Robert S. Johnson	P-47 Thunderbolt	"Double Lucky/Penrod & Sam"
Lt.Col. Clifford Jolley	F-86 Sabre	"Jolley Roger"
1st Lt. Daniel Kennedy	P-38 Lightning	"Beantown Boys"
Maj. Donald Kienholz	P-38 Lightning	"Nasa Serbska Sloboda"
Lt.Col. William King	P-51 Mustang	"Atlanta Peach"
Col. Clayton Kinnard	P-51 Mustang	"Man O War"
Maj. Marion Kirby	P-38 Lightning	"Maiden Head Hunter"
Maj. John Kirla	P-51 Mustang	"Spook"
Col. Frank Klibbe	P-47 Thunderbolt	"Little Chief"
Capt. Charles Koenig	P-51 Mustang	"Little Horse"
Capt. Kenneth Ladd	P-38 Lightning	"X Virgin"
Lt.Col. George Lamb	P-51 Mustang	"Uno Who II"
Col. John Landers	P-51 Mustang	"Big Beautiful Doll"
Capt. John Lane	P-38 Lightning	"Thumper"

NICKNAMES OF AMERICAN ACES' FIGHTER PLANES (Continued)

ACE	PLANE	NICKNAME
Col. George Laven	P-38 Lightning	"Itsy Bitsy I"
Lt.Col. Jack Lenox	P-38 Lightning	"Snookie II"
Capt. Francis Lent	P-38 Lightning	"T-Rigor Mortis III"
Col. William Leverette	P-38 Lightning	"Stingeree"
Capt. Ted Lines	P-51 Mustang	"Thunderbird"
Capt. Ray Littge	P-51 Mustang	"E. Pluribus Unum"
Col. John Loisel	P-38 Lightning	"Screamin' Kid"
Capt. Charles London	P-47 Thunderbolt	"Jeepo"
Lt.Col. Donald Lopez	P-40 Warhawk	"Lope's Hope"
Lt.Col. Marvin Lubner	P-51 Mustang	"Barfly"
Lt.Col. Carl Luksic	P-47 Thunderbolt	"Lucky Boy"
1st Lt. James Luma	DeHavilland Mosquito	"Moonbeam McSwine"
1st Lt. Stanley Lustic	P-47 Thunderbolt	"Stanley's Steamer"
Col. Charles MacDonald	P-38 Lightning	"Putt-Putt Maru"
Maj. John Mackay	P-38 Lightning	"Shoot You're Faded"
Col. Walker "Bud" Mahurin	F-86 Sabre	"Honest John/Stud"
Capt. Thomas Maloney	P-38 Lightning	"Maloney's Pony"
Lt.Col. William Mathis	P-47 Thunderbolt	"Bottom's Up"
Col. Ben Mayo	P-47 Thunderbolt	"No Guts-No Glory!"
Capt. David McCampbell	F6F Hellcat	"Minsi II"
Col. Edward McComas	P-51 Mustang	"Kansas Reaper"
Capt. Joseph McConnell	F-86 Sabre	"Beautious Butch"
Lt.Col. Norm McDonald	P-51 Mustang	"Shu-Shu"
Capt. James McElroy	P-51 Mustang	"Ridge Runner"

NICKNAMES OF AMERICAN ACES' FIGHTER PLANES (Continued)

ACE	PLANE	NICKNAME
Lt.Col. John McGinn	P-51 Mustang	"Da Quake"
Capt. John McGraw	FM-2 Wildcat	"Mah Baby"
Maj. Thomas McGuire	P-38 Lightning	"Pudgy"
Gen. John Meyer	P-51 Mustang	"Petie 2nd"
Capt. Armour Miller	P-38 Lightning	"Jinx"
Col. John Mitchell	P-38 Lightning	"Squinch"
Maj. Robert W. Moore	P-40 Warhawk	"Stinger"
Col. James Morehead	P-40 Warhawk	"L'Ace"
1st Lt. Stan Morrill	P-47 Thunderbolt	"Fats-Btfsplk"
Lt.Col. James Morris	P-38 Lightning	"Til We Meet Again"
Capt. Paul Morriss	P-38 Lightning	"Hold Everything"
Capt. Alva Murphy	P-51 Mustang	"Bite Me"
BGen. Joseph Myers	P-38 Lightning	"Journey's End"
Lt. Col. Louis Norley	P-47 Thunderbolt	"Red Dog"
Lt.Col. Jack Oberhansky	P-51 Mustang	"Iron Ass"
Lt.Col. Gilbert O'Brien	P-51 Mustang	"Shanty Irish"
Capt. William O'Brien	P-51 Mustang	"Billy's Bitch"
Col. Frank O'Connor	P-51 Mustang	"Stinky"
BGen. Robin Olds	P-38 Lightning	"Scat II"
1st Lt. John O'Neill	P-38 Lightning	"Beautiful Lass"
Col. Ernest Osher	P-38 Lightning	"Sad Sack"
Capt. Dolph Overton	F-86 Sabre	"Dolph's Devil/Devil In Disguise"
Maj. Joel Owens	P-38 Lightning	"Rum Head"
Col. Forrest Parham	P-40/P-51	"Little Jeep"

NICKNAMES OF AMERICAN ACES' FIGHTER PLANES (Continued)

ACE	PLANE	NICKNAME
1st Lt. Edsel Paulk	P-47 Thunderbolt	"Little Sir Echo"
1st Lt. Oscar Perdomo	P-47 Thunderbolt	"Lil' Meaties Meat Chopper"
Maj. Richard Peterson	P-51 Mustang	"Hurry Home Honey"
Lt.Col. Sammy Pierce	P-40 Warhawk	"The Strawberry Blond/The Hialeah Wolf"
Col. Steve Pisanos	P-47 Thunderbolt	"Miss Plainfield"
Lt Col. Pete Pompetti	P-47 Thunderbolt	"Axe The Axis"
Col. Edward Popek	P-51 Mustang	"Rollicking Rogue"
Col. Bruce Porter	F6F Hellcat	"Black Death"
Maj. George Preddy	P-51 Mustang	"Cripes A' Mighty"
Lt.Col. Jack Price	P-47 Thunderbolt	"Feather Merchant"
Col. Royce Priest	P-51 Mustang	"Eaglebeak/Weepin Deacon II"
Col. Roger Pryor	P-40 Warhawk	"Weak Eyes Yokum"
Lt.Col. John Pugh	P-51 Mustang	"Geronimo"
Col. Robert Rankin	P-47 Thunderbolt	"Wicked Wackie Weegie"
Capt. C.B. Ray	P-38 Lightning	"San Antonio Rose"
Lt.Col. Horace Reeves	P-38 Lightning	"El Tornado"
Lt Col. Leonard Reeves	P-51 Mustang	"My Dallas Darlin"
Col. Andrew Reynolds	P-40 Warhawk	"Star Dust/Oklahoma Kid"
Capt. Robert Reynolds	P-51 Mustang	".50 Calibre Concerto"
Lt.Col. Elwyn Righetti	P-51 Mustang	"Katydid"
Col. Arval Roberson	P-51 Mustang	"Passion Wagon"
Col. Eugene Roberts	P-47 Thunderbolt	"Spokane Chief"
Gen. Felix M. Rogers	P-51 Mustang	"Beantown Banshee"

NICKNAMES OF AMERICAN ACES' FIGHTER PLANES (Continued)

ACE	PLANE	NICKNAME
Capt. Gerald Rounds	P-38 Lightning	"Cadiz Eagle/Chicken Dit"
MGen. Robert Rowland	P-47 Thunderbolt	"Miss Mutt"
Col. George Ruddell	F-86 Sabre	"Mig Mad Mavis"
Lt.Col. Thomas Schank	P-38 Lightning	"Rocky Mountain Canary"
Lt.Col. Donald Scherer	P-47 Thunderbolt	"Flying Dutchman"
Col. David Schilling	P-47 Thunderbolt	"Whack/Hairless Joe"
Capt. Louis Schriber Jr.	P-38 Lightning	"Screwy Louie"
Capt. Robert Schultz	P-38 Lightning	"Golden Eagle"
Col. Harry Sealy	P-38 Lightning	"Haleakaia"
Lt.Col. William Shomo	P-51 Mustang	"The Flying Undertaker"
Col. Carroll Smith	P-61 Black Widow	"Time's A Wastin"
Lt.Gen. Donovan Smith	P-47 Thunderbolt	"Ole Cock"
BGen. Leslie Smith	P-47 Thunderbolt	"Silver Lady"
Capt. Richard Smith	P-38 Lightning	"The Japanese Sandman"
1st Lt. Virgil Smith	P-38 Lightning	"Kniption"
Maj. William Stangel	P-51 Mustang	"Stinky 2"
Lt.Col. Arland Stanton	P-40 Warhawk	"Empty Saddle"
Col. Walter Starck	P-51 Mustang	"Starck Mad Even Stevens"
Col. James Starnes	P-51 Mustang	"Tar Heel"
Lt. Col. John Storch	P-51 Mustang	"The Shillelagh"
MGen. Donald Strait	P-51 Mustang	"Jersey Jerk"
Maj. Elliott Summer	P-38 Lightning	"Blood & Guts"
Capt. Harrison Tordoff	P-51 Mustang	"Upupa Epops"
Lt. Phil Tovrea Jr.	P-38 Lightning	"Lamonica Plato"

NICKNAMES OF AMERICAN ACES' FIGHTER PLANES (Continued)

ACE	PLANE	NICKNAME
Maj. Fred Trafton Jr.	Supermarine Spitfire	"Christian Maker"
2nd Lt. Grant Turley	P-47 Thunderbolt	"Sundown Ranch"
Lt.Col. Richard Turner	P-51 Mustang	"Short Fuse Sallee"
Lt.Col. Gerald E. Tyler	P-51 Mustang	"Little Duck Foot"
Lt.Col. Robert Vaught	P-40 Warhawk	"Bob's Robin"
Gen. John W. Vogt Jr.	P-47 Thunderbolt	"Jersey Mosquito"
Col. John Voll	P-51 Mustang	"American Beauty"
Capt. Jack Warren	P-51 Mustang	"Chicago's Own"
Capt. Edward Waters	P-38 Lightning	"Mighty Mite"
Col. Darrell Welch	P-38 Lightning	"Sky Ranger"
Maj. Robert Welch	P-51 Mustang	"Wings Of The Morning"
Capt. Richard West	P-38 Lightning	"Heart Flush"
Lt.Col. Robert Westbrook Jr.	P-38 Lightning	"The Florida Thrush"
Capt. James Wilkinson	P-47 Thunderbolt	"Miss Behave"
Capt. Robert Winks	P-51 Mustang	"Trusty Rusty"
Lt.Col. Robert Woody	P-51 Mustang	"Woody's Maytag"
Maj. Robert Yaeger Jr.	P-47 Thunderbolt	"Noisy"
Col. Daniel Zoerb	P-51 Mustang	"Hey Rube!"

APPENDIX J

NOTED FIGHTER SQUADRON NICKNAMES

FIGHTER SQUADRON	NICK-NAMES	TOTAL VICTORIES
AVG-"FLYING TIGERS"		
1st Prusuit Squadron	"Adam And Eves"	98.5
2nd Prusuit Squadron	"Panda Bears"	64.5
3rd Prusuit Squadron	"Hell's Angels"	68
USAAF		
2nd FS	"Beagle Squadron"	186.33
7th FS	"Screamin' Deamons"	178
8th FS	"Black Sheep"	207
9th FS	"Flying Knights"	254
12th FS	"Dirty Dozen"	40.5
18th FS	"Blue Fox"	2
25th FS	"Our Assam Draggins"	19.75
27th FS	"Black Falcons"	187.5
35th FS	"Black Panthers"	130
36th FS	"Flying Fiends"	94

NOTED FIGHTER SQUADRON NICKNAMES (Continued)

FIGHTER SQUADRON	NICK-NAMES	TOTAL VICTORIES
USAAF		
39th FS	"Flying Cobras"	186
40th FS	"Red Devil's"	110
44th FS	"Vampires"	163.5
58th FS	"Red Gorillas"	56
59th FS	"Roaring Lion"	41
60th FS	"Fighting Crows"	35
64th FS	"Black Scorpions"	55.5
66th FS	"Exterminators"	78.5
67th FS	"Fighting Cocks"	28.5
68th FS	"Lightning Lancers"	48
73rd FS	"Barflies"	22
80th FS	"Headhunters"	213
82nd Tactical Recon	"Strafing Saints"	18
85th FS	"Flying Skull"	36
94th FS	"Hat In The Ring"	136.66
110th Tactical Recon	"Musketeers"	20
118th Tactical Recon	"Black Lightning"	71.75
314th FS	"Hawk"	50
316th FS	"Hells Belles"	37
339th FS	"Sunsetters"	163.5
345th FS	"Devil Hawk"	7
353rd FS	"Fighting Cobras"	295
355th FS	"Pugnacious Pups"	142.166

NOTED FIGHTER SQUADRON NICKNAMES (Continued)

FIGHTER SQUADRON	NICK-NAMES	TOTAL VICTORIES
USAAF		
356th FS	"Red Ass Squadron"	184.833
428th FS	"The Geyser Gang"	26.67
429th FS	"The Retail Gang"	33
430th FS	"The Backdoor Gang"	30.833
449th FS	"Lightning Tiger"	71.75
513th FS	"Basher"	33
514th FS	"Raider"	0.5
528th FS	"Dragonfly"	12
530th FS	Yellow Scorpions"	85
US NAVY		
VF-1	"High Hatters"	100
VF-2	"Chiefs/Red Rippers"	262
VF-3	"Felix The Cat"	107.5
VF-4	"Red Rippers"	62
VF-5	"Striking Eagles"	186.5
VF-6	"Shooting Stars"	121
VF-10	"Grim Reapers"	217
VF-11	"Sundowners"	157
VF-14	"Iron Angels"	138
VF-16	"Fighting Airedales"	154.5
VF-17	"Jolly Rogers"	313
VF-19	"Satan's Kittens"	155
VF-29	"Shillelagh"	114

NOTED FIGHTER SQUADRON NICKNAMES (Continued)

FIGHTER SQUADRON	NICK-NAMES	TOTAL VICTORIES
US NAVY		
VF-33	"The Hellcats"	92.5
VF-40	"The Fighting Boars"	29
VF-41	"Red Rippers"	14
VF-46	"Men-O-War"	27.75
VF-71	"Thor"	7.5
VF-72	"Blue Wasps"	44
VF-80	"Vipers"	159.5
VF-81	"Freelancers"	43
VF-84	"Wolf Gang"	92
VF-85	"Sky Pirates"	40
VF-86	"Pippers"	12
VBF-86	"Bengal Bandits"	7
VBF-88	"Game Cocks"	13
US MARINE CORPS		
VMF-111	"Devildogs"	0
VMF-112	"Wolfpack"	144
VMF-113	"Whistling Devils"	21
VMF-114	"Death Dealers"	0
VMF-115	"Joe's Jokers"	5.5
VMF-123	"Eight-Balls"	58
VMF-124	"Checkerboards"	69
VMF-213	"Hellhawks"	113
VMF-214	"Black Sheep"	126

NOTED FIGHTER SQUADRON NICKNAMES (Continued)

FIGHTER SQUADRON	NICK-NAMES	TOTAL VICTORIES
US MARINE CORPS		
VMF-215	"Fighting Corsairs"	135.5
VMF-216	"Wild Hares"	27.33
VMF-217	"Bulldogs"	19
VMF-221	"Fighting Falcons"	155
VMF-223	"Rainbow/Bulldogs"	147.5
VMF-224	"Fighting Wildcats"	111.5
VMF-311	"Hells' Belles"	71
VMF-312	"Day's Knights"	64.5
VMF-322	"Fighting Cocks"	30.5
VMF-323	"Death Rattlers"	124.5
VMF-441	"Black Jacks"	49
VMF-451	"Blue Devils"	34
VMF-452	"Sky Raiders"	4
VMF-513	"Flying Nightmares" (Korea)	10
(N) VMF-553	"Crystal Gazers"	35
(N) VMF-541	"Bat Eyes"	23
(N) VMF-543	"Night Hawks"	15

APPENDIX K

USAAF FIGHTER SQUADRONS WITH MORE THAN 100 VICTORIES

SQUADRON	TOTAL VICTORIES	SQUADRON	TOTAL VICTORIES
353rd FS	295	97th FS	149
9th FS	254	49th FS	145
487th FS	236.5	334 FIS (Korea)	143.5
61st FS	230	328th FS	143
335 FIS (Korea)	223.5	355th FS	142.167
62nd FS	221.5	94th FS	136.67
431st FS	221	74th FS	135
80th FS	213	354th FS	132
317th FS	212	35th FS	130
364th FS	211.5	4th FS	127
8th FS	207	319th FS	127
96th FS	201	76th FS	123
334th FS	200.67	342nd FS	123

USAAF FIGHTER SQUADRONS WITH MORE THAN 100 VICTORIES (Continued)

SQUADRON	TOTAL VICTORIES	SQUADRON	TOTAL VICTORIES
356th FS	200	433rd FS	121
95th FS	198	83rd FS	119.5
362nd FS	198	71st FS	115
27th FS	187.5	486th FS	114
2nd FS	186.33	358th FS	113
39th FS	186	336 FIS (Korea)	112.5
356th FS	184.833	25th FIS (Korea)	112
318th FS	180	350th FS	112
7th FS	178	370th FS	112
63rd FS	173.25	357th FS	111.5
44th FS	163.5	5th FS	111
432nd FS	167	40th FS	110
335th FS	162.167	38th FS	108
75th FS	162	37th FS	105
336th FS	161.67	82nd FS	103.5
48th FS	159	39th FIS (Korea)	103
363rd FS	155.5	351st FS	100.5

US NAVY FIGHTER SQUADRONS WITH MORE THAN 100 VICTORIES

SQUADRON	TOTAL VICTORIES	SQUADRON	TOTAL VICTORIES
VF-17	313	VF-19	155
VF-15	310	VF-16	154.5
VF-2	262	VF-27	147
VF-9	256.75	VF-14	138
VF-18	250.5	VF-83	137
VF-5	186.5	VBF-17	125
VF-31	165.5	VF-6	121
VF-30	159.83	VF-29	114
VF-80	159.5	VF-3	107.5
VF-20	158.17	VF-1	100
VF-11	157	VF-21	100
VF-8	156		

USMC FIGHTER SQUADRONS WITH MORE THAN 100 VICTORIES

SQUADRON	TOTAL VICTORIES	SQUADRON	TOTAL VICTORIES
VMF-121	204.5	VMF-214	126
VMF-221	155	VMF-323	124.5
VMF-223	147.5	VMF-213	113
VMF-112	144	VMF-224	111.5
VMF-215	135.5		

APPENDIX L

HIGHEST SCORING ACE OF EACH FIGHTER TYPE

PLANE TYPE	VICTORIES	PILOT NAME
P-38 Lightning	40	Maj. Richard Bong (America's "Ace Of Aces")
P-51 Mustang	23.83	Maj. George Preddy
P-47 Thunderbolt	28	Col. Francis Gabreski
P-40 Warhawk	14.25	Col. David "Tex" Hill
P-39 Airacobra	5	1st.Lt. William F. Fiedler (Only P-39 Ace)
F4F Wildcat	26	BGen. Joseph Foss
F6F Hellcat	34	Capt. David McCampbell
F4U Corsair	25	Lt. Robert Hanson
DeHavilland Mosquito	7	Lt.Col. Archibald Harrington
Supermarine Spitfire	13	Lt.Col. John Lynch
Hawker Hurricane	13	Wing Cdr. L.C. "Lance" Wade
Polikarpov I-16 "Rata"	5	Frank Tinker (Only I-16 Ace)
Gloster Gladiator	5.5	Maj. Sun-Shui "Buffalo" Wong
F-86 Sabre	16	Capt. Joseph McConnell Jr.
F-4 Phantom	5	BGen. Richard "Steve" Ritchie

HIGHEST SCORING ACE OF EACH FIGHTER TYPE (Continued)

PLANE TYPE	VICTORIES	PILOT NAME
F-4 Phantom	5	Cdr. Randall Cunningham
P-61 Black Widow	5	1st.Lt. Paul A. Smith
P-61 Black Widow	5	Maj. Carroll C. Smith
P-61 Black Widow	5	Capt. Eugene Axtell
P-61 Black Widow	5	1st.Lt. Herman Ernst

APPENDIX M

AMERICAN ACES THAT SHOT DOWN THE MOST DIFFERENT TYPES OF COMBAT AIRCRAFT

PILOT	FIGHTER FLOWN	TOTAL TYPES SHOT DOWN	TYPES SHOT DOWN	TOTAL VIC-TORIES
Col. Charles MacDonald	P-38 Lightning	11	(Japanese) Val/Oscar/ Zeke/Tony/Hamp/Rufe/ Topsy/Tojo/Jack/Sally/ Dinah	27
Maj. Richard Bong	P-38 Lightning	9	(Japanese) Val/Oscar/ Zero/Dinah/Betty/Tony/ Sally/Irving/Tojo	40
BGen. William Dunham	P-47 & P-51	9	(Japanese) Tony/Hap/ Pete/Val/Nell/Oscar/ Zeke/Sally/Frank	16

AMERICAN ACES THAT SHOT DOWN THE MOST DIFFERENT TYPES OF COMBAT AIRCRAFT (Continued)

		TOTAL		
		TYPES		TOTAL
	FIGHTER	SHOT		VIC-
PILOT	FLOWN	DOWN	TYPES SHOT DOWN	TORIES
Col. Neel Kearby	P-47 Thunderbolt	9	(Japanese) Betty/ Oscar/Dinah/Zeke/ Hap/Tony/Pete/Sally/ Nell	22
Maj. Thomas McGuire Jr.	P-38 Lightning	8	(Japanese) Zeke/Tony/ Val/Oscar/Tojo/Sonia/ Hamp/Jack	38
Lt.Col. John Herbst	P-51 Mustang	8	(Japanese) Oscar/ Tojo/Val/Hamp/Jake/ Nell/Tess/(German) Bf. 109	18
Col. Wiltold Urbanowicz	PZLP.XIC/ Hurricane/ P-40	8	(German) Me-110/ Ju-88/Bf.-109/Do-215/ He-111/Do-17 (Japanese) Zero (Russian) Recon A/C	18
Col. John Voll	P-51 Mustang	8	(German) FW-190/ Me-210/Ju-52/Ju-88/ Do-217/Fi-156/Bf.-109 (Italy) Mc-202	21

Appendix N

Pilots with Most Ground Strafing Victories

PILOT	PLANE FLOWN	GROUND VICTORIES
Lt.Col. Elwyn Righetti	P-51 Mustang	27
Maj. Philip Chapman	P-51 Mustang	21
Col. John Landers	(P-40/P-38/P-51)	20
Lt.Col. Edwin Heller	P-51 Mustang	16.5
Col. Gordon Compton	P-47/P-51	15
Capt. William Cullerton	P-51 Mustang	15
Maj. James Goodson	P-47/P-51	15
Col. Henry Brown	P-51 Mustang	14.5
1st Lt. Ralph Hofer	P-47/P-51	14
Lt.Col. John Elder Jr.	P-51/P-47	13
Capt. Ray Littge	P-51 Mustang	13
Gen. John Meyer	P-51/P-47	13
Maj. John Godfrey	P-47/P-51	12.67
Maj. Fred Glover	P-51 Mustang	12.5

PILOTS WITH MOST GROUND STRAFING VICTORIES (Continued)

PILOT	PLANE FLOWN	GROUND VICTORIES
Maj. Robert Welch	P-51 Mustang	12
BGen. Robin Olds	P-38/P-51	11
Col. David Schilling	P-47 Thunderbolt	10.5
Maj. Pierce McKennon	P-47/P-51	9.68
Maj. Maxwell Glenn	P-38 Lightning	9.5
Lt.Gen. Gordon Graham	P-51 Mustang	9.5
Lt.Col. Robert Ammon	P-51 Mustang	9
Maj. James E. Duffy Jr.	P-47/P-51	9
Col. John Lowell	P-38/P-51	9

Lt Col. Joseph L. Thury with (2.5) aerial victories had 25.5 ground strafing victories

APPENDIX O

AMERICAN ACES WHO SHOT DOWN ROCKET OR JET AIRCRAFT

ACE	PLANE FLOWN	TYPE AIRCRAFT SHOT DOWN	DATE OCCURRED
Capt. Robert Abernathy	P-51D Mustang	Me-262	April 10, 1945
Maj. Donald Adams	F-86E Sabre	(6.5) MiG-15s	1952 Korea
1st Lt. Dudley Amoss	P-51D Mustang	Me-262	February 15, 1945
Lt.Gen. Royal Baker	F-86E Sabre	(12) MiG-15s	1952-53 Korea
Col. Robert Baldwin	F-86E Sabre	(5) MiG-15s	1953 Korea
Maj. Richard Becker	F-86A Sabre	(5) MiG-15s	1950-51 Korea
Col. Stephen Bettinger	F-86F Sabre	(5) MiG-15s	1953 Korea
MGen. Frederick Blesse	F-86E Sabre	(10) MiG-15s	1952 Korea
Lt.Col.Wayne Blickenstaff	P-51K Mustang	Me-262	Feb. 15, 1945
Lt.Col. Donald Bochkay	P-51D/K Mustang	(2) Me-262s	Feb. 9 & April 18, 1945

293

AMERICAN ACES WHO SHOT DOWN ROCKET
OR JETAIRCRAFT (Continued)

ACE	PLANE FLOWN	TYPE AIRCRAFT SHOT DOWN	DATE OCCURRED
Lt.Col. John Bolt	F-86F Sabre	(6) MiG-15s	1953 Korea
Col. George Bostwick	P-47M Thunderbolt	Me-262	April 7, 1945
Lt.Col. Lowell Brueland	F-86E Sabre	(2) MiG-15s	1953 Korea
Lt.Col. Henry Buttelmann	F-86E/F Sabre	(7) MiG-15s	1953 Korea
Col. George Ceullers	P-51D Mustang	Me-262	April 4, 1945
Col. Van Chandler	F-86E Sabre	(3) MiG-15s	1952 Korea
1st Lt. Charles Cleveland	F-86 Sabre	(5) MiG-15s	1952 Korea
Maj. Philip Colman	F-86A/E Sabre	(4) MiG-15s	1952 Korea
Col. Gordon Compton	P-51D Mustang	(2) Me-262s	Feb. 22 & April 10, 1945
Col. Niven Cranfill	P-51D Mustang	Me-262	March 19, 1945
Col. Richard Creighton	F-86A Sabre	(5) MiG-15s	1951 Korea
Lt.Col. Donald Cummings	P-51D Mustang	(2) Me-262s	February 25, 1945
Cdr. Randall Cunningham	F4J Phantom	(1) MiG-21 & (4) MiG-17s	1972 Vietnam
Maj. Clyde Curtin	F-86F Sabre	(5) MiG-15s	1952/53 Korea
Col. William Daniel	P-51D Mustang	Me-262	March 24, 1945
Lt.Col. George Davis	F-86E Sabre	(14) MiG-15s	1951/52 Korea
Capt. William Dillard	P-51D Mustang	Me-262	March 22, 1945
Maj. Urban Drew	P-51D Mustang	(2) Me-262s	October 7, 1945

AMERICAN ACES WHO SHOT DOWN ROCKET
OR JETAIRCRAFT (Continued)

ACE	PLANE FLOWN	TYPE AIRCRAFT SHOT DOWN	DATE OCCURRED
Col. Glenn Eagleston	F-86A Sabre	(2) MiG-15s	1950/51 Korea
Col. Benjamin Emmert Jr.	F-86A Sabre	MiG-15	1951 Korea
Maj. Manuel Fernandez	F-86E/F Sabre	(14.5) MiG-15s	1952/53 Korea
Col. Harold Fischer	F-86F Sabre	(10) MiG-15s	1952/53 Korea
Col. Cecil Foster	F-86E Sabre	(9) MiG-15s	1952/53 Korea
Lt.Col. Robert Foy	P-51D Mustang	Me-262	April 19, 1945
Col. Francis Gabreski	F-86F Sabre	(6.5) MiG-15s	1951/52 Korea
Col. Vermont Garrison	F-86F Sabre	(10) MiG-15s	1950/53 Korea
Col. Ralph Gibson	F-86A Sabre	(5) MiG-15s	1951 Korea
Maj. Fred Glover	P-51D Mustang	Me-163 (rocket)	November 2, 1944
Maj. Norman Gould	P-47M Thunderbolt	Ar-234	March 14, 1945
Col. James Hagerstrom	F-86E Sabre	(8.5) MiG-15s	1952/53 Korea
Lt.Col. Edwin Heller	F-86E Sabre	(3.5) MiG-15s	1952/53 Korea
Maj. James Hockery	F-86F Sabre	MiG-15	1952 Korea
Col. William Hovde	F-86A Sabre	MiG-15	1951 Korea
Col. James Jabara	F-86A Sabre	(15) MiG-15s	1951/52/53 Korea
Col. James K. Johnson	F-86F Sabre	(10) MiG-15s	1953 Korea
Lt.Col. Clifford Jolley	F-86E Sabre	(7) MiG-15s	1952 Korea

AMERICAN ACES WHO SHOT DOWN ROCKET
OR JETAIRCRAFT (Continued)

ACE	PLANE FLOWN	TYPE AIRCRAFT SHOT DOWN	DATE OCCURRED
Col. George Jones	F-86E Sabre	(6.5) MiG-15s	1951/52/53 Korea
1st Lt. Dale Karger	P-51D Mustang	Me-262	January 20, 1945
Col. James Kasler	F-86A/E Sabre	(6) MiG-15s	1952/53 Korea
Capt. Ivan Kincheloe Jr.	F-86E Sabre	(5) MiG-15s	1952 Korea
Capt. William Lamb	F9F-3 Panther	MiG-15	1950 Korea
Capt. Robert Latshaw	F-86A/E Sabre	MiG-15	1952 Korea
Lt.Col. Brooks Liles	F-86A/E Sabre	(4) MiG-15s	1952 Korea
Col. Leonard Lilley	F-86E Sabre	(7) MiG-15s	1952/53 Korea
Capt. Ray Littge	P-51D Mustang	Me-262	March 25, 1945
Capt. Robert Love	F-86A/E Sabre	(6) MiG-15s	1952 Korea
Maj. James Low	F-86A/E/F Sabre	(9) MiG-15s	1952 Korea
Col. Walker Mahurin	F-86E Sabre	(3.5) MiG-15s	1952 Korea
Lt.Gen. Winton Marshall	F-86A/E Sabre	(6.5) MiG-15s	1951 Korea
Lt.Col. Conrad Mattson	F-86E Sabre	(4) MiG-15s	1952 Korea
Capt. Joseph McConnell	F-86E Sabre	(16) MiG-15s	1953 Korea
Gen. John Meyer	P-51D & F-86A	Ar-234 & (2) MiG-15s	Dec. 31, 1944 & 1950/51
Col. John Mitchell	F-86F Sabre	(4) MiG-15s	1953 Korea
Maj. Lonnie Moore	F-86F Sabre	(10) MiG-15s	1953 Korea

AMERICAN ACES WHO SHOT DOWN ROCKET
OR JETAIRCRAFT (Continued)

ACE	PLANE FLOWN	TYPE AIRCRAFT SHOT DOWN	DATE OCCURRED
Lt.Col. Robert H. Moore	F-86E Sabre	(5) MiG-15s	1951/52 Korea
Col. John Murphy	P-51D Mustang	Me-163 (rocket)	August 16, 1944
Lt.Col. Louis Norley	P-51D Mustang	Me-163 (rocket)	November 21, 1944
BGen. Robin Olds	F4C Phantom	(2) MiG-21s & (2) MiG-17s	1967 Vietnam
Lt. Loyd Overfield	P-51 Mustang	Me-262	April 14, 1945
Capt. Dolph Overton	F-86E Sabre	(5) MiG-15s	1953 Korea
Col. Ralph Parr	F-86F Sabre	(10) MiG-15s	1953 Korea
BGen. Robinson Risner	F-86A/E Sabre	(8) MiG-15s	1952/53 Korea
BGen. Steve Ritchie	F4E/F4D Phantom	(5) MiG-21s	1972 Vietnam
Col. George Ruddell	F-86F Sabre	(8) MiG-15s	1952/53 Korea
Col. William Shaeffer	F-86E Sabre	(3) MiG-15s	1952 Korea
MGen. Dale Shafer Jr.	P-51D Mustang	Ar-234	April 18, 1945
BGen. Harrison Thyng	F-86A/E Sabre	(5) MiG-15s	1951/52 Korea
Capt. Harrison Tordoff	P-51D Mustang	Me-262	March 3, 1945
Maj. Herman Visscher	F-86E Sabre	MiG-15	1952 Korea
Lt.Col. Robert Wade	F-86E Sabre	MiG-15	1953 Korea
Capt. Jack Warner	P-51D Mustang	Me-262	April 17, 1945

AMERICAN ACES WHO SHOT DOWN ROCKET
OR JETAIRCRAFT (Continued)

ACE	PLANE FLOWN	TYPE AIRCRAFT SHOT DOWN	DATE OCCURRED
Capt. Charles Weaver	P-51D Mustang	Me-262	April 18, 1945
Lt.Col. William Wescott	F-86E Sabre	(5) MiG-15s	1952 Korea
Maj. Ray Wetmore	P-51D Mustang	Me-163 (rocket)	March 15, 1945
Col. William Whisner	F-86A/E Sabre	(5.5) MiG-15s	1951/52 Korea
Capt. Robert Winks	P-51D Mustang	Me-262	January 15, 1945
BGen. Charles Yeager	P-51D Mustang	Me-262	November 6, 1944

APPENDIX P

EXTRAORDINARY ACHIEVEMENTS OF AMERICAN FIGHTER ACES

Capt. DONALD ALDRICH (F4U Corsair) 20 Victories

While flying with VMF-215, Capt. Aldrich scored all 20 of his victories against Japan's best single engine fighters.

Lt Col. ROBERT AMMON (P-51 Mustang) 5 Victories

Strafed and destroyed thirteen German aircraft in one mission on March 16, 1945.

1st Lt. RICHARD H. ANDERSON (P-47 Thunderbolt) 8.5 Victories

Became "Ace in a Day" in a *four* minute span on May 25, 1944 over the Southern tip of Amami O'Shima near Okinawa.

Lt Col. RUDOLPH AUGARTEN (Supermarine Spitfire) 6 Victories

Scored victories against four different fighter aircraft types while flying for the 371st IFG. Only ace pilot to score a victory over a Spitfire while flying a Spitfire. This occurred in November 1948 while flying for the newly formed Israeli Air Force.

Col. RICHARD BAIRD (F6F-5N Hellcat) 6 Victories

Became the first pure night fighting ace on June 21, 1942 while flying from Yontan Airfield with VMF(N)-533.

Maj. RAYMOND BANK (P-51 Mustang) 5 Victories

After becoming an ace in World War II, he spent three years flying 1,000 sorties in Vietnam. When Bank finally retired he had amassed more than 10,000 flying hours in 25 different types of aircraft.

1st Lt. ED BICKFORD (P-51 Mustang) 5.5 Victories

Became an ace in just his first nineteen days of combat over Germany.

Cdr. GUY BORDELON JR. (F4U Corsair) 5 Victories

Was the only Korean Ace to score all his victories in a piston engine fighter.

Maj. RICHARD BREZAS (P-38 Lightning) 12 Victories

Flying against German adversaries, Brezas shot down 12 enemy planes in a span of 49 days.

Capt. CLINTON BURDICK (P-51 Mustang) 5.5 Victories

Only father and son to become American fighter aces. Father Howard scored his victories in World War I flying Sopwith Camels and son Clinton repeated to become an ace flying his P-51 in World War II.

BGen. VICTOR CABAS (Supermarine Spitfire/P-47 Thunderbolt) 5 Victories

Cabas was decorated for bravery with the Distinguished Service Medal, Legion of Merit with one Oak Leaf Cluster, Distinguished Flying Cross with 6 OLCs, Air Medal with 41 OLCs, the French and Belgian Croix de Guerre and the Order of Leopold with Rosette.

Col. BRUCE CARR (P-51 Mustang/Focke Wulf 190) 15 Victories

Carr flew a mission on November 2, 1944 in his P-51 named "Angel's Playmate" and was shot down over a German airfield. After hiding in the woods overnight he managed to steal a FW-190 and fly it back to his base at Orconte, France nearly 200 miles away.

Became the only ace to take off in an American aircraft and return to base flying one from Germany.

During World War II, the aggressive Carr was shot down three different times by German anti-aircraft fire.

Maj. SHUI-TIN (ARTHUR) CHIN (Hawk III/Gladiator) 6.5 Victories

The Ace pilot who flew with the 5th Chinese Fighter Group was awarded an *AWE INSPIRING MEDAL* by the Chinese government.

Col. ARTHUR CONANT (USMC) 6 Victories

As a test pilot for Douglas Aircraft in 1952 he used air to air missiles to down five unmanned B-17 bomber drones. He is the only American Ace to shoot down *five* American aircraft.

2nd Lt. RAY CRAWFORD (USAAF) 6 Victories

Gained prominence in the 1950's as a race driver in the Pan Am Series and the 1955/56/58 Indy 500.

Lt Col. LOUIS CURDES (P-51 Mustang) 9 Victories

Had 7 German, 1 Japanese, 1 Italian and 1 U.S. victory flags painted on his Mustang.

While returning from a mission he saw a lost U.S. C-47 transport mistakenly try to land at a Japanese airfield. When his repeated warnings were not acknowledged he was forced to shoot out both of the cargo plane's engines to force a water ditching off the coast. All of the C-47's crew was rescued and Curdes was awarded the DFC for his quick thinking and marksmanship.

Maj. ROBERT C. CURTIS (Supermarine Spitfire/P-51 Mustang) 14 Victories

All victories were over single engine fighter aircraft

Col. ROBERT DeHAVEN (USAAF) 14 Victories

Became a test pilot for Hughes Aircraft Company in 1948 and also served as Howard Hughes personal pilot.

Maj. HARRY DORRIS JR. (USAAF) 5 Victories

Flew a memorable mission on September 28, 1951 in which he was aloft 14.25 hours in an F-80. He was refueled in flight six times and managed to successfully attack five different ground targets.

RAdm. EDWARD FEIGHTNER (USN) 9 Victories

Was a prominent member of the "Blue Angels" in the late 1950's and helped design and develop both the Navy's F-14 Tomcat and F-18 Hornet fighters.

Lt. WILLIAM FIEDLER JR. (P-39 Airacobra) 5 Victories

Fiedler was the only American P-39 Airacobra Ace in World War II.

BGen. JOE FOSS (F4F Wildcat) 26 Victories

After winning the Medal of Honor during World War II for bravery with the U.S.M.C., Foss was elected to the South Dakota House Of Representatives for two terms and then governor in 1956.

He later was the Commissioner of the American Football League and host of a popular outdoor sportsman television program.

Joe Foss was also President of the National Rifle Association from 1988 to 1990.

Maj. JAMES GOODSON (USAAF) 14 Victories

Goodson was on the way to Europe on the SS Athenia when it was torpedoed and sunk on September 3, 1939 by a German U-Boat.

After being rescued he joined the RAF and Eagle Squadron 133 to fly missions against the country that had nearly cost him his life.

Capt. JAMES GRAY JR. (USN) 6 Victories

After World War II, Gray served as a member of the Joint Chiefs of Staff in the Pentagon. He also served as Commander of three different U.S. Navy warships including the carrier USS Coral Sea.

Gen. JAMES HILL (USAAF) 5 Victories

Became Commander In Chief of the North American Air Defense Command and retired in 1980 with 54 air medals and decorations.

Gen. BRUCE HOLLOWAY (USAAF) 13 Victories

Commanded the first Air Force jet fighter group at March Field and retired in 1972 after becoming the Commander In Chief of the Strategic Air Command. He was decorated with medals from six different nations.

BGen. CLAYTON ISAACSON (USAAF) 5 Victories

Isaacson flew nearly 100 combat missions in two tours of duty in World War II, 75 missions in Korea with the 51st FG, and 50 plus additional missions flying seven different U.N. fighter aircraft.

Isaacson led the rescue of 1800 hostages held by rebels in the Congo in 1964 and Commanded the 401st Tactical Fighter Wing that led a force into Jordan during the Arab-Israeli War.

He retired with 44 decorations and medals.

Col. GERALD R. JOHNSON (USAAF) 22 Victories

The famed fighter pilot died while piloting a B-17 caught in a dangerous storm in 1945. Johnson gave his parachute to a passenger without one and rode the crippled plane into the ground.

Col. JAMES K. JOHNSON (USAF) 11 Victories

Johnson flew P-47s in World War II and the F-86 Sabre Jet in Korea. He was the Air Forces only wing commander to achieve double ace status.

As commander of the B-58 Hustler test program, Johnson achieved nine world speed records and set the non-stop speed record flying from New York to Paris in just three hours and nineteen minutes.

Col. JAMES KASLER (USAF) 5 Victories

Started his Air Force career as a B-29 gunner in World War II. He later flew multiple combat missions in both Korea and Vietnam. In August of 1966 he was shot down, captured and held as a POW in North Vietnam for nearly seven years.

Capt. IVAN KINCHELOE JR. (USAF) 5 Victories

After becoming an ace in Korea, Kincheloe earned the much coveted Mackay Trophy in 1956 flying the Bell X-2 to a record altitude of 126,000 feet. Kincheloe was one of the Air Forces top test pilots and was selected to be one of the first three original X-15 pilots.

Cdr. DEAN (DIZ) LAIRD (USN) 5.75 Victories

After becoming an ace during World War II flying F4F Wildcats and F6F Hellcats, he later served with seven different fighter squadrons from 26 different aircraft carriers.

Lt(jg) JOHN LEPPLA (SBD Dauntless & F4F Wildcat) 5 Victories

Shot down four Japanese fighters and damaged two more while flying a SBD-3 dive bomber.

Col. CHARLES MacDONALD (P-38 Lightning) 27 Victories

Was sent to the United States on forced leave for three months for letting aviation hero Charles Lindbergh fly in combat and shoot down an enemy plane.

F/Lt. JACKSON MAHON (Supermarine Spitfire) 5 Victories

The American Eagle Squadron Ace was shot down, captured and became a POW in Germany's Stalag III. Mahon worked on the tunnels used by prisoners made famous in the hit movie: *The Great Escape.*

After the war he became the head of a film production company in Hollywood and was actor Errol Flynn's manager.

Capt. DAVID McCAMPBELL (F6F Hellcat) 34 Victories

The Medal of Honor winning Navy fighter pilot shot down seven Japanese aircraft on June 9, 1944 and an additional nine more aircraft on October 24, 1944.

Lt Cdr. WILLIAM McCORMICK (F6F Hellcat) 7 Victories

Hellcat ace McCormick sank a 9,000 ton Japanese cargo ship in a low level bombing run on October 18, 1944.

Lt Col. NICHOLAS MEGURA (P-51 Mustang) 11.83 Victories

On May 22, 1944 Nicholas Megura's P-51 was mistakenly shot down by a P-38 and had to land in neutral Sweden. Megura was prohibited from combat flying for the rest of the war due to diplomatic considerations.

Gen. JOHN C. MEYER (USAAF) 26 Victories

After an astounding 24 aerial victories in World War II, Meyer took command of the 4th Fighter Interceptor Group in Korea and flew 31 more combat missions. He shot down two additional fighters, (MiG-15s), to bring his two war total to 26.

He was Commander of the Strategic Air Command before retiring from the Air Force in 1975.

MGen. WILLARD MILLIKAN (USAAF) 13 Victories

A distinguished P-51 Ace in World War II, Millikan set an East-West coast to coast elapsed time record in 1954 of four hours flying an F-86A Sabre.

Col. JOHN MITCHELL (USAAF) 15 Victories

Planned and led a 400 mile mission to shoot down Admiral Isoroku Yamamoto, the Japanese Combine Fleet Commander and brilliant tactician.

In 1943 he flew America's first successful jet (the P-80), from New York to California.

Col. Mitchell commanded the 51st Fighter Interceptor Wing in Korea and shot down four MiG-15s.

Lt(jg) JOHN MONTAPERT (F6F Hellcat) 6 Victories

On January 12, 1945 Montapert sank a Japanese destroyer escort near the Indo-China coast while flying his Hellcat fighter.

Cdr. HORACE MORANVILLE (F6F Hellcat) 6 Victories

After downing his 6th Japanese plane with his F6F, Moranville was shot down and taken prisoner by the Vichy French. He spent several months in French held Vietnamese prisons and eventually escaped and covered 300 miles in thirteen days with other downed fliers and members of the French Foreign Legion.

Lt Cdr. EDWARD (BUTCH) O'HARE (F4F Wildcat/F6F Hellcat) 7 Victories

The United States first Navy ace and also its first naval fighter Medal of Honor winner.

While patrolling in protection of his carrier the USS Lexington, O'Hare attacked 18 Japanese "Betty" bombers. He shot down five and caused the remaining planes to flee in panic, thus saving the *"Lex"* from possible disaster.

O'Hare had Chicago's "Douglas Field" airport renamed in his honor.

Lt Col. CHARLES OLDER (USAAF) 18 Victories

Became a U.S. Marine pilot in 1939 and later joined Chennaults famed *"Flying Tigers"* (AVG).

He later led a group of sixteen P-51s in an attack that shot down five aircraft and destroyed a further 72 on the ground.

After the war he became a Superior Court Judge and further added to his fame as the presiding judge in the infamous *"Manson Murder Trial"* in 1970-71.

BGen. ROBIN OLDS (P-38 Lightning/P-51 Mustang/F4 Phantom) 17 Victories

After shooting down thirteen German aircraft in World War II, Olds commanded the 8th Tactical Fighter Wing and flew his F4 Phantom to destroy a further four MiGs as a 44 year old fighter pilot in Vietnam.

He later became Commandant of the U.S. Air Force Academy.

Col. RALPH PARR (USAF) 10 Victories

F-86 Sabre pilot Ralph Parr became a double ace after destroying a Russian bomber on July 27, 1953. This coincidentally was to be the *LAST* combat victory of the Korean War.

In 1967 he flew two combat tours in Vietnam and retired with 6,000 hours logged in fighter aircraft spanning 640 combat missions.

Col. STEVE PISANOS (Supermarine Spitfire/P-47 Thunderbolt) 10 Victories

Having flown Spitfires as an original member of the *"Eagle Squadron"* Pisanos transferred to the 4th FG in 1942 and became an American citizen. He became the first person to be made an American citizen while living outside the U.S.

After scoring multiple victories in his P-47, Pisanos had to crash land behind enemy lines and was hidden and helped to escape by sixteen different French families. He worked for the French underground and the OSS sabotaging enemy war equipment.

After the war he became a renowned test pilot and also served a tour in Vietnam. Pisanos was decorated for bravery by four different allied countries.

Capt. JOHN PURDY (USAAF) 7 Victories

While leading a bombing mission against fortified bridges between Luzon and Manila in the Philippines his P-38 Lightning was shot down. Purdy was rescued and helped to escape by local guerillas. This was his fifth time shot down and his last of 184 combat missions.

After the war he was involved with the National Aviation Hall Of Fame and was President of the American Fighter Aces Association and the founder of the Fighter Aces Museum Foundation.

BGen. ROBINSON RISNER (USAF) 8 Victories

After scoring eight victories in 100 combat missions over Korea, Risner commanded the 34th Fighter Squadron and set a Trans-Atlantic speed record of 6 hours and 38 minutes flying from New York to Paris in his F-100 Super Sabre.

Risner also flew combat missions in Vietnam, was shot down and taken prisoner. After the war he flew the F4 Phantom and F-111 in various senior command positions before retiring in 1976.

BGen. RICHARD (STEVE) RITCHIE (USAF) 5 Victories

One of only two American fighter pilots to make ace in Vietnam. In 1972 he won the much sought after *"Mackay Trophy"*, *"Colonel James Jabara Award"* and the VFWs *"Armed Forces Award"* for his outstanding Air Force professionalism and leadership.

Col. HERBERT ROSS (P-38 Lightning) 7 Victories

Became known as *"Herbie the Boat Sinker"* when he dropped a bomb from his P-38 down the funnel of the Italian transport *"Rex"*.

Capt. MICHAEL RUSSO (USAAF) 5 Victories

Russo became the USAAFs *FIRST* Mustang Ace and the only A-36 (P-51 dive-bombing version), ace in World War II.

Col. DAVID SCHILLING (USAAF) 22.50 Victories

The legendary P-47 Ace also made the first non-stop F-84 jet fighter crossing of the Atlantic Ocean in 1950 and won the *"Harmon Trophy"* in 1951.

BGen. ROBERT L. SCOTT JR. (USAAF) 10 Victories

Flew lone combat missions with General Chennault's AVG in 1942 and was promoted as the 23rd Fighter Group's first commander. A most prolific author, his *"God Is My Copilot"* became a best seller and later a hit movie.

Scott continued flying jet fighters until he was in his mid 80s. The Brigadier General's life spanned nearly 100 years (1908 to 2006).

Nearly all his victories were as a lone flyer. This was the reason he was officially credited with 10 victories instead of the 22 which he personally claimed.

Lt Col. GERALD TYLER (USAAF) 7 Victories

Test flew the 1st turbo-prop fitted to a P-51 Mustang and in 1968 won the Italian Olympic Gold Medal for flying a Mustang from Newfoundland to Ireland non-stop.

Maj. HERBERT VALENTINE (USMC) 6 Victories

Valentine became an ace in World War II flying F4U Corsairs. After the war he re-enlisted as a private and finally flew dangerous L-5 Liaison missions in Korea. Valentine was shot down and rescued twice and in 1952 was given a commission for the *second* time in his military career.

Capt. STANLEY (SWEDE) VEJTASA (USN) 10.25 Victories

While flying SBD-3 dive bomber Vejtasa helped sink the Japanese aircraft carrier Shoho during the Battle of The Coral Sea in 1942. He also shot down three Japanese Zeros in his Dauntless dive bomber!

After the war he held multiple Naval Air Commands and later was Captain of the super-carrier USS Constellation.

Gen. JOHN VOGT JR. (USAAF) 8 Victories

Became a P-47 fighter Ace in World War II and later rose to the rank of Four Star General. Vogt held command positions with the Air Defense Command, Joint Chiefs of Staff, Seventh Air Force in Vietnam and finally Commander Allied Air Forces in Central Europe.

Capt. ROY (BUTCH) VORIS (USN) 7 Victories

Voris flew F4F and F6F fighters against the Japanese in World War II and became an ace during combat over Iwo Jima.

After the war he organized, trained and led the original *"Blue Angels"* Flight Demonstration Team flying Navy F8F Bearcats.

Capt. LITTLETON WARD (USN) 5 Victories

Ward became an Ace flying F6F Hellcats over Okinawa and the Japanese Home Islands in 1945.

After the war he tested new-advanced naval aircraft and later commanded the United States carriers Midway, Independence and Bon Homme Richard.

P/O CLAUDE WEAVER III (RAF) 12.50 Victories

18 year old Oklahoma youth Claude Weaver became a Spitfire Ace in his first six days of combat over Malta.

Maj. JUDGE WOLF (P-38 Lightning/P-47 Thunderbolt) 9 Victories

Wolf encountered seven *"Zekes"* over Japan and became the first American pilot to use rockets to down an enemy aircraft.

Col. SIDNEY WOODS (USAAF) 7 Victories

Sidney Woods flew and Commanded P-51 and P-38 units until he was shot down and became a POW.

He later flew combat missions during the Korean War. In 1951 he commanded and helped to organize the Air Force's famed *"Thunderbirds Aerobatic Team"*.

BGen. CHARLES (CHUCK) YEAGER (P-51 Mustang) 11.50 Victories

One of the most famous, well known and highly decorated American fighter aces. Yeager was first to break the *"sound barrier"* as a test pilot in the Bell X-1A.

He commanded several fighter squadrons, became Commandant of the Aerospace Research Pilot School and flew 127 missions in Vietnam.

As Air Force Director of Safety he was probably the only pilot ever granted the *privilege* to fly any plane, at any time, at any Air Force base of his choosing.

Col. MICHAEL YUNCK (USMC) 5 Victories

Michel Yunck flew F4F and F4U fighters to become an ace in World War II. After the war Yunck became a top test pilot and commanded numerous Marine Air Wing units. In 1963 he was named *"Marine Aviator of the Year"* and awarded the prestigious *Alfred A. Cunningham* Trophy.

Appendix Q

ACE MEDAL OF HONOR RECIPIENTS FROM WORLD WAR II/KOREA

LIEUTENANT COLONEL HAROLD BAUER (U.S. Marine Corps)
VMF-212   F4F Wildcat   11 Victories

Citation: "For extraordinary heroism and conspicuous courage as Squadron Commander of Marine Fighting Squadron 212 in the South Pacific Area during the period 10 May to 14 November 1942. Volunteering to pilot a fighter plane in defense of our positions on Guadalcanal, Lt Col. Bauer participated in two air battles against enemy bombers and fighters outnumbering our force more than 2 to 1, boldly engaged the enemy and destroyed 1 Japanese bomber in the engagement of 28 September and shot down 4 enemy fighter planes in flames on 3 October, leaving a fifth smoking badly. After successfully leading 26 planes on an over-water ferry flight of more than 600 miles on 16 October, Lt Col. Bauer, while circling to land, sighted a squadron of enemy planes attacking the U.S.S. McFarland. Undaunted by the formidable opposition and with valor above and beyond the call of duty, he engaged the entire squadron and, although alone and his fuel supply nearly exhausted, fought his plane so brilliantly that 4 of the Japanese planes were destroyed before he was forced down by lack of fuel. His intrepid fighting spirit and distinctive ability as a leader and an airman, exemplified in his splendid record of combat achievement, were vital factors in the successful operations in the South Pacific Area."

MAJOR RICHARD BONG (U.S. Army Air Corps)
49 FG   P-38 Lightning   40 Victories

Citation: "For conspicuous gallantry and intrepidity in action above and beyond the call of duty in the Southwest Pacific area from 10 October to 15 November 1944. Though assigned to duty as gunnery instructor and neither required nor expected to perform combat duty, Maj. Bong voluntarily and at his own urgent request engaged in repeated combat missions, including unusually hazardous sorties over Balikpapan, Borneo, and in the Leyte area of the Philippines. His aggressiveness and daring resulted in his shooting down 8 enemy airplanes during this period."

MAJOR GREGORY BOYINGTON (U.S. Marine Corps Reserve)
VMF-214   F4U Corsair   24 Victories

Citation: "For extraordinary heroism and valiant devotion to duty as commanding officer of Marine Fighting Squadron 214 in action against enemy Japanese forces in the Central Solomons area from 12 September 1943 to 3 January 1944. Consistently outnumbered throughout successive hazardous flights over heavily defended hostile territory, Maj. Boyington struck at the enemy with such daring and courageous persistence, leading his squadron into combat with devastating results to Japanese shipping, shore installations, and aerial forces. Resolute in his efforts to inflict crippling damage on the enemy, Maj. Boyington led a formation of 24 fighters over Kahili on 17 October and, persistently circling the airdrome where 60 hostile aircraft were grounded, boldly challenged the Japanese to send up planes. Under his brilliant command, our fighters shot down 20 enemy craft in the ensuing action without the loss of a single ship. A superb airman and determined fighter against overwhelming odds, Maj. Boyington personally destroyed 26 of the many Japanese planes shot down by his squadron and, by his forceful leadership, developed the combat readiness in his command which was a distinctive factor in the Allied aerial achievements in this vitally strategic area."

MAJOR GEORGE A. DAVIS JR. (U.S. Air Force)
348 FG/4 FIW   P-47D/F-86E   21 Victories

Citation: "Maj. Davis distinguished himself by conspicuous gallantry and intrepidity at the risk of his life above and beyond the call of duty. While leading a flight of 4 F-86 Sabrejets on a combat aerial patrol mission near the Manchurian border, Maj. Davis' element leader ran out of oxygen and was forced to retire from the flight with his wingman accompanying him. Maj. Davis and the remaining F-86's continued the mission and sighted a formation of approximately 12 enemy MiG-15 aircraft speeding southward toward an area where friendly fighter-bombers were conducting low level operations against the Communist lines of communications. With selfless disregard for the numerical superiority of the enemy, Maj. Davis positioned his 2 aircraft, then dove at the MiG formation. While speeding through the formation from the rear he singled out a MiG-15 and destroyed it with a concentrated burst of fire. Although he was now under continuous fire from the enemy fighters to his rear, Maj. Davis sustained his attack. He fired at another MiG-15 which, bursting into smoke and flames, went into a vertical dive. Rather than maintain his superior speed and evade the enemy fire being concentrated on him, he elected to reduce his speed and sought out still a third MiG-15. During this latest attack his aircraft sustained a direct hit, went out of control, then crashed into a mountain 30 miles south of the Yalu River. Maj. Davis' bold attack completely disrupted the enemy formation, permitting the friendly fighter-bombers to successfully complete their interdiction mission. Maj. Davis, by his indomitable fighting spirit, heroic aggressiveness, and superb courage in engaging the enemy against formidable odds exemplified valor at its highest."

CAPTAIN JEFFERSON DeBLANC (U.S. Marine Corps Reserve)
VMF-121   F4F-4 Wildcat   9 Victories

Citation: "For conspicuous gallantry and intrepidity at the risk of his life above and beyond the call of duty as leader of a section of 6 fighter planes in Marine Fighting Squadron 112, during aerial operations against enemy Japanese forces off Kolombangara Island in the Solomons group, 31 January 1943. Taking off with his section as escort for a strike force of dive bombers and torpedo planes ordered to attack Japanese surface vessels, 1st Lt. DeBlanc led his flight directly to the target area where at 14,000 feet, our strike force encountered a large number of Japanese Zeros protecting the enemy's surface craft. In company with the other fighters, Lt. DeBlanc instantly engaged the hostile planes and aggressively countered their repeated attempts to drive off our bombers, preserving in his efforts to protect the diving planes and waging fierce combat until, picking up a call for assistance from the dive bombers, under attack by enemy float planes at 1,000 feet, he broke off his engagement with the Zeros, plunged into the formation of float planes and disrupted the savage attack, enabling our dive bombers and torpedo planes to complete their runs on the Japanese surface disposition and withdraw without further incident. Although his escort mission was fulfilled upon safe retirement of the bombers, 1st Lt. DeBlanc courageously remained on the scene despite a rapidly diminishing fuel supply and, boldly challenging the enemy's superior number of float planes, fought a valiant battle against terrific odds, seizing the tactical advantage and striking repeatedly to destroy 3 of the hostile aircraft and to disperse the remainder. Prepared to maneuver his damaged plane back to base, he had climbed aloft and set course when he discovered 2 Zeros closing in behind. Undaunted, he opened fire and blasted both Zeros from the sky in a short, bitterly fought action which resulted in such hopeless damage to his own plane that he was forced to bail out at a perilously low altitude atop trees on enemy-held Kolombangara. A gallant officer, a superb airman, and an indomitable fighter, 1st Lt. DeBlanc had rendered decisive assistance during a critical stage of operations, and his unwavering fortitude in the face of overwhelming opposition reflects the highest credit upon himself and adds new luster to the traditions of the U.S. Naval Service."

CAPTAIN JOSEPH FOSS (U.S. Marine Corps Reserve)
VMF-121   F4F-4 Wildcat   26 Victories

Citation: "For outstanding heroism and courage above and beyond the call of duty as executive officer of Marine Fighting Squadron 121, 1st Marine Aircraft Wing, at Guadalcanal. Engaging in almost daily combat with the enemy from 9 October to 19 November 1942, Capt. Foss personally shot down 23 Japanese planes and damaged others so severely that their destruction was extremely probable. In addition, during this period, he successfully led a large number of escort missions, skillfully covering reconnaissance, bombing, and photographic planes as well as surface craft. On 15 January 1943, he added 3 more enemy planes to his already brilliant successes for a record of aerial combat achievement unsurpassed in this war. Boldly searching out an approaching enemy force on 25 January, Capt. Foss led his 8 F4F Marine planes and 4

Army P-38's into action and, undaunted by tremendously superior numbers, intercepted and struck with such force that 4 Japanese fighters were shot down and the bombers were turned back without releasing a single bomb. His remarkable flying skill, inspiring leadership, and indomitable fighting spirit were distinctive factors in the defense of strategic American positions on Guadalcanal."

MAJOR ROBERT E. GALER (U.S. Marine Corps)
VMF-244   F4F-4 Wildcat   13 Victories

Citation: "For conspicuous heroism and courage above and beyond the call of duty as leader of a marine fighter squadron in aerial combat with enemy Japanese forces in the Solomon Islands area. Leading his squadron repeatedly in daring and aggressive raids against Japanese aerial forces, vastly superior in numbers, Maj. Galer availed himself of every favorable attack opportunity, individually shooting down 11 enemy bomber and fighter aircraft over a period of 29 days. Though suffering the extreme physical strain attendant upon protracted fighter operations at an altitude above 25,000 feet, the squadron under his zealous and inspiring leadership shot down a total of 27 Japanese planes. His superb airmanship, his outstanding skill and personal valor reflect great credit upon Maj. Galer's gallant fighting spirit and upon the U.S. Naval Service."

LIEUTENANT COLONEL JAMES H. HOWARD (U.S. Army Air Corps)
AVG/354 FG   P-40C/E/P-51B   8.33 Victories

Citation: "For conspicuous gallantry and intrepidity above and beyond the call of duty in action with the enemy near Oschersleben, Germany, on 11 January 1944. On that day Col. Howard was the leader of a group of P-51 aircraft providing support for a heavy bomber formation on a long-range mission deep in enemy territory. As Col. Howard's group met the bombers in the target area the bomber force was attacked by numerous enemy fighters. Col. Howard, with his group, and at once engaged the enemy and himself destroyed a German Me-110. As a result of this attack Col. Howard lost contact with his group, and at once returned to the level of the bomber formation. He then saw that the bombers were being heavily attacked by enemy airplanes and that no other friendly fighters were at hand. While Col. Howard could have waited to attempt to assemble his group before engaging the enemy, he chose instead to attack single-handed a formation of more than 30 German airplanes. With utter disregard for his own safety he immediately pressed home determined attacks for some 30 minutes, during which time he destroyed 3 enemy airplanes and probably destroyed and damaged others. Toward the end of this engagement 3 of his guns went out of action and his fuel supply was becoming dangerously low. Despite these handicaps and the almost insuperable odds against him, Col. Howard continued his aggressive action in an attempt to protect the bombers from the numerous fighters. His skill, courage, and intrepidity on this occasion set an example of heroism which will be an inspiration to the U.S. Armed Forces."

COLONEL NEEL KEARBY (U.S. Army Air Corps)
348 FG   P-47D Thunderbolt   22 Victories

Citation: "For conspicuous gallantry and intrepidity above and beyond the call of duty in action with the enemy. Col. Kearby volunteered to lead a flight of 4 fighters to reconnoiter the strongly defended enemy base at Wewak. Having observed enemy installations and reinforcements at 4 airfields, and secured important tactical information, he saw an enemy fighter below him, made a diving attack and shot it down in flames. The small formation then sighted approximately 12 enemy bombers accompanied by 36 fighters. Although his mission had been completed, his fuel was running low, and the numerical odds were 12 to 1, he gave the signal to attack. Diving into the midst of the enemy airplanes he shot down 3 in quick succession. Observing 1 of his comrades with 2 enemy fighters in pursuit, he destroyed both enemy aircraft. The enemy broke off in large numbers to make a multiple attack on his airplane but despite his peril he made one more pass before seeking cloud protection. Coming into the clear, he called his flight together and led them to a friendly base. Col. Kearby brought down 6 enemy aircraft in this action, undertaken with superb daring after his mission was completed."

COMMANDER DAVID McCAMPBELL (U.S. Navy)
VF-15   F6F-3/5 Hellcat   34 Victories

Citation: "For conspicuous gallantry and intrepidity at the risk of his life above and beyond the call of duty as commander, Air Group 15, during combat against enemy Japanese aerial forces in the first and second battles of the Philippine Sea. An inspiring leader, fighting boldly in the face of terrific odds, Cmdr. McCampbell led his fighter planes against a force of 80 Japanese carrier-based aircraft bearing down on our fleet on 19 June 1944. Striking fiercely in valiant defense of our surface force, he personally destroyed 7 hostile planes during this single engagement in which the outnumbering attack force was utterly routed and virtually annihilated. During a major fleet engagement with the enemy on 24 October, Cmdr. McCampbell, assisted by but 1 plane, intercepted and daringly attacked a formation of 60 hostile land-based craft approaching our forces. Fighting desperately but with superb skill against such overwhelming airpower, he shot down 9 Japanese planes and, completely disorganizing the enemy group, forced the remainder to abandon the attack before a single aircraft could reach the fleet. His great personal valor and indomitable spirit of aggression under extremely perilous combat conditions reflect the highest credit upon Cmdr. McCampbell and the U.S. Naval Service."

MAJOR THOMAS McGUIRE JR. (U.S. Army Air Corps)
475 FG   P-38 Lightning   38 Victories

<u>*Citation:*</u> "He fought with conspicuous gallantry and intrepidity over Luzon, Philippine Islands. Voluntarily, he led a squadron of 15 P-38's as top cover for heavy bombers striking Mabalacat Airdrome, where his formation was attacked by 20 aggressive Japanese fighters. In the ensuing action he repeatedly flew to the aid of embattled comrades, driving off enemy assaults while himself under attack and at time outnumbered 3 to 1, and even after his guns jammed, continuing the fight by forcing a hostile plane into his wingman's line of fire. Before he started back to his base he had shot down 3 Zeros. The next day he again volunteered to lead escort fighters on a mission to strongly defended Clark Field. During the resultant engagement he again exposed himself to attacks so that he might rescue a crippled bomber. In rapid succession he shot down 1 aircraft, parried the attack of 4 enemy fighters, 1 of which he shot down, single-handedly engaged 3 more Japanese, destroying 1, and then shot down still another, his 38th victory in aerial combat. On 7 January 1945, while leading a voluntary fighter sweep over Los Negros Island, he risked an extremely hazardous maneuver at low altitude in an attempt to save a fellow flyer from attack, crashed, and was reported missing in action. With gallant initiative, deep and unselfish concern for the safety of others, and heroic determination to destroy the enemy at all costs, Maj. McGuire set an inspiring example in keeping with the highest traditions of the military service."

LIEUTENANT EDWARD (BUTCH) O'HARE (U.S. Navy)
VF-3/VF-6   F4F Wildcat/F6F Hellcat   7 Victories

Citation: "For conspicuous gallantry and intrepidity in aerial combat, at grave risk of his life above and beyond the call of duty, as section leader and pilot of Fighting Squadron 3 on 20 February 1942. Having lost the assistance of his teammates, Lt. O'Hare interposed his plane between his ship and an advancing enemy formation of 9 attacking twin-engine heavy bombers. Without hesitation, alone and unaided, he repeatedly attacked this enemy formation, at close range in the face of intense combined machinegun and cannon fire. Despite this concentrated opposition, Lt. O'Hare, by his gallant and courageous action, his extremely skillful marksmanship in making the most of every shot of his limited amount of ammunition, shot down 5 enemy bombers and severely damaged a sixth before they reached the bomb release point. As a result of his gallant action—one of the most daring, if not the most daring, single action in the history of combat aviation—he undoubtedly saved his carrier from serious damage."

MAJOR WILLIAM A. SHOMO (U.S. Army Air Corps)
71 TRG   F6D-10 Mustang   8 Victories

Citation: "For conspicuous gallantry and intrepidity at the risk of his life above and beyond the call of duty. Maj. Shomo was lead pilot of a flight of 2 fighter planes charged with an armed photographic and strafing mission against Aparri and Laoag airdromes. While en route to the objective, he observed an enemy twin engine bomber, protected by 12 fighters, flying about 2,500 feet above him and in the opposite direction. Although the odds were 13 to 2, Maj. Shomo immediately ordered an attack. Accompanied by his wingman he closed on the enemy formation in a climbing turn and scored hits on the leading plane of the third element, which exploded in midair. Maj. Shomo then attacked the second element from the left side of the formation and shot another fighter down in flames. When the enemy formed for counterattack Maj. Shomo moved to the other side of the formation and hit a third fighter which exploded and fell. Diving below the bomber he put a burst into its underside and it crashed and burned. Pulling up from his pass he encountered a fifth plane firing head on and destroyed it. He next dived upon the first element and shot down the lead plane; then diving to 300 feet in pursuit of another fighter he caught it with his initial burst and it crashed in flames. During this action his wingman had shot down 3 planes, while the 3 remaining enemy fighters had fled into a cloudbank and escaped. Maj. Shomo's extraordinary gallantry and intrepidity in attacking such a far superior force and destroying 7 enemy aircraft in one action is unparalleled in the southwest Pacific area."

MAJOR JOHN L. SMITH (U.S. Marine Corps)
VMF-223   F4F-4 Wildcat   19 Victories

Citation: "For conspicuous gallantry and heroic achievement in aerial combat above and beyond the call of duty as commanding officer of Marine Fighting Squadron 223 during operations against enemy Japanese forces in the Solomon Islands area, August-September 1942. Repeatedly risking his life in aggressive and daring attacks, Maj. Smith led his squadron against a determined force, greatly superior in numbers, personally shooting down 16 Japanese planes between 21 August and 15 September 1942. In spite of the limited combat experience of many of the pilots of his squadron, they achieved the notable record of 83 enemy aircraft destroyed in this period, mainly attributable to the thorough training under Maj. Smith and to his intrepid and inspiring leadership. His bold tactics and indomitable fighting spirit, and the valiant and zealous fortitude of the men of his command not only rendered the enemy's attacks ineffective and costly to Japan, but contributed to the security of our advance base. His loyal and courageous devotion to duty sustains and enhances the finest traditions of the U.S. Naval Service."

LIEUTENANT JAMES SWETT (U.S. Marine Corps Reserve)
VMF-221   F4F-4 Wildcat/F4U-1 Corsair   15.5 Victories

Citation: "For extraordinary heroism and personal valor above and beyond the call of duty, as division leader of Marine Fighting Squadron 221 with Marine Aircraft Group 12, 1st Marine Aircraft Wing, in action against enemy Japanese aerial forces in the Solomon Islands area, 7 April 1943. In a daring flight to intercept a wave of 150 Japanese planes, 1st Lt. Swett Unhesitatingly hurled his 4-plane division into action against a formation of 15 enemy bombers and personally exploded 3 hostile planes in midair with accurate and deadly fire during his dive. Although separated from his division while clearing the heavy concentration of antiaircraft fire, he boldly attacked 6 enemy bombers, engaged the first 4 in turn and, unaided, shot down all in flames. Exhausting his ammunition as he closed on the fifth enemy bomber, he relentlessly drove his attack against terrific opposition which partially disabled his engine, shattered the windscreen and slashed his face. In spite of this, he brought his battered plane down with skillful precision in the water off Tulagi without further injury. The superb airmanship and tenacious fighting spirit which enabled 1st Lt. Swett to destroy 7 enemy bombers in a single flight were in keeping with the highest traditions of the U.S. Naval Service."

FIRST LIEUTENANT KENNETH WALSH (U.S. Marine Corps)
VMF-124/VMF-222   F4U-1 Corsair   21 Victories

Citation: "For extraordinary heroism and intrepidity above and beyond the call of duty as a pilot in Marine Fighting Squadron 124 in aerial combat against enemy Japanese forces in the Solomon Islands area. Determined to thwart the enemy's attempt to bomb Allied ground forces and shipping at Vella Lavella on 15 August 1943, 1st Lt. Walsh repeatedly dived his plane into an enemy formation outnumbering his own division 6 to 1 and, although his plane was hit numerous times, shot down 2 Japanese dive bombers and 1 fighter. After developing engine trouble on 30 August during a vital escort mission, 1st Lt. Walsh landed his mechanically disabled plane at Munda, quickly replaced it with another, and proceeded to rejoin his flight over Kahili. Separated from his escort group when he encountered approximately 50 Japanese Zeros, he unhesitatingly attacked, striking with relentless fury in his lone battle against a powerful force. He destroyed 4 hostile fighters before cannon shellfire forced him to make a dead-stick landing off Vella Lavella where he was later picked up. His valiant leadership and daring skill as a flier served as a source of confidence and inspiration to his fellow pilots and reflect the highest credit upon the U.S. Naval Service."

APPENDIX R

WORLD WAR II FIGHTER AIRCRAFT PERFORMANCE INFORMATION

	Speed	Ceiling	Range		Rate of Climb	
WWII Fighters	**(mph)**	**(feet)**	**Miles**	**HP**	**(ft/min)**	**Armament**
Bell P-39 Airacobra (D)	368	32,100	800	1,150	2,240	(1) 37mm/ (2).50 cal./ (4).30 cal.
(Q)	385	35,000	650	1,200	2,240	(1) 37mm/ (2).50 cal./ (4).30 cal.
P-63 Kingcobra	408	43,000	450	1,325	-	(1) 37 or 20mm can./ (4) mg
Supermarine Spitfire Mk.1	355	34,000	500	1,030	2,190	(8) .303 mg
Mk. VB	374	37,000	470	1,440	2,667	(2) 20mm can./(4) .303 mg
Mk. IX	408	44,000	434	1,565	2,985	(2) 20mm can./(4) .303 mg

WORLD WAR II FIGHTER AIRCRAFT PERFORMANCE
INFORMATION (Continued)

| | | | | | Rate of | |
| | Speed | Ceiling | Range | | Climb | |
WWII Fighters	(mph)	(feet)	Miles	HP	(ft/min)	Armament
Mk. XIV	450	44,500	460	2,050	2,857	(2) 20mm can./(4) .303 mg
Messerschmitt Bf. 109 (E)	342	34,450	410	1,050	3,100	(1) 15mm can./(2)mg
(F)	373	36,000	440	1,200	4,350	(1) 20mm can./(2) mg
(G)	406	39,370	528	1,475	3,346	(1) 20mm can./(2) mg
(K)	452	41,000	356	2,000	4,823	(2) 15mm can./(1) 30mm can.
Mitsubishi Reisen A6M2	332	33,150	1,930	950	3,100	(2) 20mm can./(2) mg
A6M3	338	35,220	1,477	1,130	2,461	(2) 20mm can./(2) mg
A6M5	351	36,745	1,194	1,130	2,565	(2) 20mm can./(2) mg
A6M8	355	38,400	1,200	1,500	2,857	(2) 20mm can./(2) mg
North Amer. P-51 Mustang (A)	390	31,500	750/ 2,350	1,200	2,198	(4) .50 cal. mg
(B)	440	42,000	550/ 2,200	1,620	2,857	(4) .50 cal. mg
(D)	437	41,900	950/ 2,080	1,695	2,740	(6) .50 cal. mg

WORLD WAR II FIGHTER AIRCRAFT PERFORMANCE INFORMATION (Continued)

| | | | | | Rate of | |
| | Speed | Ceiling | Range | | Climb | |
WWII Fighters	(mph)	(feet)	Miles	HP	(ft/min)	Armament
Curtiss P-40 Warhawk (B)	352	32,400	940	1,040	1,960	(2) .50 cal. mg/(4) 30 cal. mg
(E)	354	29,000	700	1,166	1,960	(6) .50 cal. mg
(F)	364	34,400	375	1,300	2,083	(6) .50 cal. mg
(N)	378	38,000	240	1,360	2,083	(6) .50 cal. mg
Republic P-47 Thunderbolt (C)	433	42,000	550/ 1,250	2,000	2,780	(8) .50 cal. mg
(D)	428	42,000	475/ 1,800	2,000	2,120	(8) .50 cal. mg
Vought Corsair (F4U-1)	417	36,900	1,015	2,000	2,890	(6) .50 cal. mg
(F4U-1D)	425	37,000	1,015	2,000	2,990	(6) .50 cal. mg
Grumman Wildcat (F4F-3)	331	37,500	845	1,200	3,050	(4) .50 cal. mg
(F4F-4)	318	34,900	770	1,200	2,190	(6) .50 cal. mg
(FM-2)	319	-	780	1,350	2,122	(4) .50 cal. mg
Grumman Hellcat (F6F-3)	376	38,400	1,090	2,000	2,260	(6) .50 cal. mg
(F6F-5)	386	37,300	1,040	2,200	3,240	(6) .50 cal. mg

WORLD WAR II FIGHTER AIRCRAFT PERFORMANCE
INFORMATION (Continued)

| | | | | | Rate of | |
| | Speed | Ceiling | Range | | Climb | |
WWII Fighters	(mph)	(feet)	Miles	HP	(ft/min)	Armament
Focke Wulf FW-190 (A-1)	389	34,775	497	1,600	-	(2) 20mm can./(4) mg
(A-3)	382	34,775	497	1,700	3,450	(4) 20mm can./(2) mg
(D-9)	426	32,810	520	1,770	2,773	(2) 20mm can./(2) mg
Lockheed P-38 Lightning (F)	395	39,000	450/ 1,780	1,325 x (2)	3,200	(1) 20mm can./ (4) .50 cal. mg
(J)	414	44,000	450/ 2,260	1,475 x (2)	2,200	(1) 20mm can./(4) .50 cal. mg

*The second listing under "range" catagory is for aircraft with external fuel tanks fitted

Appendix S

Total Production of World War II Aircraft

COUNTRY	PRODUCTION
UNITED STATES—FIGHTERS	
North American P-51 Mustang	15,686
Republic P-47 Thunderbolt	15,683
Curtiss P-40 Warhawk	13,733
Vought F4U Corsair	12,681
Grumman F6F Hellcat	12,272
Lockheed P-38 Lightning	9,923
Bell P-39 Airacobra	9,558
Grumman F4F Wildcat	8,000
Bell P-63 King Cobra	3,303
Northrop P-61 Black Widow	700
UNITED STATES—BOMBERS/TRANSPORTS/RECON	
Consolidated B-24 Liberator	18,188
Douglas C-47 Skytrain	13,000
North American B-25 Mitchell	11,000

TOTAL PRODUCTION OF WORLD WAR II AIRCRAFT (Continued)

COUNTRY	PRODUCTION
UNITED STATES—BOMBERS/TRANSPORTS/RECON	
Grumman TBF Avenger	9,836
Boeing B-17 Flying Fortress	8,685
Douglas A-20 Havoc	7,385
Curtiss SB-2 Helldiver	7,002
Douglas SBD Dauntless	5,936
Martin B-26 Marauder	5,157
Boeing B-29 Superfortress	3,970
Consolidated PBY Catalina	3,290
Curtiss C-46 Commando	3,200
Douglas A-26 Invader	2,446
Lockheed Hudson	2,000
Lockheed PV-1 Ventura	1,600
Lockheed PV-2 Harpoon	1,600
Vultee A-35 Vengeance	1,528
Vought OS2U Kingfisher	1,519
Douglas C-54 Skymaster	1,100
Martin PBM Mariner	1,000
Consolidated PB4Y-2 Privateer	977
Curtiss SC Seahawk	576
Lockheed C-56 Lodestar	325
Consolidated PB2Y Coronado	216

TOTAL PRODUCTION OF WORLD WAR II AIRCRAFT (Continued)

COUNTRY	PRODUCTION
GREAT BRITAIN—FIGHTERS	
Supermarine Spitfire	20,351
Hawker Hurricane	14,233
deHavilland Mosquito (All Variants)	6,439
Bristol Beaufighter	5,562
Hawker Typhoon	3,330
Supermarine Seafire	2,089
Boulton Paul Defiant	1,064
Hawker Tempest	800
Fairey Firefly	658
Fairey Fulmar	602
Gloster Gladiator	527
GREAT BRITAIN—BOMBERS/TRANSPORTS/RECON	
Vickers Wellington	11,461
Avro Lancaster	7,366
Handley Page Halifax	6,176
Bristol Blenheim	5,213
Fairey Barracuda	2,572
Fairey Swordfish	2,391
Short Stirling	2,371
Fairey Battle	2,185
Armstrong Whitworth Whitley	1,814

TOTAL PRODUCTION OF WORLD WAR II AIRCRAFT (Continued)

COUNTRY	PRODUCTION
GREAT BRITAIN—BOMBERS/TRANSPORTS/RECON	
Handley Page Hampden	1,430
Bristol Beaufort	1,121
Fairey Albacore	800
Armstrong Whitworth Albermarie	600
Avro York	257
SOVIET UNION—ALL TYPES	
Ilyushin Il-2	35,000
Yakovlev Yak-1	30,000
Polikarpov I-16	20,000
Lavochkin La-5	15,000
Tupolev SB-2	6,439
Ilyushin Il-4	5,000
Mikoyan-Gurevich MiG-1	2,100
Beriev MBR-2	1,500
Tupolev TB-3	800
GERMANY—ALL TYPES	
Messerschmitt Bf. 109	35,000
Focke Wulf FW-190	20,000
Junkers Ju-88	14,980
Heinkel He-111	7,450
Messerschmitt Bf. 110	6,050

TOTAL PRODUCTION OF WORLD WAR II AIRCRAFT (Continued)

COUNTRY	PRODUCTION
GERMANY—ALL TYPES	
Dornier Do-217	1,905
Messerschmitt Me-262	1,430
Heinkel He-177	1,169
Messerschmitt Me-410	1,160
Junkers Ju-188	1,076
Junkers Ju-86	870
Henschel Hs-129	866
Dornier Do-17	500
Heinkel He-115	300
Dornier Do-24	220
Messerschmitt Me-323	198
JAPAN—ALL TYPES	
Mitsubishi A6M Reisen	10,449
Nakajima Ki-43 Hayabusa	5,919
Nakajima Ki-84 Hayate	3,514
Nakajima Ki-27	3,399
Kawasaki Ki-61 Hien	3,078
Mitsubishi G4M	2,446
Mitsubishi Ki-51	2,385
JAPAN—ALL TYPES	
Mitsubishi Ki-21	2,064
Yokosuka D4Y Suisei	2,038

TOTAL PRODUCTION OF WORLD WAR II AIRCRAFT (Continued)

COUNTRY	PRODUCTION
JAPAN—ALL TYPES	
Kawasaki Ki-48	1,977
Kawasaki Ki-45 Toryu	1,701
Aichi D3A	1,495
Kawanishi N1K1-J Shiden	1,435
Tachikawa Ki-54	1,368
Nakajima B6N Tenzan	1,268
Nakajima Ki-44 Shoki	1,225
Nakajima B5N	1,149
Yokosuka P1Y Ginga	1,098
Mitsubishi A5M	1,094
Mitsubishi G3M	1,048
Kawasaki Ki-32	854
Yokosuka MXY7 Ohka	852
Nakajima Ki-49 Donryu	819
Mitsubishi Ki-67 Hiryu	698
Mitsubishi Ki-57	507
Kawasaki Ki-56	121
ITALY—ALL TYPES	
Fiat C.R.42	1,781
SIAI Marchetti S.M.79	1,217
Macchi M.C.200	1,151

TOTAL PRODUCTION OF WORLD WAR II AIRCRAFT (Continued)

COUNTRY	PRODUCTION
ITALY—ALL TYPES	
Macchi M.C.202	1,100
SIAI Marchetti S.M.82	875
Fiat G.50	782
Cant Z.1007 bis	560
SIAI Marchetti S.M.81	534
Fiat B.R.20	514
Reggiane Re.2002	225
FRANCE—ALL TYPES	
Potez 630	1,100
Morane Sauinier M.S.406	1,081
Dewoitine D.520	775
Liore' et Olivier LeO 451	602

APPENDIX T

AMERICAN ACE VICTORY TALLIES OVER OPPONENTS

Japan produced 30,447 fighters and 15,177 bombers during World War II. Japan's engine output was 116,577 during this same time period. Along with Axis powers Germany and Italy, Japan suffered through a lack of fuel, lubricants and quality pilots due to the relentless Allied attacks against their homeland.

JAPAN		
VICTORY TALLIES FOR AMERICAN ACE PILOTS VERSUS JAPAN IN WORLD WAR II. TOTAL AIR VICTORIES—5,305		
MITSUBISHI AIRCRAFT CORP		
		AMERICAN ACE
AIRCRAFT	CODE NAME	VICTORIES
A6M REISEN	ZERO	608.5
A6M-3/A6M-5/A6M-8	ZEKE	1,877
G3M	NELL	15.33
G4M	BETTY	217.33

AMERICAN ACE VICTORY TALLIES OVER OPPONENTS (Continued)

A5M	CLAUDE	14.33
Ki-51	SONIA	12
F1M	PETE	32.5
Ki-21	SALLY	47
Ki-46	DINAH	22.25
Ki-57	TOPSY	18
J2M RAIDEN	JACK	26
Ki-67 HIRYU	PEGGY	2.75
K3M	PINE	11

KAWASAKI AIRCRAFT CORPORATION

		AMERICAN ACE
AIRCRAFT	**CODE NAME**	**VICTORIES**
Ki-56	THALIA	2
Ki-45 TORYU	NICK	57.25
Ki-48	LILY	29.5
Ki-61	TONY	274
Ki-32	MARY	1

YOKOSUKA AIRCRAFT CORPORATION

		AMERICAN ACE
AIRCRAFT	**CODE NAME**	**VICTORIES**
K5Y	WILLOW	5.5
D4Y SUISEI	JUDY	103.75
P1Y1 GINGA	FRANCES	21.25

NAKAJIMA AIRCRAFT CORP.

AMERICAN ACE VICTORY TALLIES OVER OPPONENTS (Continued)

AIRCRAFT	CODE NAME	AMERICAN ACE VICTORIES
Ki-43 HAYABUSA	OSCAR	621.75
Ki-44 SHOKI	TOJO	222.25
Ki-27	NATE	86
B5N	KATE	125.5
A6M2	RUFE	60
Ki-84 HAYATE	FRANK	38
C6N SAJUN	MYRT	10.83
B6N TENZAN	JILL	58
E8N	DAVE	9.5
G5N SHINZAN	LIZ	1
Ki-49 DONRYU	HELEN	6.5
J1N GEKKO	IRVING	9

AICHI AIRCRAFT CORPORATION

AIRCRAFT	CODE NAME	AMERICAN ACE VICTORIES
D3A1	VAL	379.75
E13A	JAKE	12
E-16A ZUIUN	PAUL	4

KAWANISHI AIRCRAFT CORPORATION

AIRCRAFT	CODE NAME	AMERICAN ACE VICTORIES
H6K	MAVIS	13
NIK1-J SHIDEN	GEORGE	85.5

AMERICAN ACE VICTORY TALLIES OVER OPPONENTS (Continued)

OTHER COMBAT TYPES CONFIRMED DESTROYED		
		AMERICAN ACE
AIRCRAFT	**CODE NAME**	**VICTORIES**
KOKUSAI Ki-16	STELLA	1.5
	TESS	8
	RUTH	1
	HAMP	115.75
ACES REPORTS OF UNIDENTIFIED FIGHTERS SHOTDOWN		
	17.5	
ACES REPORTS OF UNIDENTIFIED BOMBERS SHOT DOWN		
	18.25	

GERMANY

VICTORY TALLIES FOR AMERICAN ACE PILOTS VERSUS GERMANY IN WORLD WAR II. TOTAL AIR VICTORIES—3,760.25		
GERMANY produced 120,400 aircraft during World War II. Of this total there were (35,000) Me-109s, (20,001) FW-190s and (6,050) Me-110s.		
MESSERSCHMITT A.G.		
		AMERICAN ACE
AIRCRAFT		**VICTORIES**
Me-(Bf.-109)		1,888.83
Me-(Bf.-110)		164
Me-410		58.25
Me-108		6.5

AMERICAN ACE VICTORY TALLIES OVER OPPONENTS (Continued)

Me-262		31
Me-210		43
Me-309		1
Me-209		5
Me-163		6

JUNKERS FLUGZEUG & MOTORENWERKE A.G.

		AMERICAN ACE
AIRCRAFT		**VICTORIES**
Ju-88		89.33
Ju-52		96.25
Ju-87		43.5
Ju-188		12
Ju-34		2

ARADO FLUGZEUGWERKE GmbH

		AMERICAN ACE
AIRCRAFT		**VICTORIES**
Ar-234		4
Ar-196		1.5

OTHER COMBAT TYPES CONFIRMED DESTROYED

FIESELER Fi-167	2	
BLOHM & VOSS Bv-138	1	
FW-190/Ju-88 (MISTEL)	6	

FOCKE WULF FLUGZEUGBAU GmbH

AMERICAN ACE VICTORY TALLIES OVER OPPONENTS (Continued)

AIRCRAFT		AMERICAN ACE VICTORIES
FW-190		1,199.50
FW-190/290 (long nose) "DORA"		24
FW-189		1
FW-200		4.75
FW-44		1.5
FW-187		1

ERNEST HEINKEL A.G.

AIRCRAFT		AMERICAN ACE VICTORIES
He-111		18.83
He-177		3.33
He-126		4
He-51		2

ERNEST HEINKEL A.G.

AIRCRAFT		AMERICAN ACE VICTORIES
He-156		10
He-115		0.25

DORNIER WERKE GmbH

AIRCRAFT		AMERICAN ACE VICTORIES

AMERICAN ACE VICTORY TALLIES OVER OPPONENTS (Continued)

Do-17		1
Do-215		4
Do-217		18

ACES REPORTING OTHER UNIDENTIFIED PLANES SHOT DOWN—6

ITALY

ITALY produced 11,508 aircraft before the armistice on September 8, 1943. By then only 877 planes had survived in usuable condition. Italy had neither the fuel, spare parts or trained pilots that were needed to continue fighting. Total air victories—111.50

AMERICAN ACE VICTORY TOTALS

SIAI MARCHETTI AIR-CRAFT

AIRCRAFT	**AMERICAN ACE VICTORIES**	
S.M.79	2	
S.M.82	4	
S.M. TRANSPORTS	5	

CANTIERI RIUNITI dELL'ADRIATICO

AIRCRAFT	**AMERICAN ACE VICTORIES**	
CANT Z.1007 bis	3	
CANT Z.506 (B)	2	

AMERICAN ACE VICTORY TALLIES OVER OPPONENTS (Continued)

AERONAUTICA MACCHI S.p.A.		
	AMERICAN ACE	
AIRCRAFT	**VICTORIES**	
M.C.200	8	
M.C.202	42	
M.C.205	6	
FIAT S.A. AIRCRAFT		
	AMERICAN ACE	
AIRCRAFT	**VICTORIES**	
Cr.32	8.5	
G.50	11	
G.55	1	
OTHER AIRCRAFT TYPES CONFIRMED DESTROYED		
SOCIETA ITALIANA CAPRONI Ca.313		1
REGGIANE Re.2001		7
UNIDENTIFIED AIRCRAFT SHOT DOWN		11
THE FOLLOWING AIRCRAFT FROM OTHER NATIONS WERE SHOT DOWN BY U.S. ACES IN WORLD WAR II		
CURTISS H.75 (A)	3	
BRITISH SPITFIRES	2	
FRENCH BLOCH 174	1	
FRENCH DEWOITINE D.520	4	

AMERICAN ACE VICTORY TALLIES OVER OPPONENTS (Continued)

UNIDENTIFIED FRENCH Bi-plane	1	
DAKOTA transport	1	

THE FOLLOWING RUSSIAN/CHINESE AIRCRAFT WERE SHOT DOWN DURING THE KOREAN WAR BY U.S. ACES

MiG-15	346.5	
WWII RUSSIAN recon	1	
La-7	1	
La-9	5	
Yak-9	3	

THE FOLLOWING RUSSIAN/CHINESE AIRCRAFT WERE SHOT DOWN DURING THE VIETNAM WAR BY U.S. ACES

MiG-17	6	
MiG-21	8	
Tu-2	3	
Yak-18	2	

AMERICAN FIGHTER ACES FOR EACH WAR

WAR	TOTAL ACES	TOTAL AIR VICTORIES
WORLD WAR I	116	959
RUSSIAN CIVIL WAR	1	5

AMERICAN ACE VICTORY TALLIES OVER OPPONENTS (Continued)

WORLD WAR II	1,314	9,187.75
KOREA	40	356.5
VIETNAM	2	19*

*Includes victories by aces who also fought in World War II or Korea

NEARLY 50% OF ALL AIR COMBAT VICTORIES WERE SCORED BY JUST 5% OF THE FIGHTER PILOTS

TOTAL U.S. ACES FROM ALL CONFLICTS	**1,473**
TOTAL PLANES SHOT DOWN BY U.S. ACES IN ALL CONFLICTS	**10,527.25**
AVERAGE VICTORIES PER ACE PILOT	**7.15**

APPENDIX U

AMERICAN FIGHTER PILOTS THAT SHOULD BE GIVEN "ACE" STATUS

Different aviation historians often disagree on which American fighter pilots should be given "ace" status. New evidence is constantly being reviewed and analyzed. New findings have resulted in some new pilots being given "ace" status. My research for this book indicates that the following 37 pilots should be granted this elite honor. Each of these combat aviators deserves inclusion and has earned the right to be honored and called an "American Fighter Ace".

NAME	FIGHTER GROUP	PLANE FLOWN	TOTAL VICTORIES
Lt.Col. Wyman Anderson	79th	P-40 Warhawk	6
Lt.Cdr. Redman Beatley	VF-18	F6F Hellcat	6
Cdr. Foster Blair	VF-5/VF-6	F4F Wildcat/ F6F Hellcat	5
Col. Victor Bocquin	361st	P-51 Mustang	5
Capt. Jasper Brown	51st	P-40 Warhawk	5

AMERICAN FIGHTER PILOTS THAT SHOULD BE GIVEN
"ACE" STATUS (Continued)

NAME	FIGHTER GROUP	PLANE FLOWN	TOTAL VICTORIES
1st Lt. Charles Cleveland	334 FIS/4 FIW	F-86 Sabre	5
Col. Oscar Coen	71st FS/4th FG/ 356th FG	Spitfire/P-47 Thunderbolt	5.5
Maj. William Collins	359th	P-51 Mustang	5
Col. Lucian Dade Jr.	56th	P-47 Thunderbolt	5
V.Sqn.Ldr. Parker Dupouy	AVG	P-40	6.5
V.Adm. James Flatley Jr.	VF-42/VF-10	F4F Wildcat/ F6F Hellcat	6
Lt. Frank Foltz	VF-18	F6F Hellcat	6
Col. Robert Fry	365th	P-47 Thunderbolt	7
Capt. William Garry	368th	P-47 Thunderbolt	6
Capt. Walter Haas	VF-42/VF-3	F4F Wildcat	6
1st Lt. Ivan Hasek	354th	P-51 Mustang	6
Col. Donald Hillman	365th	P-47 Thunderbolt	5
Col. Wallace Hopkins	361st	P-51 Mustang	6
Lt.Col. A.T. House Jr.	49th FG	P-40 Warhawk	5
Lt.Col. Joseph (Wayne) Jorda	82nd	P-38 Lightning	5
Cdr. Leslie Kerr Jr.	VF-23	F6F Hellcat	6.75
Capt. Melvin Kimball	51st	P-40 Warhawk	5
Capt. Wiltold Lanowski	56th	P-47 Thunderbolt	6

AMERICAN FIGHTER PILOTS THAT SHOULD BE GIVEN "ACE" STATUS (Continued)

NAME	FIGHTER GROUP	PLANE FLOWN	TOTAL VICTORIES
Maj. Michael McPharlin	71st FS/4th FG	Spitfire/P-51 Mustang	5.5
Cdr. Robert Merritt	VF-72/VF-6	F4F Wildcat/ F6F Hellcat	7
Col. Raymond Myers	355th	P-47/P-51	5.5
Lt.Col. Lawrence Powell Jr.	339th	P-51 Mustang	5.5
Maj. Frank Presley	VMF-121	F4F Wildcat	5
W/Man Robert Raines	AVG	P-40	5
Col. Ben Rimerman	353rd	P-47 Thunderbolt	7
Col. Charles Sawyer	AVG/23rd FG	P-40 Warhawk	5.25
Lt.Cdr. Carl E. Smith	VF-14	F6F Hellcat	5
Lt.Cdr. John F. Sutherland	VF-72/VF-10	F4F Wildcat	7
Lt.Cdr. William (Paul) Thayer	VF-26	F4F Wildcat	6.5
Capt. John W. Wainwright	404th	P-47 Thunderbolt	6
Cdr. Ed "Wendy" Wendorf	VF-16	F6F Hellcat	6.5
1st Lt. Warren M. Wesson	78th	P-47 Thunderbolt	5

GLOSSARY

AA	Anti-aircraft guns
A/D	Airdrome (airfield)
Adm.	Admiral
AILERONS	Moveable hinged trailing edge section of aircraft wing for controlling the rolling movements of an airplane
API	Armor Piercing Incendiary
AVG	American Volunteer Group
BANDIT	Enemy aircraft
BEAT-UP	Strafing a ground target
Bf	German aircraft designation indicating planes produced by the Bayerische Flugzeugwerke. Throughout World War II even the '109s' and '110s' produced by Messerschmitt A.G. late in the war were still officially referred to as "Bf." in German documents and official reports.
BGen.	Brigadier General
BOGEY	Unidentified aircraft
BOLT	P-47 Thunderbolt

BREAK!	Quick turn away from the enemy
CAP	Combat Air Patrol
Capt.	Captain
CBI	China/Burma/India Theatre of operation
Cdr.	Commander
CEILING	Maximum altitude of a particular aircraft
CG	Center of gravity
CO	Commanding officer
Col.	Colonel
COMPRESSIBILITY	The resulting changes in airflow on an airplane wing as the speed of sound is approached. During a high speed dive, lift characteristics change dramatically. Air flowing over the top of the wing is accelerated, thus changing the lift qualities. This affect normally causes a nose-down trim that in many cases cannot be corrected.
CV	Aircraft carrier
CVE	Aircraft carrier escort
CVL	Aircraft carrier light
DECK	The ground
DITCH	Forced landing in the water
DFC	Distinguished Flying Cross
D/F STATION	Direction finding station
DIVISION	A formation of four aircraft flying in two sections
DOGFIGHT	Aerial combat
E/A	Enemy aircraft

Ens.	Ensign
FIG	Fighter Interceptor Group
FIW	Fighter Interceptor Wing
FLAK	Anti-aircraft fire
FLAPS	A moveable airfoil used to increase lift or drag
F/Ldr.	Flight Leader
F/O	Flight Officer
FORM 5	Monthly report of pilot's flights
FS	Fighter Squadron
FRAG	Fragmentation bomb
FUSELAGE	Body of an airplane
Gen.	General
G-FORCE	(Force of gravity) Pull of centrifugal force on a plane and pilot while in curved flight
HARDSTAND	Concrete or metal parking area for aircraft
JUG	P-47 Thunderbolt
IMMELMANN	Maneuver where aircraft is half-looped to an upside-down Position and then half rolled back to normal upright flight
IP	Initial Point
(jg)	junior grade
KAMIKAZE	Suicide aircraft
KIA	Killed In Action
KIFA	Killed In Flying Accident
KILL	Aerial combat victory

KNOT	Nautical measure of speed. One KNOT equals 1.15 statute Miles.
LSO	Landing Signal Officer (Helps land carrier aircraft)
Lt.	Lieutenant
LUFBERY	Defensive tight circling maneuver with group of aircraft following each other for mutual protection. Named for World War I ace Raoul Lufbery.
MAG	Magneto
Maj.	Major
Me	General term used to denote German aircraft designed by the legendary Professor Willy Messerschmitt.
MGen.	Major General
MIA	Missing In Action
MTO	Mediterranean Theatre of Operation
MUSHING	Flying at a high angle of attack (nose angle), close to a stall
NAAS	Naval Auxiliary Air Station
NFS	Night Flying Squadron
OPS	Operations
P/O	Pilot Officer
PRG	Photo Recon Group
PSP	Pierced steel planking used as artificial runway
RAdm.	Rear Admiral

REX	Large Italian luxury liner converted to Axis troop carrier
R & R	Rest and Relaxation
SNAP ROLL	Quick aircraft maneuver where plane rotates quickly around its longitudinal axis
Sqn Ldr.	Squadron Leader
SPLIT-S	An aircraft maneuver where plane half-rolls onto its back and then dives vertically
STALL	Condition where there is a loss of lift and an increase in drag that causes an aircraft to drop or go out of control
TAC	Tactical Air Command
TRACER	Ammunition that emits a glowing light while in flight
USAAF	United States Army Air Force
USAF	United States Air Force
USMC	United States Marine Corps
USN	United States Navy
VB	Dive bomber or squadron
VERTIGO	Sensation of dizziness, disorientation or a feeling that you or an object around you is whirling out of control
VF	Naval Fighter Squadron
VMF	Marine Fighter Squadron
VT	Torpedo aircraft or squadron
W/Man	Wing Man

BIBLIOGRAPHY

Anderson, Clarence E. with Joseph P. Hamelin. *To Fly and Fight*. Pacifica: Pacifica Military History, 1990.

Angelucci, Enzo and Paolo Matricardio. *World War II Airplanes Volume 1*. Chicago: Rand McNally and Company, 1978

Angelucci, Enzo and Paolo Matricardio. *World War II Airplanes Volume 2*. Chicago: Rand McNally and Company, 1978.

Barker, A.J. *Stuka Ju-87*. London: Bison Books Limited, 1980.

Bauer, Dan. *Great American Fighter Aces. Osceola: Motorbooks, 1992*.

Bell, Dana. *Air Force Colors Volume 1, 1926-1942*. Carrollton: Squadron/Signal Publications, 1979.

Bergerud, Eric M. *Fire In The Sky*. Boulder: Westview Press, 2001.

Bishop, Patrick. *Fighter Boys-The Battle of Britain, 1940*. New York: Viking, Penguin Group, 2003.

Blesse, Frederick C. *Check Six, A Fighter Pilot Looks Back*. Mesa: Champlin Fighter Museum Press, 1987.

Boyce, J, Ward (editor). *American Fighter Aces Album*. Mesa: The American Fighter Aces Association, 1996.

Boyne, Walter J. *Clash Of Wings, World War II In The Air*. New York: Touchstone/ Simon & Schuster, 1994.

Caidin, Martin. *Zero Fighter*. New York: Ballantine Books, 1970.

Caras, Roger A. *Wings of Gold. The Story of the U.S. Naval Aviation.* Philadelphia: Lippincott Company, 1965.

Caswell, Dean. *Fighting Falcons-The Saga of Marine Fighter Squadron 221.* Austin: VMF-221 Foundation, 2004.

Caygill, Peter. *Flying to the Limit.* South Yorkshire: Pen & Sword Aviation, 2005.

Cecil, Robert. *Hitler's War Machine.* New York: Chartwell Books, 1975.

Coen, Oscar with Mildred Coen Robeck. *Oscar-His Story.* Pittsburgh: Dorrance Publishing Company, 2000.

Cooper, Bryan and John Batchelor. *Fighter.* New York: Ballantine Books, 1973.

Davies, Peter E. *USAF F-4 Phantom II, MiG Killers 1965-68.* Oxford: Ospry Publishing, 2002.

Davies, Peter E. *U.S. Navy F-4 Phantom II, MiG Killers 965-70.* Oxford: Ospry Publishing, 2001.

Deighton, Len. *Blood, Tears And Folly.* Edison: Castle Books, 1999.

Doerr, Robert F. with Jon Lake and Warren Thompson. *Korean War Aces.* London: Ospry Publishing, 1995.

Doll, Thomas E. with Berkley R. Johnson and William A. Riley. *Navy Air Colors.* Carrollton: Squadron/Signal Publications, 1983.

Dupuy, Trevor Nevitt. *The Air War In the West, September 1939-May 1941.* New York: Franklin Watts, 1963.

Eden, Paul with Soph Moeng. *Aircraft Anatomy of World War II.* Edison: Chartwell Books, 2003.

Elward, Brad with Peter Davies. *U.S. Navy F-4 Phantom II, MiG Killers 1972-73.* Oxford: Ospry Publishing, 2002.

Ethell, Jeffrey L. with Robert T. Sand. *World War II Fighters.* St. Paul: MBI Publishing Company, 2002.

Ford, Daniel. *Flying Tigers: Claire Chennault & the American Volunteer Group.* Washington: Smithsonian Institution Press, 1991.

Foster, Cecil G. with David K. Vaughn. *Mig Alley To Mu Ghia Pass.* Jefferson: McFarland & Company, 2001.

Galland, Adolf. *The First and the Last.* Bristol: Cerberus Publishing Limited, 2005.

Goebel, Robert J. *Mustang Ace.* Pacifica: Pacifica Military Press, 1991.

Grant, Newby. *P-51 Mustang.* London: Bison Books limited, 1980.

Green, William. *Famous Fighters of the Second World War.* New York: Doubleday & Company, 1957.

Green, William. *Famous Fighters of the Second World War (Second Series).* Garden City: Doubleday & Company, 1969.

Green, William with Gordon Swanborough. *U.S. Navy and Marine Corps Fighters.* New York: Arco Publishing Company, 1977.

Green, William with Gordon Swanborough. *Japanese Army Fighters (Part 1).* New York: Arco Publishing Company 1977.

Gurney, Gene with Mark P. Friedlander. *Five Down and Glory.* New York: Arno Press, 1972.

Halpert, Sam. *A Real Good War.* St. Petersburg. Southern Heritage Press, 1997.

Heiferman, Ron. *Flying Tigers (Chennault in China).* New York: Ballantine Books, 1971.

Hess, William N. *The Allied Aces of World War II.* New York: Arco Publishing Company, 1966.

Hess, William N. *The Allied Aces of World War II and Korea.* New York: Arco Publishing Company, 1968.

Hinchliffe, Peter. *The Other Battle.* Edison: Castle Books, 2001.

Holmes, Tony. *Aircraft of the Aces (Legends of the Skies).* Oxford: Osprey Publishing Company, 2004.

Holmes, Tony. *Aircraft of the Aces (Legends of World War II).* Oxford: Osprey Publishing Company, 2003.

Humble, Richard. *War in the Air 1939-1945.* London: Salamander Books Limited, 1975.

Ilfrey, Jack with Max Reynolds. *Happy Jack's Go-Buggy.* Hicksville: Exposition, 1979.

Ireland, Bernard. *The Aircraft Carrier.* Sacaucus: Chartwell Books, 1979.

Jackson, Robert. *Air Aces of World War II.* Wiltshire: The Crowood Press, 2003.

Johnson, Frederick A. *Weapons of the Eighth Air Force.* St. Paul: MBI Publishing Company, 2003.

Johnson, J.E. 'Johnnie'. *Full Circle.* London: Cassell & Company, 2001.

Kershaw, Andrew (editor). *1939-1945 Warplanes.* London: Marshall Cavendish USA, 1973.

Killen, John. *A History of Marine Aviation 1911-68.* London: Frederick Muller, 1969.

Macintyre, Donald. *Aircraft Carrier, The Majestic Weapon.* New York: Ballantine Books, 1971.

Mason, Francis K. *British Fighters of World War II.* Windsor: Hylton Lacy, 1969.

Mason, Herbert M. *Duel For The Sky.* New York: Grosset & Dunlop, 1970.

McLachlan, Ian. *USAAF Fighter Stories-A New Selection*. Gloucestershire: Sutton Publishing Limited, 2005.

McWhorter, Hamilton with Jay A. Stout. *The First Hellcat Ace*. Pacifica: Pacifica Military History, 2000.

Mellinger, George with John Stanaway. *P-39 Airacobra Aces of World War 2*. Oxford: Osprey Publishing, 2004.

Mondey, David. *American Aircraft of World War II*. Edison: Chartwell Books, 2002.

Mondey, David. *Axis Aircraft of World War II*. Edison: Chartwell Books, 2002.

Molesworth, Carl. *P-40 Warhawk Aces of the CBI*. Oxford: Osprey Publishing, 2003.

Molesworth, Carl. *P-40 Warhawk Aces of the MTO*. Oxford: Osprey Publishing, 2002.

Molesworth, Carl. *P-40 Warhawk Aces of the Pacific*. Oxford: Osprey Publishing, 2003.

Morehead, James B. *In My Sights Completed*. Petaluma: James Bruce Morehead, 2003.

Morgan, Hugh with John Weal. *German Jet Aces Of World War 2*. Oxford: Osprey Publishing, 2004.

Munson, Kenneth. *Aircraft of World War II*. London: Ian Allan Limited, 1962.

Munson, Kenneth. *Fighters and Bombers of World War II*. New York: Blandford Press Limited, 1983.

Olmsted, Merle. *Aircraft Armament*. New York: Crown Publishing, 1970.

Olynyk, Frank. *Stars & Bars*. London: Grub Street, 1995.

Patton, Wayne W. *Aces*. Carrollton: Squadron/Signal Publications, 1998.

Patton, Wayne W. *Aces 2*. Carrollton: Squadron/Signal Publications, 2004.

Patton, Wayne W. *Aces 3*. Carrollton: Squadron/Signal Publications, 2004.

Pitt, Barrie. *The Military History of World War II*. New York: The Military Press, 1986.

Robertson, Bruce. *Aircraft Camouflage and Markings 1907-1954*. Letchworth: Harleyford Publications Limited, 1956.

Ross, Herbert E. *Adventures of a P-38 Ace*. Stockton: Graphics West Printing, 2006.

Sakaida, Henry. *Imperial Japanese Navy Aces 1937-45*. Oxford: Osprey Publishing, 2004.

Scott, Robert Lee. *God Is My Co-Pilot*. New York: Charles Scribner's Sons, 1943.

Scutts, Jerry. *P-47 Thunderbolt Aces of the Eighth Air Force*. Oxford: Osprey Publishing Company, 1998.

Scutts, Jerry. *P-47 Thunderbolt Aces of the Ninth and Fifteenth Air Forces*. Oxford: Osprey Publishing, 2002.

Scutts, Jerry. *P-51 Mustang Aces of the Eighth Air Force*. Oxford: Osprey Publishing, 2002.

Scutts, Jerry. *P-51 Mustang Aces of the Ninth and Fifteenth Air Forces and RAF*. Oxford: Osprey Publishing, 2004.

Spick, Mike. *Luftwaffe Fighter Aces*. Mechanicsburg: Stackpole Books, 1996.

Stafford, Gene B. *Aces of the Southwest Pacific*. Warren: Squadron/Signal, 1977.

Stafford, Gene B. with William N. Hess. *Aces of the Eighth. Warren: Squadron/Signal, 1973*.

Stanaway, John. *Mustang and Thunderbolt Aces of the Pacific and CBI*. Oxford: Osprey Publishing, 2003.

Stanaway, John. *P-38 Lightning Aces of the ETO/MTO.* Oxford: Osprey Publishing, 1998.

Stanaway, John. *P-38 Lightning Aces of the Pacific and CBI.* Oxford: Osprey Publishing, 2001.

Styling, Mark. *Corsair Aces of World War 2.* Oxford: Osprey Publishing, 2003.

Thomas, Andrew. *Mosquito Aces of World War 2.* Oxford: Osprey Publishing, 2005.

Tillman, Barrett. *Hellcat Aces of World War 2.* Oxford: Osprey Publishing, 2002.

Tillman, Barrett. *Wildcat Aces of World War 2.* Oxford: Osprey Publishing, 1995.

Toliver, Raymond F. *Fighter Aces of the U.S.A.* Fallbrook: Aero Publishing, 1979.

Townsend, Peter. *A Duel of Eagles.* Edison: Castle Books, 2003.

Vander, John. *Spitfire.* New York: Ballantine Books, 1969.

Wandry, Ralph H. *Fighter Pilot.* New York: Careton, 1979.

Wilhelm, David C. *Fly Boy/Experiences of a Fighter Pilot.* David C. Wilhelm, 2005.

Willmont, H.P. *Zero A6M.* London: Bison Books Limited, 1980.

Wooley, Charles with Bill Crawford. *Echoes of Eagles.* New York: Penguin Group (USA), 2003.

*I wish to extend a special note of appreciation to the following American fighter aces for granting me permission to use information from their own published works in the preparation of this text.

Col. Clarence E. Anderson: *To Fly and Fight.*

MGen. Frederick C. Blesse: *Check Six, A Fighter Pilot Looks Back.*

Col. Dean Caswell: *Fighting Falcons–The Saga of Marine Fighter Squadron 221.*

Col. Cecil G. Foster: *Mig Alley To Mu Ghia Pass.*

Lt Col. Robert Goebel: *Mustang Ace.*

Cdr. Hamilton McWhorter III: *The First Hellcat Ace.*

Maj. Ralph H. Wandry: *Fighter Pilot.*

Capt. David C. Wilhelm: *Fly Boy/Experiences of A Fighter Pilot.*

A FINAL THOUGHT

All of the fighter aces I have met, interviewed and corresponded with over the years, to a man, believe they are not *'heroes'*. I have been consistently told that *'we were only doing the job that had to be done and were trained to do.'* Fighter aces believe that the real *'heroes'* are the pilots they flew with that didn't make it back home.

Be that as it may, to be a successful fighter pilot that faced and survived the dangers of aerial combat, took a great measure of courage and skill. Regardless of what pilots say, the results were often times *'heroic'*.

Naval Ace, Commander LeRoy (Robby) Robinson wrote me and stated: "Aces are only a small part of our great heritage. The men who carried rifles and went virtually unprotected against great amounts of ordinance are the real heroes of freedom. Imagine going ashore at Normandy Beach!"

I concur with Commander Robinson.

From the author's point of view, anyone who has defended our countries freedom, regardless of branch of service or rank, deserve our deepest gratitude and sincere respect. They are the true "HEROES", one and all!

978-0-595-70912-0
0-595-70912-5

Printed in the United States
107493LV00004BB/5/A

9 780595 709120